Yes! Ordinary

people ***can***

make a difference!

WHAT THEY SAW

Telling the truth could cost them their freedom!

Monica Bennett-Ryan

IN HIS NAME
PUBLISHING

WHAT THEY SAW

ISBN: 978-0-9943256-3-1

Printed in Australia

Email: monica@inhisname.com.au

IN HIS NAME
PUBLISHING

IN HIS NAME Publishing
PO Box 148
Waterford Qld 4133

www.inhisname.com.au

Graphic Design

BRONWEN RUSSELL
www.bronsdesign.com.au

God has chosen

the foolish things of the world

to confound the wise;

and the weak things of the world

to shame the strong.

(Bible: 1Cor.1:27)

CONTENTS

FOREWORD

It's been said, "Truth is stranger than fiction". This was never truer than in the Defence debacle I had the dubious pleasure of sharing with Monica Bennett-Ryan.

My brief stay within the Defence Intelligence and Security Authority was packed with gasping surprise, almost on a daily basis.

Monica has captured the essence of the horror that continually shocked us. Using known facts and hidden details from emails, transcripts and official reports, she has managed to bring this truly unbelievable part of Australian Defence history out into the open as accurately as possible.

When I read through the first finished draft, several years after coming out of the horror, it took me to a dark place of remembering things from which I'd since recovered. That her words were able to take me there again shows the accuracy of her portrayal of our experience.

Read these pages and see what I mean...but a caution! When you start muttering, "This is far-fetched! Unbelievable! It can't be true!" remember that is exactly what we were muttering continually while we were living through this whole sorry saga…

Janice Weightman

PREFACE

This story is true. For that reason, the names of the people I worked with in the Defence Intelligence and Security Authority (DSA) Brisbane have been changed. Though many were honourable people who stood with we three whistleblowers as we revealed the corruption, even more would have been glad to see us spend time in jail for revealing their secrets.

The organisation itself, DSA Brisbane, no longer exists, and the building I describe is no longer used by Defence Intelligence. After our story broke, DSA Brisbane was given a new name and moved to a different location. It is now known as the Australian Government Security Vetting Authority (AGSVA), and the new, bigger and brighter AGSVA building is not located on, or anywhere near, the monstrosity I describe in the grounds of Victoria Barracks in Brisbane.

So, despite the fact this story is true, the book is referring to unidentifiable people in places which no longer exist. How very cloak and dagger!

The conversations reported are not meant to be taken as exact quotes. They are mostly the products of memory and hindsight, yet the facts they represent are correct.

The facts of this book are backed up by dated emails, letters, television interviews, newspaper articles, comments from Ministers, Senate documents and official reports which have been made public. Though, for the sake of those who simply wish to read a story, I've only included a few references in this publication.

When we first saw the corruption and decided to put our lives and freedoms on the line by going public, we had absolutely no proof the corruption existed. Unlike most whistleblowers, we weren't able to provide paper evidence because paper evidence alone was useless. For the corruption to be seen, the paper evidence would need to be checked against digital data entries held on highly secured Defence computers. So, at the time we went to air, the only proof our allegations were true was hidden within a secure facility; completely inaccessible to anyone outside Australia's powerful intelligence organisation.

The big question for us was, "How are we going to get Defence to admit guilt, open the DSA files and investigate this corruption?" It was an impossible task for three ordinary people, who at the time of going to air, no longer worked within the Department.

We couldn't have done what we did without the help of some exceptional people, notably:

- ABC *Lateline* reporter and producer, John Stewart, who's foresight, professionalism, integrity and sensitivity was evident in all his reporting. He always kept his word to us and never betrayed our trust.
- The Former Labor member for Forde, Brett Raguse, who assisted us as we took our first 'baby' steps in exposing the corruption and explained the process.
- Our unofficial barrister, Dayle Smith B.A. L.L.B. L.L.M. PhD, who generously offered his extensive expertise free of charge at the very time we most needed legal advice.
- Liberal Senator David Johnston who asked the hard questions in the Senate and greatly assisted in exposing the enormity of the problem the Labor Government of the day kept trying to either flatly deny or play down.

- The invisible army of unsung current and ex DSA permanent and temporary staff (many more than Defence knew about) who bravely risked their jobs to secretly confirm to the ABC the truth of our story, and who still wish to remain anonymous.

- All our praying friends, and family members, who supported and encouraged us during this long battle.

- And finally, God himself, who stepped in on several occasions in such a dramatic way, we could only stand in awe and praise Him for the victory he was bringing.

Many whistleblowers are crushed by the experience of standing up for what is right against increasing pressure to hide the truth, and many take a long time to recover from their ordeal. Our heart goes out to them, but that was not our experience. We three whistleblowers, all dedicated Christians, were not crushed; not for a minute.

This journey took us three and a half years, and during that time we were carried by the Lord as we stood on his word. Occasionally we could see God's miraculous hand at work, and when we saw him work, we knew with deep confidence he would have the victory. And He did!

Personally, the most practical thing I took from this experience and would like to pass on is that bullying is just a ruse, a red herring, to cover the real corruption. If you are suffering bullying in your workplace, don't attack the bullying, start looking behind the bullying for the other laws being broken. You'll find them! Then all you have to do is get your proof and a few trustworthy witnesses and take action. That's how you fight the bullies - and win!

Monica Bennett-Ryan

INTRODUCTION

In March 2010, whistleblowers wrote to three government ministers through their local Labor member, the former member for Forde in Queensland. They set out a pattern of conduct in the granting and administration of security vetting that involved a number of things, including bullying and harassment. They also raised the issue of corrupted vetting practices.

Defence's response and the response of the members of parliament was to simply ignore them. But worse still the Defence report went on to treat them as if they were cranks in a most arrogant and offhand way.

It was not until the *Lateline* program, in May 2011, raised these issues that the whistleblowers were taken seriously and the Defence administrators and, indeed those people higher up the chain, were brought to any form of account to set out what had been going on.

We now know that more than 20,000 security vettings have been compromised—that is, people who work in the Prime Minister's office, people who work with the Minister for Defence, people who guard bases. And let us not forget what happened with respect to the terrorism plot over Holsworthy. These compromised vettings include people who guard embassies, embassies that can be troubled in terms of their current and previous political histories.

The Secretary of Defence, when this was raised with him in estimates, slapped it down, flicked it away and said that he was totally oblivious to the significance of the issue.

He said on the record that a flaw in the data input did not necessarily lead to a flaw in the security clearance.

We now know that the flaws in the clearances from Defence went all the way into the ASIO system. This department's maladministration not only corrupted its own processes but also, through the electronic transfer, corrupted the ASIO understanding and capacity to review who is who out there doing sensitive and important security based jobs.

There are 5,000 top-secret security clearances that have been compromised. The simple question that we all must ask is: who is accountable? Who is responsible? There is nobody that this government has pointed to as being responsible. It is always a review, adverse findings and 'we'll fix it now'. Nobody is accountable. This is an absolute disgrace.

These whistleblowers were treated with contempt. They have now received the Inspector-General's report. The first line of that report is that there should be an acknowledgement that what the whistleblowers said from day one was true and correct.

We owe them a debt of gratitude. The parliament owes these three brave people a great debt of gratitude for coming forward in the circumstances. They were derided and treated as cranks.

The Prime Minister was asked to commission this report because these three might have been in breach of the law disclosing what they disclosed. The Inspector-General has the power of a royal commissioner. The Prime Minister had to convene this review and, as I say, it is damning.

The evidence has been overwhelming that there has been endemic, entrenched maladministration. This report makes fascinating reading as to a level of incompetence that is Olympic gold medal class.

I seriously cannot believe this is not front-page news in most newspapers. There are 5,000 top secret security vets that have been compromised. Several thousand of them have been worked through, but we are two or three or four years away from resolving what has gone on here.

It beggars belief, and the minister was on television last night saying, 'Look, people have made mistakes and we all bat on.' It is just appalling, and it fits wholly and solely into the track record and the performance standards of this government. It is just a disgrace.

Senator David Johnston

Ministerial Statement given to the Senate in the Parliament of Australia on 9 February 2012 by Senator David Johnston, Shadow Minister for Defence.

Didn't they know
the law applied
to them?

CHAPTER ONE

Australian law? Irrelevant!

Over the space of two years, between 2009 and 2011, Australia's National Security was severely compromised. This was not an accident. It was not a misunderstanding of procedure. And it was not poor management. It was calculated and deliberate.

The Queensland branch of the Defence Intelligence and Security Authority (DSA) was responsible for doing background checks on people applying for security clearances at all levels; restricted, confidential, secret, top-secret and above. The people being checked were applying to work in secure areas like Military Bases, Airports, Embassies and Government.

Approved security checks were, of necessity, slow and methodical, so the only way to speed the processes was to introduce shortcuts. The shortcuts chosen by the management of DSA were not approved and therefore not legal, yet they were introduced and enforced anyway.

In order to introduce these illegal processes, an elaborate web of deception needed to be created. The plan was that half the staff would uphold correct procedure while the other half would be trained in the illegal shortcuts. For this deception to work, the two groups had to remain totally separate from one another. If their worlds ever collided, the deception would be discovered.

Highly trained Defence analysts continued to uphold correct procedure while temporary employees were brought in to do the illegal shortcuts. Neither group knew what the other was doing. The strict social barrier created between these two groups was so effective Defence analysts generally had no idea why the turnover of temporary agency staff was so high.

The new DSA temps had to be prevented from finding out what they were doing was illegal, so from the very start, they were subjected to sudden and intense brutality, experiencing isolation, segregation, discrimination, harassment, bullying and persistent threats, as 'encouragement' to do as they were told without question. These threats were jointly enforced by DSA management and the employment agency who found the temps for DSA. Despite being Australian citizens, agency staff suddenly found themselves in a place where the protection of Australian law was completely irrelevant.

Have you ever noticed how much extra work goes into a cover-up? Children give us plenty of examples. When my eldest son was six years old, he decided not to eat his vegetables. Leaving them on the plate for me to see wasn't an option, so he developed a plan. He knew no one wanted to remain at the table waiting for him to finish his meal and that little bit of knowledge was all he needed to bring his plan to life and cover his sneaky deed.

He learned to dawdle, playing with his food until everyone else had given up waiting and left the table. Then when no one was looking, he would quietly take his plate from the table, scrape all but one vegetable into the kitchen tidy bin and return quickly to his chair. When he caught my eye, he would manufacture a perfect hang-dog expression and ask, "Can I leave the table please?" Stupidly, I always fell for it! When I saw my sweet little darling had eaten most of his veggies, I would smilingly excuse him and watch him skip away from the table like a wild thing set free from an enclosure.

His plan was working! His rouse was successful! Until one day, that is, when someone was in the right place at the right time to see exactly what he was doing. His plan had been working for several weeks before he was caught out, but after that, he was not left alone at the table and had to eat his vegetables for real.

There is not much difference between a child who wants to cover wrongdoing and an adult who wants to cover wrongdoing. The process is basically the same no matter how old one becomes. First comes the distraction, which covers the sneaky deed, then comes the discovery, followed closely by feigned innocence and fake submission to authority. The trouble is, deception is fleeting and only lasts for a time because there is always someone in the right place at the right time to see what is really going on.

We three whistleblowers just happened to be three experienced parents in the right place at the right time to see the deception being played out by people who, like children, thought their deception would never be discovered.

The constant threats of dismissal, along with intimidation, segregation, isolation, bullying, harassment and general harsh treatment of staff were the not-so-nice distraction. The inappropriate and thoroughly illegal vetting processes were the sneaky deed, and feigned innocence and fake submission to authority were the first reactions after they were found out.

In the right place at the right time

I didn't plan to work for the Defence Intelligence and Security Authority. I didn't even apply for it! Australia tripped, and I sort of fell sideways through an open door. I don't know how it affected you, but the 2009 Global Financial Crisis (the world disaster over which Australia tripped) affected me directly. I lost the best job I'd ever had.

I'd been working as a full-time temporary employee of the Queensland State Government for several years in their Home Water Wise Rebate Scheme. People who purchased water saving devices to assist the State in conserving our limited water resources were rewarded with rebates for their purchases. It was a great job; filled with friendly people. There were very few disgruntled customers but plenty of happy rebate receivers, and it was a pleasure doing business with happy people.

This atmosphere of contentment permeated the whole office, and the workers got along so well that for years after the Scheme was forced to close, many of us still met for 'catch-up' luncheons a couple of times a year.

The point though is the Rebate Scheme was shut down six months ahead of time, due that pesky Global Financial Crisis, and so sixty of my colleagues and I suddenly found ourselves out of a job. Typically, long term temporary government staff would be absorbed into other State government departments, but that too became impossible. Money was tight! At the same time the Water Wise Scheme closed, other government departments were ordered to amalgamate.

That put the whole of the Queensland State Government into what is called 'caretaker mode' which meant no new person could be hired unless someone else was willing to vacate their position. Yes, well! Who in their right mind would give up a secure government position in the middle of a recession? Virtually no-one! So suddenly, at the end of June 2009, I found myself without a job at a time when jobs had become very hard to find.

Needless to say, things were looking grim. I was the sole breadwinner for my family. My two older children were married and starting families of their own, but my youngest son was still in high school, and I needed to keep a roof over our heads. If I didn't have a job, I couldn't pay the rent, and my son and I would be homeless. I didn't want to end up destitute but without a reasonable wage coming in that was now, for the first time in my life, a nasty reality. There was no time to sit around. I had to find a job, and I had to find one fast. So the day after leaving my supposedly secure State government employment, I hustled to a recruitment agency, one which specialised in finding government positions, and went through the humiliation of registration.

I was met by a short, round, congenial looking woman in her late forties. I later discovered this sweet looking recruitment agent also doubled as the one and only, not so nice, DSA staff liaison officer. I explained my predicament and asked if I could be placed on the agency register.

"Can you type?" she asked.

I handed her my resume and told her I had about 30 years secretarial experience, to which she responded, "You'll need to take a test."

I assumed from her response my experience was irrelevant, that 30, 50 or even 100 years experience would never be enough. I was right! It was soon apparent my years of experience would be compacted into one ability; data entry. In other words, I had to prove I knew how to work a computer. I took the test and waited to see if my results would be good enough to compete with the computer savvy younger generation. About an hour later I was told I passed the test and had been placed on their books. I breathed a sigh of relief.

Then she told me the truth. "We don't have any jobs at the moment, the government is not hiring."

Surprised by her sudden candour, I looked at the smiling face in front of me dumbfounded. Why had I just spent all day going through this time-consuming rigmarole if there were no jobs to be had?

"No jobs at all?" I questioned, returning her professional smile.

“None!” she said, and I knew this was her final word. She wasn’t even going to try to find me a job.

Without thinking, words tumbled from my mouth, “I really need a job. I don’t want to walk the streets, destitute.”

She shrugged her shoulders. There was nothing more she could say.

I left her office thinking I had just wasted a whole day when I could have been looking for work in more efficient ways, though I didn’t have a clue what those more efficient ways might be, and I started to realise getting work this time might be harder than I’d thought. I didn’t want to start feeling defeated, so I did what I was accustomed to doing at times like this, I prayed. I handed the situation over to God, asked him to help, and left it with him.

The next morning I received a phone call from the congenial recruitment agent, let’s call her Dora, asking me to come back into the office.

“I’ve a job for you, Monica,” she said, sounding pleased with herself, “all you need to do is come in and sign some official paperwork.”

When I arrived at the agency, Dora took me into her office and told me what had happened.

“I couldn’t sleep last night...at all...because of you.” She settled herself into the leather swivel chair behind her desk. She wasn’t smiling. “You haunted me all night.”

“Pardon?” I asked, taken aback.

“I kept tossing and turning, trying to avoid your face.” She was using her hands as she spoke. “I saw images of you in rags, destitute on the street, begging for food, and I couldn’t stand the look on your face.” She paused. “All I could think of was that you needed a job...and I had to get you one.”

I was astounded! Had God just answered my prayer?

“So when I got up this morning I knew what I had to do,” she said. “There were four people I was thinking of firing anyway, so first thing this morning, I fired them. You can have one of their positions.”

My mouth dropped open, but only for a second. “You said four positions?”

“Yes!”

“Can I bring three friends?”

“Yes,” there was a slight pause, but then Dora added, “as long as they’re registered with this agency, there won’t be a problem.”

“I know one person already registered with you.” I waited while Dora picked up her pen. “Janice Weightman,” I said as Dora wrote, “she was a Senior Administration Officer. There are several others, we all lost our jobs at the same time.” I rattled off a few names, “I’m not sure if they are registered with you yet. I’ll contact them.”

The words ‘stunned’, ‘ecstatic’, ‘incredulous’, even when put together, were inadequate to describe how I felt at that moment. I was over the moon! And I couldn’t help smiling at God’s sense of humour. He’d turned my face into a nightmare to get Dora’s attention. That was not quite the image I had of myself, but very funny, and creatively effective. In doing that one little thing, God had not only provided a job for me but for three of my friends as well. Amazing! I felt like I was floating.

“Just fill this in,” Dora said as she handed me another application form. “You’ll be working for the Defence Department at Victoria Barracks, so you’ll need a restricted clearance to gain access to the Base.”

I came back-to-earth and filled in the form as she continued, “There are a few things you need to be aware of...” her voice trailed off as she reached over to a box of chocolates sitting on the far corner of her desk. To my surprise, she opened the box and offered me a treat.

"I need a pick-me-up," she said, urging me to take one. "I have no energy. I didn't sleep much last night."

"No, thank you," I said, feeling slightly surreal.

Dora continued. "Defence is a different culture." She was munching on chocolate, but her tone of voice had become official. "Its workplace rules are different from other places, and so from our point of view, there are certain actionable offences. They include; office gossip, office politics, complaining, criticism of Defence management or not showing up for work. Any of these actions will bring instant dismissal."

She began searching through layers of paperwork as she continued. "The four people I fired this morning had been gossiping and complaining about the management for a while. Their criticism was not acceptable under the terms of their employment."

Ouch! Sudden death! It sounded a bit harsh. Was this normal practice, I wondered?

Dora must have guessed my thoughts because she looked up from the paperwork, and her tone became confidential. "This is a long-term position, Monica. One of the four has only worked eleven full weeks in the last eighteen months, he was only turning up for work four days a week instead of five...so he had to go."

I began to relax again. That sounded reasonable. Eighteen months was a long time, maybe this position had real long term potential. I later learned Dora's confidential tone was a flashing amber light which screamed, 'warning, warning, you are about to be lied to...'

"The job is not high-pressure," Dora continued, "it's just processing information packs for soldiers. The information simply needs to be entered into a database."

Convinced this simple little role could be exactly what I needed, I indicated I was willing to take the position. "Sounds perfect!" I said.

Dora nodded and continued. "When they first work for Defence, most people experience a kind of 'culture shock'. She suddenly smiled. "You will. It's normal. You'll get used to it."

My mind flicked back to my experience the last time I'd worked for Defence...decades ago...when I was young and employed as a secretary to the Air Commodore commanding RAAF Wagga. I'd loved that job, even though it was strange and difficult to get used to.

In Defence, I'd discovered, the standard rules of written grammar and language didn't apply. Time was expressed differently, and everyone spoke in acronyms; there were so many to master it was like learning a foreign language. There were no margins for error; everything had to be exact. There was a place for everything, and everything was held neatly in its place. On top of that, as a civilian, I was aware I was an outsider and would never be part of the 'in' crowd. I didn't have a problem with any of those things. I was as proud of our military then as I am proud of it now, and I was happy to do my small and limited part.

Remembering my previous experience, I felt confident I understood what Dora meant by 'culture shock' so I responded almost immediately, "It won't be a problem, Dora. I've worked in Defence before. I know what it's like."

She smiled. I smiled. It was a done deal.

She saw me to the door. "As soon as your clearance comes through, you'll start immediately."

I had no idea I'd just been lied to. I found out later, nothing I'd been told was true. I was entering into a high-pressure situation which was not run by the military but by civilians; a huge difference, of mammoth proportions! The information packs for soldiers were actually security clearances for the military as well as for embassy employees, government officials and civilians, and the data I was entering would end up in the ASIO database, no less.

I wasn't told I would be working for the Defence Intelligence and Security Authority, would be sworn to secrecy or would be required to undergo an intense examination of the last ten years of my life just to gain the correct level of clearance I needed to do this 'simple' job. In fact, I had absolutely no idea what I was walking into. Dora, it seemed, was short for Pandora. The position she presented was nothing like the nightmare I was about to experience.

When first impressions prove accurate

I first saw Victoria Barracks on a beautiful, warm, sunny winter's day. It was the first day of my new job, and these old barracks were a quaint surprise. Located on a rise in the middle of cosmopolitan Brisbane, hidden behind a high brick wall, was a snapshot relic of the convict era. Heritage listed stone and red brick buildings with hand painted rust-red corrugated iron roofs and white painted cedar window frames, some still displaying their original mouth-blown glass, sat amongst vivid green lawns, ancient trees and well-kept gardens. It gave the impression of order, pride, honour, safety, endurance and care; things which were, in my experience, normal for Australia's military.

My father had been in the military all his adult life, and he died in service. Reminiscent of every Base I had grown up on or visited every other day or week until I was in my twenties, this neatness was familiar territory. It was like coming home. I felt safe.

After being met by Dora at the guard house, nestled behind the white-painted boom-gates, I was escorted along a sealed road, past a neatly manicured grass assembly quadrant, to a building which, without any stretch of the imagination, was entirely out of place. Discordant would be one way to describe it. Out of harmony with its surrounds, definitely! There was no other way to say it really, it was just plain ugly! And neglected as well, which was a surprise given its surroundings.

The grim-looking two-storey facade was square and windowless, and it's dirty, unpainted grey concrete walls dripped with rust marks from the short antennas which adorned its flat top. Like a discarded, oversized building block, it sat alone and disconnected from the other buildings. There was no warmth, no welcome, no pleasantness about it. Off to the side, amongst unremarkable garden shrubbery, a short stand-alone sign read 'Defence Intelligence and Security Authority', and beside the sign half a dozen unadorned cement stairs led up to the entry; a single, double-glazed, glass security door.

As we climbed the stairs, I questioned Dora, "Intelligence and Security?"

Her only response was a non-committal smile.

I held my breath, not knowing what to expect. Intelligence! This was the stuff of television, and despite my best efforts to suppress them visions of neatly suited British secret agent types in modern buildings with 'state of the art' equipment began to invade my thinking.

The door opened, and a tall, red-haired man of military bearing greeted us, holding the door ajar for Dora and me to enter.

"A new staff member for you Doug," Dora said as we bustled through the door and into the small glass foyer. It was tiny. We three filled a third of the room.

Doug punched a code into the second, more solid, security door, opened it, and stood back to allow us to walk through.

As I began to pass through the doorway, Dora turned to me, "I have someone to see, so I'll be leaving you now." She smiled at Doug, "Chao!" and abruptly left the building.

I was a little surprised by her sudden departure. I hadn't been introduced to this Doug person, nor he to me. I had no idea of his role or what I should expect next.

This turned out to be my first, nothing-subtle-about-it lesson in DSA staff relationships. I was not important enough to be greeted, let alone introduced.

They say first impressions count. Well, this first impression is something which will stay with me for the rest of my life. I had just come from the happiest workplace on earth, a place of light, order, diligence and humour. What I was entering now was precisely the opposite. My life had just swung like a pendulum from one extreme to the other. I had enjoyed workplace harmony, now I had a sinking feeling I was about to become familiar with chaos.

Looking around all I could see was darkness and shadows. There were no windows. The only light came from filtered neon bulbs in the high ceilings. The walls were covered with old grey paint which was chipped, scraped and dirty looking. Small, dark, three-person cubicles, known as 'pods' and filled with messy clutter, adorned every inch of space on each side of a central stairway. The people in those pods were dressed as untidily as their workspaces, in what could only be described as scruffy BBQ casual; and there was not one smiling face to be seen.

The heavy, depressive, unwelcoming atmosphere ripped the 'pleased to meet you' smile off my face, but before I could begin to wonder why everyone was so unhappy, Doug spoke. "I'm going to take you to orientation," he said and closed the security door firmly behind us. He didn't ask my name, nor did he seem interested in what it may be. Walking past me he said over his shoulder, "Follow me," and began descending the central stairway.

The 1940s style two-person wide stairs were steep and narrow, so I gripped the railing as I followed him for fear of stumbling. As we neared the landing on the next floor, I was surprised to see an open bank vault door blocking part of the stair exit. It was the old fashioned kind, the type you see in classic movies; around 30cm thick and made of solid grey steel with a circular turning handle on the front.

Squeezing through the gap between the vault door and the stair rail, I immediately did what most people do in such circumstances; I looked into the space on the other side of the open vault door.

Another dirty room! A large one though! From the ripped vinyl flooring, worn down to the black backing in patches, to a row of small, grubby, unwashed windows set high on one wall, it was just plain sad, the type of place you would want to avoid. Wall to wall it was choked full of filing cabinets, the old kind, army surplus, ex-World War II; scratched, dented, grey of course, and adorned here and there with stuck-on bits of partly lifting paper.

I found it strange the only windows I had seen so far were in a vault. And I began to wonder why anyone would put such a heavy security door on a room with windows. Surely, if someone wanted to break in, they would not need to struggle with a security door when they could just smash a window. But hey, what did I know? This was intelligence! Smarter minds than mine had thought this one through!

Where was Doug? I looked around and saw him in a room on the other side of the landing, opposite the vault door. He was standing at the end of what appeared to be a large table, sorting through some paperwork. It only took a second for me to negotiate my way, without tripping, around the high pile of discarded boxes and bags of shredded paper spilling out willy-nilly from underneath the stairwell, and enter the room with the table.

No windows here either, but at least the walls looked clean. I was right about the table, it was huge; it could comfortably seat twenty people. This long rectangular room was the conference room, which I found out later, also doubled as the staff lunch room. A wall at one end was covered from floor to ceiling with shelving which was filled with boxes of stationery. So I guess this room could be more accurately described as a conference room / lunch room / stationery cupboard.

"Take a seat," said Doug to no one in particular.

I sat down next to the only other seated person in the room, a very pretty young Islander lady with long, straight, black hair and greeting in her eyes. She was well dressed in smart office attire. I could tell she was new and this was her first day because she was as overdressed as I was. We both attempted a courteous half smile, but neither of us said a word. Speaking didn't seem like the-thing-to-do.

"Welcome to DSA," Doug said without a smile.

He was still standing as he handed each of us a well worn blue vinyl ring-binder containing about 60 pages. "Just familiarise yourselves with the contents of these folders. When you've finished reading, I'll get you to sign some paperwork." Then he looked up directly into our faces and for the first time smiled. Well, sort of smiled. He tried. I gathered he wasn't used to smiling because his attempt didn't last long.

"I'm Doug," he said, holding out his hand.

I took his hand and shook it. "Hello Doug, I'm Monica." I still didn't know who this man was or what I should say to him. Was he from personnel? Was he a security guard? I had no idea.

"I'm Sara," said the pretty Islander lady, reaching past me to shake his hand.

"I'm going to leave you to it," Doug said. The faint hint of a smile was completely gone, and he was already starting to move towards the doorway.

My eyebrows shot up, but I tried not to appear shocked he was leaving.

Doug continued, "I'll be back in about an hour to take you to your work area." Then he turned and walked out the door.

Scratch personnel! Scratch security guard!

More stunned than surprised at this new turn of events, Sara and I looked at each other a bit nonplussed. Alone for an hour? What kind of orientation was this? We didn't speak. I had the strangest feeling we were going to be 'caught' if we said anything. I could only guess Sara had the same feeling because neither of us said a word. We had only been in the building five minutes, and we were already being squeezed into the DSA mould.

When Doug returned, he wasn't alone. A slender, pink-shirted, dark-haired man, of Greek extraction, came buzzing through the door behind him with a fixed smile and face agog with artificial excitement.

"Hello ladies," he said in a sing-song voice, letting the s's hang in the air. "I'm Con, your agency team leader."

"Hello, Con," Sara and I responded in unison. I was grateful to be able to speak again; the 'cone of silence' thing was all a bit much.

"Just fill in and sign this paperwork," said Doug, handing us each an Official Secrecy Acknowledgement form, "then Con will take you to your work area."

I took a moment to read the form, "information...not to disclose...not to be published...during or after service... any breach...liable to prosecution." Hmm, not a problem! I'd signed one of these in a previous position when I worked as secretary to a Member of Parliament. No issues here! I completed the form and handed it back to Doug.

"Follow me, ladies," said Con who proceeded to lead us, mincing walk and all, out through the door, past the over-flowing rubbish and back up the stairs. We passed the depressive main entrance landing and continued to ascend to the top floor.

Now, this was more like it! There was light everywhere. I breathed a sigh of relief; at least I didn't have to work in the dark, depressive atmosphere downstairs.

Large windows ran the full length of the building along each of the side walls. The whole floor was flooded in natural light. The walls themselves were a clean shade of cream, and the floor was covered with freshly vacuumed grey-blue carpet. Beyond the windows, the tops of gently moving trees provided the welcome appearance of green shrubbery. It all looked very civilised, and I guessed, correctly, this was where the executives worked.

Sara and I were led to the third, of a line of five, small, only partly cluttered, two-person cubicles. "Make yourselves at home, ladies," said Con as he stood back to allow us to enter our new workspace.

The far side of the pod was all windows from desktop to ceiling, giving a feeling of openness and order. Outside the window, a sunlit tree top brushed the window ledge at desk height as it swayed in the breeze, and beyond the tree top, red painted rooftops gave way to a panoramic sky view. Maybe working here wouldn't be so bad after all.

Sara took the desk by the aisle, and I was left with the undraped window seat. Bliss! I settled in and stood for a moment, enjoying the view.

"Are you sure you don't want this window, Sara?" I asked. I felt like I was getting the better position in the pod.

Sara smiled, and her smile was genuine. "No, you take it, I can still see the tree from here if I want to."

We began to chat - girl chat - the usual 'get to know you' things like, where we lived, how many children we had, and how we ended up in this job. We didn't notice no one else around us was talking.

Con bustled into the pod. "Ladies, ladies, pel-ease!" He was smiling his excited smile, but he had both hands in the air waving them like he was trying to stop an accident. He lowered his voice to an almost confidential whisper. "Talking is not allowed. You're here to work. Not to talk."

Oops! I looked at Sara. Her face was showing that 'peace and good-will', 'getting to know you' glow. I was hoping my face showed the same. I decided to say something. "We're just getting to know each other, Con," I said gently.

"I know, sweetie," he said, and his voice seemed full of understanding. Then suddenly he changed and his smile completely disappeared, "But it's my job to make sure you understand all the rules, so here goes."

He proceeded to rattle off a list of rules which were, I found out as time went by, ruthlessly enforced.

"Number one," he was still not smiling. "Agency staff do not talk to other agency staff about work or any other subjects during the course of a workday. If you wish to talk you can talk to the team leaders, either myself or any of the Defence team leaders."

I wasn't sure I'd heard him correctly. "Do you mean, Con, I can't speak to the person I sit beside all day, even about work?"

"Number two," he continued as if I had not said anything. "Agency staff will not talk to Defence Staff about work or any other subjects unless the Defence staff member opens the conversation. These two rules are not negotiable. Any breach of these rules will bring instant dismissal."

My mouth dropped open. Surely this wasn't right. I closed my mouth and tried to make sense of what I was hearing. Okay, this is intelligence. Maybe they have to operate like this. "Is this for security reasons?" I asked, hoping my question would also show my compliance.

No response. Ignored again!

"Number three. Agency staff will not ask questions." Con was looking directly at me as he spoke.

Ouch! Talk about Jekyll and Hide.

"Everything here is on a 'need to know' basis," he continued. "Everything you need to know will be told to you. If you need to refresh your memory about anything you've been told, you can go to a team leader. Any breach of this rule will bring instant dismissal.

Later I discovered Con had been nick-named 'the smiling assassin', apparently not without reason.

"Number four."

More? How many more could there be? This was brutal. Did I really want to work in such a place?

"Agency staff will not complain about the way DSA management conducts its business or any decisions the management makes. To do so will bring instant dismissal."

My head began to spin. Did this mean no one was allowed to complain about the rubbish flowing out from under the stairs? Was that why everything around us was so dirty and messy?

"Number five." Con sounded disconnected like he had said all of this many times before. "Agency staff will arrive five minutes before start time and be seated at your desk with your computer up and running before 800 hours. Three minutes late and your pay will be docked 15 minutes. "He paused, but he wasn't finished, there was still more. "Agency staff will leave the premises at exactly 1600 hours. If you are found on the premises after that time, you will be considered a trespasser and instantly dismissed."

For goodness sake! What had I gotten myself into?

"Number six. There'll be no unscheduled breaks, you'll choose a break time and stick to it." Con handed us both a mini questionnaire. "You'll have a choice of one of two time-slots for morning tea and one of two time-slots for lunch. Once you choose your break time, you can't change it. If you are found on breaks outside the times you have nominated you'll be instantly dismissed."

What did personal meal breaks have to do with security? Instant dismissal? Why such a hefty penalty for such an insignificant offence?

"Number seven. Agency staff positions at DSA are temporary and highly sort after. There are plenty more people waiting in line to take your place."

I glanced at Sara. She was no longer smiling. Her eyes were lowered and she was studying the floor. I guessed we wouldn't be friends after all. As it turned out, I was right. From that time on, though we shared a pod for eight hours a day, we were never more than nodding acquaintances.

Con continued, "Any un-requested day off will be regarded as a resignation. And any requested leave will be given on the understanding this position may not be here for you when you wish to return. Any sickness must be proven by a medical certificate, but even so, return to employment within DSA will not be guaranteed."

I had never heard anything like this in any workplace in Australia in all my years of working. I was appalled.

"As agency staff, Defence is only required to give you one hours notice prior to dismissal." Con suddenly smiled. His face was beaming and agog with excitement again like it was at our first meeting. "But the good news is," he paused, taking a long deep breath, as if he was going to say something wonderful, "you, also, only have to give one hours notice if you don't like working here."

That was the good news? How horrible! There was something very wrong with this whole picture. Scary wrong! I just didn't know what it was. I felt like running, but I knew I couldn't, there were no jobs out there. Besides, this was an answer to prayer for me. Deep down inside, in that place where faith lives, I believed there was a reason God had gone to such great lengths to place three of my friends with me in these strange surroundings, so despite my growing misgivings, I decided to stay.

The optional nature of training and procedures

Formal training, if anyone could call it that, began the next morning and it was as disjointed and surreal as orientation. The first thing which struck me as strange was that Sara and I were taught separately, even though the training was done at our desks and we were being taught by the same person. I assumed we were learning the same thing, but as Sara and I were taught individually, I began to wonder if that was actually the case.

The second strange thing was the lack of procedures. Nothing was written down. We had to rely entirely on memory, which was ridiculous, considering the importance of the work and how much there was to learn. But I reminded myself this was an intelligence agency, I had to expect things to be different. Nevertheless, I found it difficult to adjust.

How does a person learn without asking questions, without reading notes, without following someone else's example? In every other training situation I'd experienced, I could say to a fellow worker, "what are we supposed to put in this field?" They would reply, "Oh, you just put this..." The light of understanding would come on, and I would continue my work with a hearty, "Thanks."

That was not the case in this role. We were not allowed to communicate - at all! So with no discussion, no written procedures, Betty, our trainer, seated on a different floor, and instant dismissal for unscheduled breaks (like going downstairs to talk to a team leader) learning was exceedingly difficult. In fact, it just didn't make sense to me. I had to keep telling myself this was intelligence. There had to be a reason they wanted things run like this. And anyway, who was I to question the way things were being done?

After learning how to enter restricted, confidential, secret and top-secret data into the specialised security database, I was told I would be sent for further training on how to enter data into the general military database, but this new training would be conducted by the military.

Early that afternoon, Sara and I joined with a larger group of around six people. We weren't introduced, because we weren't allowed to talk to each other. So, without a word, we were led out of the cement building block, along a pretty flower-filled garden path, to one of the iconic red brick buildings which so beautifully complimented the green lawns of Victoria Barracks.

We were met at the entrance to the building by a female army officer who asked us to follow her down a long, long hall to her office. I expected computer training to be conducted in a training room with desks and computers, but no, it wasn't. Instead, we all crowded around the officer's desk and watched over her shoulder as she explained the ins and outs of the system via her personal computer. There was so much to take in; I thought my brain would explode. Then towards the end of our session, the officer made the most amazing statement.

"I can't show you how to operate the programs you use because I don't have the clearance," she said, not realising she had just dropped an almighty bombshell.

What? Did I hear right? This highly skilled military officer, who specialised in IT training, thought my clearance was higher than hers?

My mind went into overdrive. The questions came thick and fast, and none of them had any answers. Who did she think she was training? My clearance level was only 'restricted', the bottom level, no higher than a cleaner. Didn't she know that? Would she have shown me the things she did if she had known? How could I, with a lower clearance than a military officer, access data she was not allowed to access?

I couldn't grasp the enormity of what I had just heard. It just wouldn't compute. I had inadvertently discovered the work I was doing on a lowly restricted clearance, I should not have been doing at all. Yet, despite my lack of clearance, my job was to use classified systems to enter classified information up to and including top-secret level.

This was too deep for me. Surely smarter minds than mine had thought this through. I certainly hoped they had. Or was it planned by the same minds who'd put a vault door on a room with windows? Scary thoughts!

In the end, I put it down to my own ignorance and moved on. After all, how was I supposed to know how 'intelligence' worked? I had only been on the job for two days. The trouble was, like everything else I'd encountered at DSA so far, this just didn't feel right. It nagged at me, but I didn't know what to do about it.

A tranquil oasis in the midst of chaos

The cavalry arrived in the form of three of my ex-State government employment friends. I so needed friends I could talk to about all this, yet I couldn't talk to anyone who didn't have the right clearance. Janice arrived first, starting the week after I did. Cassandra and Jennifer arrived in my third and fourth weeks, respectively. Having friends around me was such a blessing. We didn't waste any time finding a nice quiet place to have lunch together, away from everyone else, and away from prying ears.

The place we found was gorgeous. Perfect! Quiet! Empty! It was as secluded as a 'secret garden', but huge, like a park. A long rolling green lawn dotted with mature trees of different kinds was fully edged with meandering garden beds held in place by chunks of sandstone and backed on one side by a ten-foot-high sandstone wall which ran down half its length.

The entry to this delight, hidden by parked cars, was behind the flagpole on the far side of the quadrant, a mere hundred metres from the cement building block. Two short flights of spacious sandstone steps led down to a wide garden path which, after five meters, took a 90° turn around a huge shady tree and suddenly revealed a paved picnic area. This rather large area was home to five, weather-worn, cedar picnic tables and a double brick bar-b-que which was next to, surprisingly, an extremely tall and elegant antique lamp post.

The view from the picnic area down the sweeping expanse of lawn gave a sense of peace and tranquillity. Just what we needed!

Since no one else used this spot, not even the military in the buildings beside it, we had our pick of the tables, and I decided to add a little humour and civilisation to our lunchtimes by adding a round, butter-yellow tablecloth.

At first, it gained a few odd looks from military passers-by, but after a while the yellow cloth became familiar. The passing regulars would give us a smile and a wave, and we would smile and wave in return. Lunchtimes were wonderful; it was like we had entered a different world.

I discovered DSA staff avoided this particular place because of 'the lizards'. What lizards, I wondered? In all the time I was at Victoria Barracks I only ever saw one rock lizard. And who is afraid of lizards anyway? I couldn't understand why anyone would prefer to eat in a windowless lunchroom / conference room / stationery cupboard instead of out here, in paradise.

"This is so beautiful," said Cassie as she took a deep breath of the fresh air. "I love coming out here."

"It's nice to be normal for a few minutes," said Jennifer. She didn't have to expand, we knew what she meant.

This was a place where we could relax and be ourselves. We could talk to each other about anything; whether work or home or family. We could laugh and joke and discuss forbidden topics, like our horrific work conditions and the management practices of DSA.

We were friends, we'd known each other for years. We'd previously worked together in the best work environment any of us would ever experience. We trusted each other and were confident we could discuss everything we were banned from talking about inside the walls of DSA

"So you didn't get fired?" asked Jennifer.

I shook my head and smiled, "No, not this time."

"What happened?" asked Cassie.

"I couldn't stand working under that freezing air conditioning any longer, I had to choose between my health and my job. So I bit the bullet and made a complaint." I took a sip of my drink. "I fully expected to be fired."

"Monica's been rugged up with a coat, scarf and gloves for weeks," said Janice, filling in the details.

"It's like an arctic blast over my chair...way too cold for me...and it's only in that one spot," I said, "It got so bad I couldn't use my fingers to type...they were all stiff."

"The air-con technicians have been in, but they can't fix it," said Janice.

"I was expecting 'instant dismissal' but, to my surprise, Con told me I would be moved to the middle floor instead. I'm now down in the dingy area with the analysts."

"So, they don't mean what they say," said Cassie.

"I think they do," said Janice without emotion. "Donna was fired yesterday."

Slightly built, with long fading red hair and a polished English accent, Janice reminded me a little of Agatha Christie's Miss Marple character, who also had a habit of coming straight to the point.

"That pretty woman with the long curly blond hair," I questioned, "the one who's always pleasant and smiling?"

"Yes, she's the one," Janice said simply.

"Oh, she was such a ray of sunshine!" I remembered seeing Donna on every trip down to the vault-window filing room. In the midst of drab, dirty disorganisation, this slim, always busy young woman wore crisp, bright colours and red lipstick. She always wore red lipstick. It made her perfect smile seem even brighter.

"What excuse did they use this time?" I asked.

"She worked past 4.00pm. She was on the premises after hours," said Janice. "It didn't seem to matter that she had permission from her team leader who was working back with her. Erik and Dora decided to fire her."

Erik was the top boss. He was a middle-aged Scandinavian man of medium build and balding grey/red hair. He totally ignored agency staff. When we passed him on the stairs, it was as if we didn't exist. He would not shift his path to acknowledge there was an individual on the stairs with him. He didn't speak to us, nor did he make eye contact. Even so, he was a micro-manager who controlled everything in the cement building block by emailing orders from behind closed doors. We called him the puppet-master because he pulled all the strings.

"I heard she quit," said Cassie, softly.

"She tried to, but they wouldn't let her," said Janice. "When she came in to work the next day, she got taken straight up to Erik's office and grilled. When the grilling was over, she told Con she was quitting, but Dora didn't give her the chance. She fired her and escorted her off the premises. Donna didn't even get to say goodbye to anyone."

"How can you be fired for working after hours with permission?" asked Jennifer.

"You can't!" said Cassie.

"She was!" said Janice.

"So much for being conscientious," said Jennifer. "Why did she work back when it was against policy?"

"She was given a job which needed to be completed that day, but completing it meant going over time," Janice said.

"Ah! Catch 22!" said Jennifer.

"Dora and Erik didn't even question the team leader who gave her the task and stayed back with her," Janice continued, making sure we were aware of all the facts.

“Sounds like a set-up,” said Jennifer.

“It does!” agreed Cassie.

“But she was such a good worker!” I was puzzled. “Why do they throw away so many good people?”

Jennifer frowned as she looked at me. “How many have been let go since you started?”

“Well, let’s see,” I said. “There are the four of us, plus Sara who started with me and Zelda who started with Janice.

“So if six were hired, six were fired,” said Jennifer.

“Six in four weeks,” said Janice.

“With those figures, they would be going through around seventy staff per year,” I said. “Could that be right?”

“One thing we can be sure of,” Jennifer predicted, “we won’t last long...our turn is coming.”

We all nodded in agreement. We had seen enough in a few weeks to know what Jennifer was saying was true. Donna was living proof, good workers were not immune.

“Maybe we should just talk to Dora, you know, reason with her,” Cassie suggested.

The rest of us slowly shook our heads. We knew by now Dora was the enemy. No mistake about it. DSA said ‘hit them’ and Dora said ‘how hard?’

Cassie was such a sweetie, and her quiet observations invariably made us smile. A mother of three children she was about 6’ tall, and slender with softly curled auburn hair falling to her shoulders. She spoke slowly and softly and always had a quiet smile on her face. She was as gentle as she was tall, yet her serene manner belied her ability. She had been a Project Officer at Home WaterWise. Her DSA position was a definite backward step for her career.

Jennifer was still frowning, “Seriously though, is there anywhere we can go to make an official complaint?”

The most qualified of us all, Jennifer had worked as a Technical Officer for the CSIRO for twenty years before taking a position as an IT Project Officer for the Queensland Government. Slim and pretty with short-cropped, dark brown hair and intelligent brown eyes, she was not one to mince words, "I have never experienced such outrageous working conditions. Worker's here have no rights at all!"

"We can't go to Dora, and we can't go to Defence so where do we go?" I asked, "there must be somewhere."

We sat in silence for a moment munching on our lunches and considering the possibilities. Yes, where could we go to complain? Agency staff were the 'meat in the sandwich' so to speak. We didn't work for Defence directly; they didn't pay us so we couldn't go through any of their channels to make a complaint. Neither did we work for the agency directly because our work was classified and we couldn't tell them about it; which meant we couldn't go through any of their channels to make a complaint. We couldn't go to any outside agency, like the Ombudsman, because it would be a breach of the Secrecy Act.

"I think we're in a bit of a pickle," said Janice.

We all chuckled, a sad, involuntary, hopeless kind of chuckle. She was right. We *were* in a pickle!

Despite my unusual reprieve, instant dismissal was a constant threat, and Dora had let us know, in no uncertain terms, those who were 'replaced' would not be considered by her to be eligible for any future position elsewhere. In other words, we were doomed if we complained and we were doomed if we didn't.

"I still don't have a desk," Janice suddenly blurted out. "I've been in that idiotic conference room for three weeks. At lunchtimes, and whenever there are meetings, I'm booted out and have nowhere to sit. I have to carry all my work and supplies around in a box and use any desk I find unoccupied for a short amount of time. I can't always find an empty desk, but I am still frowned on if I don't do my work in time. Where do I go to complain about that?"

She was angry. And rightly so!

"Two other people started after me, and they've been given desks." Her logic was undeniable. "It seems to me they don't want to give me a place to sit."

"Surely that's not the case," said Cassie.

Janice turned to Cassie, "you started after me, Cass, and you have a desk." Janice looked around the group and then back at Cassie, "Do you know that military database training you've all just done?"

We nodded.

"I asked Doug when I'd be receiving my training, and he told me he'd heard I wouldn't be here very long." Janice sighed and looked down at the drink bottle she was absently twiddling. "I think they want me to resign," Janice said softly. Her anger was now gone. "I think I'm next."

Cassie put a comforting hand on her friend's arm, "do you want to resign?" she asked. Her question was like a warm hug. She had such a soft way about her.

"I don't have anything to lose by resigning," Janice suddenly frowned, "but if I have to go down that road, I want to do it on my terms, not theirs."

"What do you mean?" I asked.

"I don't want to be escorted out in shame," said Janice with determination, "I want to go out with my head up."

Jennifer dropped back into her chair. "So you might be gone tomorrow?" The fragile nature of agency positions in DSA had just hit her.

Cassie shook her head. There were no words.

I often felt a pang of guilt I'd involved my friends in this horror story. What a nightmare we'd all stumbled into. If any of us had known in advance the horrors which lurked behind DSA's coded doors, we would've turned away and looked for work elsewhere.

Nevertheless, being together was a God-send. Our lunchtime chats helped clarify what our eyes were seeing and provided a forum for questions which may not have otherwise been asked.

Through our candid lunchtime conversations, we all came to realise there was no easy way out of this situation for us or any other agency contractor. The simplest solution was to find another job, which was complicated by the fact new employers wanted a referee from the most current former employer and we were not likely to get a referral from either Defence or Dora. But then, there were no jobs anyway; the global recession had made sure of that. So, we quickly realised all we could do was put our heads down, do our work, obey the rules, and wait for the hammer to fall.

Seeing the gulf between military and Defence

Those first few weeks at DSA were like an emotional roller-coaster. Working there was exhausting! Like every other agency worker, I didn't know, from one day to the next, if I would keep my job, or if my friends would keep their jobs. In a few short weeks, I'd become used to being isolated, constantly threatened, and made to feel as disposable as a used tissue. All I knew for sure was, something was very wrong, and everything seemed upside down.

I no longer had the protection of Australian law; it didn't seem to apply within DSA.

I couldn't trust Con, my agency team leader; I'd learned that everything any of us did and said was reported by him to Dora. If a look could be construed as criticism Con made sure it was, or if a light-hearted comment could be mistaken as dissent Con made sure it was, he surely was a smiling assassin.

I couldn't trust Dora, she was just a puppet on one of Erik's strings; her whole motivation was to please Defence.

I couldn't trust Defence personnel for I'd discovered their smiles were just masks which hid daggers. I was safe as long as one of them didn't smile at me. If they smiled, I knew I was about to be deceived, used, or fired; a smile meant I was in big trouble. Now I understood why no one smiled - why Doug didn't smile during orientation. In DSA, smiles were deadly, and misery and mayhem were the order of the day. How twisted! How insane!

There was nothing normal about any of this behaviour. But what I couldn't understand was why. Why were they like this? This was not the Defence I'd grown up with. My father would have been horrified by this behaviour. But he was military - this was not!

Suddenly the light came on. That was it! That was the difference! I suddenly understood.

I'd always held Defence in high esteem. Like most Australians, I believed Defence was our protector; there to keep us safe and protect our rights as Australians. That long-held belief had just been shattered into a million pieces. Like a pin bursting a bubble, my fantasy world had been blown apart before my eyes.

This Defence was not my protector; it was not keeping me safe, and it was definitely not protecting my rights as an Australian. This Defence was the opposite of everything I'd always loved about our military. Until that moment, I didn't realise Defence and our military were worlds apart. But the glaring reality was - these people were *not* military!

Before my experience with DSA, I tended to lump Defence and the military together. I had put them both way up there on a pedestal. This was mainly because of my father and the respect for the military he'd instilled in his children. I grew up proud in the knowledge our military were never aggressors, only defenders; clothed in honour, hard-earned and well-deserved.

The trouble with my pedestal fantasy was that, in reality, the military only made up a small part of Defence.

The majority of those working under the Defence banner seemed to know how to manipulate military protocols and illegally use them to coerce civilian workers in order to further their own agenda's. They'd learned to use the light of military glory to cover their inglorious actions.

When the bubble burst, it swept the non-military off my pedestal. Our military is still up there and always will be, but the non-serving civilians working under the Defence banner do not deserve the same honour as those in the military itself. Our military is our protector, and always will be, but these people - these people were a disgrace.

There was no honour in DSA. It was easy to see really, like black against white. The stark contrast was obvious from the moment I arrived at Victoria Barracks. Everything in the hands of the military was neat and ordered while everything in the hands of the DSA civilians was disorganised to the point of chaos.

I'd never been treated cruelly by any member of the military at any time in my life. In my experience they'd only ever been helpful to civilians in times of trouble, lending a helping hand and going the extra mile whenever possible. The news coverage of the soldier holding a toddler during the 2010 Queensland floods is a perfect example. He was taking the child to a helicopter but wasn't just transporting the child, he had his hands over the child's ears, protecting the little one from the noise and wind of the rotors. Beautiful! That's our military!

In predictable polarity, cruelty was the order of the day within DSA. Human dignity was a foreign concept to them. I'd discovered the hard way that many of the civilian bureaucrats within DSA who ride on the back of military honour have no honour at all.

But I hadn't seen the worst. I'd only dipped my toe into this foul swamp. There was more to come – much more.

> *Defence Minister Stephen Smith says an internal Defence Department review has found serious maladministration flaws.* (ABC News 21 Sept. 2011)

Didn't they care

about

the consequences?

CHAPTER TWO

No facts? Use fiction!

During 2009 to 2011 the management of DSA Brisbane forced its agency staff to falsify official data and pass that data on to ASIO as if it were checked and accurate. No facts? Pretend there are! Make it up!

> *A Defence review found that procedural errors led to false information being passed to ASIO.* (ABC News 21 Sept. 2011)

When news of this corruption finally emerged in the media in 2011, people were incredulous. They were not only shocked by the allegations against Australia's Defence Intelligence and Security Authority, they couldn't believe their Defence Department would order their workers to do such a thing. Further, they couldn't understand how so many people could claim they didn't know what they were doing was wrong.

The implications for Australia's National Security were enormous. Many security clearances, from restricted right through to top-secret, were apparently granted even though they were based on false information.

Considering these clearances covered people who worked in highly secure places like military bases, embassies, government offices and airfields the real potential for disaster, particularly during visits by overseas dignitaries, like Queen Elizabeth or President Obama, was disturbing, to say the least.

Once it was exposed to the media, this appalling breach of security was finally acted on. As a result, the slow and cumbersome wheels of resolution began to turn.

Clearances done during those two years were counted and put aside to be rechecked with the promise that, as they were rechecked, the potential threat would grow smaller each day. Yet, despite action being taken to reverse the damage, the original question remained. How could so many people falsify data, for so long, without knowing that was what they were doing? I believe the answer to that question can only be found by looking at the deliberate and calculated nature of the callous deception of staff.

At first, I didn't know what I was doing was wrong. It took a long time, nearly seven months, for me to see what was actually going on; and I was only able to do so then because of the multiple exceptional circumstances in which I found myself. If events had not unfolded for we three whistleblowers as they did, none of us would have seen through the deception.

How and when the deception began

I, and my friends, just happened to join DSA at the right time. I know the timing wasn't an accident, and I marvel at God's ways. His timing is always perfect. I arrived in time to see the beginning of the deception and how it was subtly and forcefully introduced. It was not an accident. It was not an administration flaw. It was, as I mentioned earlier, deliberate and calculated.

I arrived three weeks before the deception began. For the first three weeks, everything was done by what could only be called typical government department process. It was my job to check new applications to see if all the required information was present and do one of two things:

1. If any documentation was missing, it was my job to reject the application and return it to the applicant in the afternoon mail. Simple! Normal public service procedure! Familiar ground! I'd followed exactly the same process for years in both my State and Federal government employment.
2. If all the documentation was present, it was my job to enter the details into the database, leaving gaps where any data was missing, then pass the application on to a DSA analyst for follow-up. Simple!

It was the DSA analyst's job to check the accuracy of the information provided and phone the applicant to obtain all missing information before sending a report about the completed application to ASIO. The report to ASIO signalled the completion of the DSA process for this was only supposed to be done once all the data being sent to them had been verified as accurate. This, I understood, was correct procedure. Normal! Simple! It made sense! The trouble was - it didn't last!

Three weeks after I started at DSA, this correct procedure was done away with and replaced with what would turn out to be the cause of the greatest security scandal in Australia's history.

The new procedures puzzled me. They didn't make sense at all, but I wasn't allowed to ask questions, and nothing was explained. There was no training given, and nothing was written down. However, we were constantly reminded to do as we were told, on pain of dismissal.

Agency staff were suddenly ordered not to reject any applications; nothing was to be sent back to the applicant. Whether they had complete data or not, the information provided on all applications for 'Restricted', 'Confidential', 'Secret' or 'Top-Secret' level clearances were to be entered into the database and finalised by us; that included the sending the completion report to ASIO.

I had no idea this new process had been set up to bypass the analyst check; that what we were actually doing was sending reports to ASIO as complete before information had been checked, or even received. DSA management cleverly hid that little bit of very important information from both the agency staff and the analysts, though it didn't remain hidden for long.

Within a few days of their implementation, everyone could see there was a huge problem with these new procedures, which I could only call vault-window mentality in action.

The ASIO database would not accept reports with gaps in information. This meant, if there was even one 'field' left unfilled in the electronic report, it would reject the whole report as an 'error'. Since most of the reports being sent by agency staff under the new procedures had a lot of missing information, the number of bounce back 'errors' suddenly skyrocketed.

I was amazed DSA management didn't know this would happen! What amazed me more was that even after they saw the new procedures were causing problems with the ASIO database, they defied logic and all reason and insisted we use the new procedures anyway! Unbelievable!

This was the direct 'cause' which produced the 'effect' of the greatest security scandal Australia has ever seen. There was nothing accidental about it! It was not only deliberate, it was enforced with threats!

"Ya makin' too many errors, Monica," I jumped! I didn't know Jack had walked into the pod and was standing behind me.

Jack, a short pompous bulldog of a man in his late forties, had been given the job of training people in the new procedures; and he did this loudly with humiliation as his preferred training method.

"What ar'ya gunna do about it?" he bellowed at the back of my head loud enough for the whole floor to hear.

“I’m sorry,” I said, turning my chair around to face him, “I’ll correct them now.” At this stage, I didn’t know rejected ASIO reports were called ‘errors’. So, thinking he meant typing errors, or data entry mistakes, I held out my hand expecting him to give me the files which needed correcting.

“Errors never come back to the person who makes them,” he blustered, it was obvious he wanted everyone to hear what he was saying. “But we keep a record of how many are made...and if y’make too many you’ll be replaced.”

Oh, no! My heart sank. I was getting the sack.

“You’ve got till the end of the week.” Why was he so angry? “If y’can’t get y’errors down by then you’ll be replaced.” With no further explanation, Jack left the pod.

I was devastated. Replaced was the DSA word for fired. I’d seen this happen to others so many times. I guessed I was going to be the next one given one-hours notice and escorted off the base like a criminal. Oh, well! I suppose it had to happen sometime! I spent the rest of the day being super careful, double checking all my entries. It slowed me down, but what else could I do?

The next day was the same. “Ya still makin’ too many errors, Monica,” Jack announced loud enough for everyone on the floor to hear him berating me. “And ya’need to get y’speed up. Yesterday y’didn’t process enough applications.”

I scanned my memory, searching for something I may have missed. There wasn’t anything. I knew my work was accurate. I had double checked all my data entries. I couldn’t let this accusation pass. I had to speak up. I was losing my job anyway.

“Jack, I made sure my data-entry was accurate. I double-checked everything.” My voice had an edge to it; this humiliation thing was actually starting to make me feel angry. “That’s why the number of applications dropped a little. I was just trying to be accurate. I don’t understand how I could still be making errors.”

It was difficult to communicate when I couldn't ask a simple question like 'what errors am I making?' Not being allowed to ask questions was just plain stupid, right up there with vault-window mentality.

Thankfully, Jack let his guard down and told me what the errors were. "The errors aren't in y'typing or accuracy they're in y'data entry – y'not fillin in all the fields."

Oh! This was different, I hadn't heard this before. I sat back in my chair and waited for him to continue.

"If all the fields arn't filled in – when y'send the ASIO report – it'll bounce back – those bounce backs are called 'errors'. He seemed pleased with his explanation. "Y'makin' too many errors of this kind." He paused to let what he had said sink in then continued. "Y've got one more day, if y'don't get it right tomorrow, y're out the door." As he turned to walk away, I stopped him.

"Jack," I said, "I need a list of the fields the ASIO database is sensitive to so I can keep it beside the computer to check my data-entry."

He stepped back and laughed, a kind of shocked half laugh, then shook his head like he couldn't believe what he was hearing and walked out of the pod.

A few seconds later, I heard him talking loudly with Betty in his own one-person pod at the far end of the room, about forty metres away. They were laughing, and I heard my name mentioned. "Oh, what?" boomed Betty for the whole floor to hear; and they both laughed again.

I stood up and looked over the top of the pod dividers in the direction of the voices. Jack was walking away from Betty, his face red from laughing, but his parting comment to Betty was loud enough for me to hear clearly four pods away. "As if we'd write anything down!" he bellowed, and they both laughed again. Jack looked across the tops of the pods and fixed his eyes on mine. There was no laughter in his eyes. Then he turned and continued on his way.

I sat back down. I guessed I was not going to get my list. Why would I? He was right, they didn't write anything down. Not orientation instructions. Not procedure notes. Certainly not lists!

My job was on the line, I had to work this out. I sorted my files into those which had all their information and those which didn't, entering each of them into the database. I didn't have a clue which fields were safe to leave blank and which fields would cause an error. But this was life and death for me now - job wise - so I changed the rules.

If an application had complete information, I sent the report to ASIO. If it didn't, and around 30 to 40 per cent didn't, I held back the ASIO report, wrote out the missing information onto a yellow sticky note, stuck it on the front of the file, and took the file to an analyst so the applicant could be contacted for information.

Then I waited to see what would happen; if I would still have a job the next day.

The next day was a Friday, and it was not until just before knock off time that Jack came to my pod. I'd spent the whole day not knowing what management had decided, and wondering if I'd have a job to come back to on Monday.

"Look what y'can do when y'try," Jack said. "Y'didn't make any errors yesterday." He was smiling at me. This was not good!

"Do I still have a job?" I asked, forgetting I wasn't supposed to ask questions.

"The jury is still out on that one," he said. "Erik hasn't made up his mind, so y'll find out on Mond'y." He was smiling as he walked away.

Great! I had the whole weekend to continue not knowing, wondering, worrying. Fantastic!

This, I'd discovered, was another one of their nasty little habits. Something they did simply because they could.

They would save their worst news for Friday afternoon, knowing it would ruin our weekend. It gave them a lot of pleasure. It gave us a lot of pain. Like children torturing insects, they were just plain mean. No wonder Jack was smiling.

Ordered to fill in the blanks

Janice and I travelled to and from work together on the same bus. The walk to the bus that afternoon gave us the opportunity to chat.

"What did they say?" She looked at me with concern in her eyes.

"They did the Friday afternoon torture trick," I said.

"Oh, no!" She shook her head. "So you have to go through the whole weekend not knowing?"

"Yep!" I nodded.

"What's wrong with these people?" She asked, not expecting an answer. "This is not normal."

"Tell me about it," I said and grinned. "They're not going to ruin my weekend. I've got other things to think about...nice things."

We both chuckled and walked on for a bit in silence.

"I sort of hesitate to tell you what's going on in my world," Janice ventured, "you've enough on your plate."

"Spit it out..."

"All right, well, umm...I'm a little concerned about what happened today," she stopped walking and turned to me. "Would you like to have a coffee? Let's have coffee... we never have coffee. We can't talk about this on the bus."

"Okay, where would you like to go?" We were at Brisbane's Roma Street Bus Terminal, and there was a food mall upstairs, so we rode the escalator to the mezzanine floor, chose a quiet corner and ordered our coffees.

"I was told to delete data today," Janice said simply.

"What?" I was shocked. "What do you mean?"

"Well, you know they've given me the job of clearing the backlog of top-secret files."

I nodded.

"I'm supposed to enter them and then send the ASIO report, right?"

I nodded again.

"They keep bouncing back because of the gaps in information."

"Yes, that's normal," I said, waiting for Janice to get past the background information. She was good at making sure she was understood; though I sometimes felt I wanted to speed up the process.

"I usually attach a yellow slip to those which have blanks and give them to an analyst – to Francine."

"Yes," I agreed. "I started doing that today."

"Great minds..." she laughed a short laugh, then looked serious again. "Well," she paused and sighed, "they don't want us to do that. I was told to fill in the blanks."

"What?"

"Francine told me the analysts do it all the time."

"Well, yes, that's their job," I said, puzzled why this would be a problem. "They contact the applicants, get the details and fill in the blanks."

"I know that, but that's not what I mean." Janice took a sip of coffee. "She said they fill in the blanks without referring to the applicants." Her eyes were searching my face waiting for my reaction. "Monica, I'm worried the applicants could get into trouble later for giving false information - information they never actually gave!"

"No!" I shook my head in disagreement. I couldn't believe what I was hearing.

"She told me...if I didn't have all the birthdates for siblings I should just delete all reference to the siblings, then the report would go through without an error."

My mouth dropped open. "No way!" I was stunned. "How can they delete data?"

"I told her I wasn't comfortable doing that and so I would continue handing the incomplete files to an analyst." Janice paused, waiting for my response.

"That can't be right, Janice. She's telling you the wrong thing." I was searching for reasons. "Maybe she's just fobbing you off." I certainly hoped she was.

"Well, she *was* getting annoyed because I was giving her so many files with yellow slips," Janice conceded.

"There you go then," I said, "she doesn't want the extra work. She's making it up, but why would she tell you to do such a terrible thing? Why would she want to get you into trouble? Can you take them to someone else?"

"I could take some to Betty, I suppose, but that's not the worst of it," Janice took a sip of her now cold coffee and grimaced, "this afternoon, I came across an application which had children's names but no birthdates."

"So you deleted the kids?" I grinned, and raised my eyebrows, trying to be light-hearted.

"No, no, no." Now it was Janice's turn to look shocked. "I...I would never..."

"Sorry," I said, "keep going."

Janice nodded. "Anyway, Helga was there, you know, one of the team leaders from the top floor. So I tried to ask her what I should do. She didn't want to talk about it, so when Jack walked through the door, she called him over and told me I should speak to him."

A stranger walked past our table, and not wanting to be overheard, Janice lowered her voice and continued. "He sat down at my computer and began entering false birthdates for the children."

My eyes widened. "False birth dates?"

"I swear!" She put her hand over her heart, "yes, false birth dates. And he explained how he was calculating the dates so I could do the same."

"What do you mean?" I couldn't believe my ears. This was bad – very bad.

"He said I should check the birth dates of the parents and calculate a reasonable date for the birth of each of the children from their parent's birth dates." She could see the astonishment on my face. "They were completely made up, Monica. Totally fabricated!"

"What did you do?" I whispered, shocked.

"I told him this was false information and I didn't feel right giving false information to ASIO."

"And?" I whispered. My brain was numb. I was holding my breath.

"He said ASIO had no problem with it. They knew the database was too sensitive and they would be able to pick up any discrepancies at their end. He said it was just up to DSA processors to get them through the database."

I sighed with relief. "Okay, so it's not so terrible," I could breathe again. "If ASIO has approved this, who are we to buck the system?" I thought about it for a minute. "This is intelligence, Janice. We're at the bottom of the pile. How can we possibly know what decisions have been made at high levels?"

"We can't," she agreed.

"Smarter minds than ours, Janice," An image of the vault-window room flashed through my mind. This time I pushed it aside, "What do we know?"

At that point in time, I couldn't imagine DSA would lie to us about something as important as intelligence. I couldn't believe DSA would encourage its staff to deceive ASIO, I couldn't believe our Defence Department would order staff to compromise our National Security, and in my wildest dreams, I would never have thought anyone working for Australia's Defence would deliberately place so many Australian lives in jeopardy. I couldn't believe any of that, and so later, I could easily understand how hard it was for the Australian public to believe it when the story broke.

I knew DSA were sloppy and dirty and messy and just plain nasty, but I didn't believe for a minute they would betray Australia or Australians. Not for a minute!

I thought we were being told the truth. So did Janice. So did all the other agency staff. But the cold, hard reality was, we were all being deceived, and being trained to deceive.

Every one of us was kept isolated from the other. We were all taught separately and were not allowed to talk to each other so that we couldn't compare notes. We were always under constant threat of job loss, which served to deter us from questioning what we were being ordered to do. And the disposable nature of our short-term positions kept us bowing to the assumed wisdom of the established long-term, supposedly know-what-they-are-talking-about, Defence staff. Added to that, anyone who came close to finding out the truth was fired.

In the beginning, I thought the sloppiness, mess, filth, disorganisation and chaos was just poor management or lack of discipline. But when I discovered the truth, I realised there was nothing accidental or undisciplined about it.

This was indeed a well-planned operation; executed with military precision. Isolation, segregation, intimidation, threats, bullying, malice and deceit were all openly mixed into a cocktail of organised chaos which served as an elaborate distraction to take our minds off what was actually going on.

The fly in the ointment for them, so to speak, and one of the major reasons for their eventual exposure, was our little group; hand-selected by God. When we got together, we compared notes. We discussed what we saw, and we started to plan what we could do about it. The first big mistake DSA made was hiring four people at the same time who had already worked well together for years.

Our little group had a long established history together. We trusted each other. We all understood our workplace rights. We'd all held positions of authority. We all understood how government departments worked or were supposed to work. And not one of us was afraid to speak openly about things which concerned us.

Despite what it looked like, small and insignificant, our little group was the beginning of the end for their plans. They just didn't know it at the time. Neither did we.

Expanding our circle of influence

After the shocking discussion I'd had with Janice that Friday afternoon, I was not able to stop thinking about DSA. The more I tried to forget, the more I remembered, and so despite my best efforts, I couldn't concentrate on anything else. My whole weekend was ruined, and by Monday I was drained and exhausted.

When I dragged myself to work on Monday morning, I was fully expecting to be told to turn around and go straight back home - jobless. But, to my great surprise, that didn't happen. Shortly after I arrived and began my work, Jack came to the pod.

"Erik has decided to keep ya'on for a while longer." His face was expressionless...a good sign. "Y'didn't make any errors on Friday."

I breathed a sigh of relief and quietly thanked God for my second reprieve in as many weeks.

"By the way," he continued. "Con has been relocated from the top floor to the basement. He'll be commencin' in a new role and won't have the time he used to have to deal with agency staff matters."

I wondered what new job Con was doing. But I knew better than to ask, so I kept my mouth firmly closed, even though I was bursting with curiosity.

Jack read my face - interesting that he did, I would have to watch that. "Con's been placed in charge of correctin' all the ASIO errors. When y'make a mistake, he's the one who fixes it," he explained. "He's flat out at the moment, so don't contact him unless y'need to."

He turned to leave but then paused like he had something else to say. "If everyone adjusts as well as you, he won't be flat out for long."

Was that a compliment? Shock of shocks!

Without waiting for my response, he turned away again, and as he left he bellowed in a commanding, almost threatening tone, "Keep it up!"

Hmmm, yes, well, that was more like it!

I couldn't wait to tell the girls I'd had a reprieve. They were as anxious to know as I was. When lunchtime came around, I bolted out the door, set up the yellow cloth in our usual spot and was soon surrounded by friendly faces.

"You look happy," Cassie said.

"It must be good news," echoed Janice.

"Yes, yes, yes," I said, grinning from ear to ear, as we started unwrapping our lunches.

"I'm glad for you, Monica," Jennifer said, "but I'm furious! These people are barbarians! I don't know how they can get away with treating people like this."

We stopped unwrapping our lunches and looked at her. "They've told Beryl that if she does jury duty, she'll be fired."

"What?" I said. Beryl was an older lady who had only been at DSA a few weeks. She worked on the top floor just down from Jennifer and Cassie, who now shared a pod.

"Beryl was notified last week," Jennifer explained. "She brought the letter in and showed it to Con, who took it to Erik. When he returned, he told her if she took time off for jury duty she wouldn't have a job to come back to." Jennifer opened her soft drink with a snap. "I'm livid," she said and took a long swig of iced tea.

"I thought bosses were supposed to exempt staff called to jury duty." I looked around at the others. They were nodding in agreement.

"How dare they use threats to stop people from doing jury duty!" Jennifer continued, "I thought we were living in Australia, not some jack-boot, fascist dictatorship."

"What's she going to do?" asked Janice.

"She's upset about having her job threatened," said Cassie in her always soothing manner. "When I spoke to her at morning tea, she didn't know what to do."

Jennifer began to calm down. "I advised her to write a letter to the court telling them about her situation, including that her job had been threatened if she attended."

"That'll do it, Jennifer," I said

"I hope they take some kind of action!" said Cassie.

"Probably not!" said Jennifer still agitated. "This is Defence. They're too powerful."

My mind flashed to the Maralinga, HMAS Voyager, Vietnam Vets, Agent Orange, F111 de-seal/re-sealers and Navy asbestos claims, to name just a few of the nasty, difficult, long, strung-out battles for justice which had been fought by countless military personnel against Defence bureaucrats in my lifetime. Most of them taking so long the people fighting for justice grew old and died, or died young of the terminal illness they were complaining about, before ever seeing justice.

The military versus Defence – it was an old and on-going story. Not even our military was able to win against the all-powerful Defence machine.

I nodded my agreement with Jennifer, "Yes, you know the old saying, Jennifer, 'no one wins against Defence'."

At that moment, two of our fellow agency workers, Owen and Jim, came down the path and around the shady tree, lunches in hand and great big smiles on their faces.

"Well, doesn't this look civilised," said Jim, pulling up a bench seat and plonking his lunch on the table.

"A bit too posh for me," laughed Owen. "Do you mind if we join you ladies?"

"Oh, I'm so glad you could make it," said Janice smiling her most welcoming smile. Turning back to us she said, "Jim and Owen work in the dungeon with me. I invited them ages ago." She turned back to the men. "But this is the first time you've deigned to show."

I was already on smiling terms with Owen and nodding terms with Jim. Cassie had worked with both of them when she worked in the dungeon, before being relocated to the top floor. Only Jennifer needed to be introduced. Jennifer shook hands across the table, and we began to eat our lunches. The dynamic had just shifted. We were glad to have them, they were glad to be with us, but no one was sure what to say.

"You were right Janice. This garden is beautiful," Owen began. He was eating his lunch, and his gaze was taking in the broad expanse of lawn with its long-established trees and well-kept gardens. "This has got to be the nicest place in these barracks. How come there's no one else here?"

"Apparently the lizards frighten them away," Cassie drawled, and we all laughed. The ice was broken.

We chatted for a while, getting to know the guys, letting them get to know us.

Owen was a Samoan Australian, a family man, father to two young children and husband to a very, very pretty young wife. He pulled out his wallet and showed us a picture. So proud! We found out he was a devout Christian, a joker and someone who didn't know how to walk around without a genuine smile on his face.

Jim was a tall, slender, quietly spoken, young, good-natured university student who had taken a break from uni and was planning on going back to full-time study in 2010.

We discovered after a bit of testing, these two men thought the same way we did. They were seeing what we were seeing; they didn't like it either.

"We won't be in the dungeon for much longer," said Jim, beginning to open up, "Owen's, going to the middle floor, where Monica is, and I'm going upstairs."

"It should be your turn soon, Janice," said Owen.

"Oh, I don't think I'll be going upstairs," said Janice. "It seems they don't think I'm able to do the job."

"That's not right..." Cassie said softly.

"Of course you can do the job..." I said.

"It's not rocket surgery..." laughed Owen.

"You're breathing aren't you? You're qualified!" said Jennifer, munching on her sandwich.

"Leave your intelligence at the door!" Jim concluded, summing up the way we all felt.

"It's not about what you can do, Janice," said Owen trying to be both blunt and gentle at the same time. "It's whether they like you or not."

"What do you mean?" asked Janice.

Owen turned to Jim, "Do you remember what happened to Kylie?"

Jim nodded to Owen and explained to us, "it was just before you all started."

"Kylie was fired because she didn't say 'hello' properly," Owen said with a hint of disgust in his voice.

"No way!" We chorused, all shaking our heads.

"Uh, huh," Jim nodded. "She came in one morning... said hallo...but didn't smile submissively as she said it."

"The smiling assassin reported her for bad workplace attitude," Owen continued.

"Dora came in and fired her that day," Jim concluded.

"That's not anywhere near legal!" said Jennifer.

"Who's going to know?" asked Jim

"Secret organisation and all that..." said Owen

"Con didn't like her," said Jim, "so she lost her job."

"It had nothing to do with her skills or work performance," Owen concluded.

"So they don't like me," said Janice. "Is that what you're saying?"

The men said nothing but their gentle eyes said it all.

"Who is 'they'?" asked Cassie.

"'They' is Con," said Jim. "He's the one who decides who stays or goes."

"Is that why you call him 'the smiling assassin'?" drawled Cassie.

Jim nodded. "He's vicious!"

"Todd got the bullet today," said Owen, "another one bites the dust."

"Yeah," confirmed Jim. "He was, talking to me, telling me a joke. I saw Con coming, and I signalled him to stop, but he just kept going. Anyway, the punch line had a swear word in it, and Con heard."

"Oh, no!" We all groaned.

"Con must've disliked him. He went straight upstairs to Erik and dobbed him in," Jim continued.

"Dora came in today and fired him," Janice said. "The official reason was 'negative workplace attitude'."

"Poor guy," said Owen."He'd only been at DSA three weeks. He probably didn't know what hit him."

"They're all such hypocrites," said Jennifer. "We're surrounded by Defence personnel who swear all day."

"That's true," I nodded, "I'm amazed it's allowed."

Owen laughed, "They don't seem to know how to talk without swearing."

"No fear of being sacked!" said Janice.

"Todd probably thought it was acceptable," said Jim.

As strong as we tried to be, the pressure was getting to all of us. It was so hard to maintain a positive attitude when all we could think about was how we were being treated, when we were going to be sacked, what excuse they were going to use and who was going to disappear next.

"See the stains on the wall over there?" Owen asked with a face full of mischief. He was looking across to the ten-foot-high sandstone wall, so we followed his gaze. There was a section without plants where the chopped wood for the bar-b-que was stored. In several places, the iron in the sandstone had 'bled' leaving long, dark, rust-red streaks running down the wall. They could have been mistaken for old blood stains.

"You know the people who disappear don't actually go home," he said, trying to keep a straight face.

We knew what was coming and we all started to chuckle. He had fired our imaginations.

"They get shot at dawn," he continued.

We burst out laughing.

Jim put his finger across his lip and pretended to be Hitler. "You vill not speak, you vill not joke, you vill not svear, you vill not complain and you vill not ask ze qvestions - ve vill ask ze qvestions!" he spat out, in a terrible, but hilarious, attempt at a German accent. "If you do any of zis, you vill be shot!"

Jim wasn't finished. He suddenly started looking around, in a jerky, secretive manner. "Vere do you zink zey buried za bodies?" He asked us.

Owen was ready for it. "The bodies are buried in the garden - that's why the flowers look so healthy."

We all roared with laughter. We were holding our sides and tears were streaming down our faces. The guys had struck a chord. And it felt so good to laugh at our antagonists.

Our tranquil oasis was a life saver. It gave us a kind of out-of-body experience; a place where we could detach ourselves from the reality of our daily horror story, catch our breath and be ourselves again.

That first day, just as we were about to go back to work, Owen suddenly pulled up the tablecloth, reached under the table and began patting around as if he was looking for something. "Did you check for bugs?" he asked.

We all chuckled, and warned him the eight-legged bugs under the table might bite! But we understood where he was coming from. He had verbalised something each of us had secretly wondered about but never put into words. Were our conversations being monitored? We didn't know. He was joking, of course, we all knew that, but there was an uncomfortable reality in what he was implying. Yep, here was a man we could trust.

The first of three significant events

During the next week, the first of three significant events happened. The other two events would happen later, and they each played a major part in opening my eyes to the corruption the DSA managers were trying so hard to hide.

I was suddenly moved into a cubicle with three analysts. This was a silly move by DSA for it meant I would be sitting next to people who followed the vetting procedure approved by Parliament. Correct procedure! It would only be a matter of time before I discovered the double standard.

I had three pod-fellows; Crystal, who despite the inhuman rules attached to agency staff was to become a firm friend, Linda, who turned out to be a trusted ally and Cleo, who seemed to be related to Attila-the-Hun.

After being introduced to my three new pod-fellows, I was basically left alone. So I sat quietly in my corner, doing my work, minding my own business and pretending I didn't exist. I must admit, I felt a little jealous that these three people around me had the freedom to chat with each other about whatever came into their heads; office gossip, office politics, jokes, swearing (which was accepted...how bizarre!), hobbies, their families, what they did on the weekend and all the other usual things people talk about at work, while I had to force myself not to listen, not to enter in and not to offer up my thoughts as well.

This was particularly hard for me when a question was being asked to the group about something work-related like how to spell a particular word or the location of some building in the city. If I knew the answer I still, with great difficulty, had to keep my mouth shut. It was like having an annoying itch and not being allowed to scratch. Argh! So frustrating! The only way to kill the frustration was to shut out the chit-chat by not listening to anything at all, which I learned to do pretty quickly.

Nevertheless, my first real insight into the personalities of these three analysts presented itself a few days after my move. Another new agency person had begun, and as he would be carting files for the analysts, he was brought to the pod by Con and introduced.

"Hello ladies," beamed Con, exuding his usual fake excitement and enthusiasm.

Linda and I were seated with our backs to the aisle, so we turned around, Crystal looked up and was smiling a genuine welcoming smile, but Cleo didn't move.

"This is Brian!" Con gushed as if he was Brian's best friend. "He has just started today and will be bringing you your allocations, so you'll be seeing quite a bit of him."

"Nice to meet you, Brian," Crystal was gracious in her welcome, "I'm Crystal."

"I'm Linda, welcome to DSA," Linda offered.

"Hi! Bye!" Cleo said, facing her computer screen. Then suddenly she turned, and looking directly into Brian's face, laughed at him. It was a mean, challenging laugh.

Everyone was stunned. Brian didn't know what to do. Con stopped smiling and whisked Brian away. Crystal's jaw was almost on the floor. Linda was the first to speak.

"Cleo!" she was shocked, and her face was showing anger. "What a nasty thing to say!"

Cleo was still laughing.

"How could you be so mean?" Crystal was going pink in the face, "why did you say that?"

Cleo looked over at me and was still laughing as she spoke. "They never stay long." She was looking directly into my eyes and pointedly referring to me but speaking as if I wasn't there. "I figure I'll get my good-bye's in early."

Not nice! This was personal. Cleo obviously resented sharing her work-space with a common agency staffer.

Crystal and Linda looked over to me to see if I was upset. I wasn't. I had come to expect this attitude from DSA personnel. Though I could see Crystal and Linda looking at me, my eyes were on Cleo. She was laughing into my face, but her eyes were as hard as nails. I held her gaze until she stopped laughing. What a nasty piece of work – well, at least I know!

Linda and Crystal watched me. It was like time was standing still. Then, when Cleo stopped laughing, Linda gave Crystal a knowing look, turned her back to Cleo and went on with her work.

Crystal was mortified. "I'm so sorry, Monica," she said softly. "We're not all like that." She was searching my face for a response.

"I can see that, Crystal," I said and smiled into her eyes. Here was someone with a heart. I liked her from that moment. That was the beginning of our friendship.

Cleo probably didn't understand what had just happened. Bullies usually aren't too bright. But we three understood the dynamic in the pod had just changed. Now it was Crystal, Linda and me. Cleo had just become the odd-one-out.

That same day, Owen arrived on my floor. He was moved up from the dungeon to the desk I had vacated and was beginning to process applications. This gave each of us added support because it allowed both of us to see first hand how the other was being treated. I finally had a truly friendly face on my floor.

The timing of his move was perfect, for chaos was about to erupt, big time!

The new procedures were suddenly changed again, and both Owen and I were now in the position to hear what the DSA analysts thought about the changes. Unlike agency staff, the analysts *were* allowed to complain about management decisions.

The implementation of the previous new procedures had caused an uproar amongst the analysts who, to my surprise, had not been told about them. They were insulted that their professional responsibility had been passed to untrained agency staff. And they complained long and loud that agency staff had now been placed in the position of telling them what to do.

That was fair comment, and it made them despise us even more. I'd thought we couldn't be despised any more than we already were, but apparently, I was wrong!

The offending procedures had made agency staff responsible for everything from entering data at the beginning, to sending the ASIO report at the end, excluding analysts by making sure there were no blanks in the data for them to check. From start to finish agency staff had been given the task of streamlining applications so they would be accepted by ASIO without an analyst needing to do anything except sign off the physical file.

This deliberate exclusion of analysts from the vetting process was a time-saving approach deliberately put in place by DSA management, which would allow more applications to be processed in a shorter time, making DSA more money. Yes, money! The bottom line, as usual, was money!

Clearances cost money. The people who wanted them had to pay for them. The higher the clearance, the more they cost. So, logically, the more clearances DSA could process in a year, the more money Defence could make in a year. Not just pennies, I'm talking multiple tens of millions! Clearances are a multi-million dollar business. We were in a Global Economic Crisis, and this was DSAs solution.

The problem was, Janice, myself and other conscientious agency staff thought our roles involved keeping Australia safe, silly us! So instead of going along with their illegal 'streamlining concept' we had been sending applications with missing information to the analysts instead of completing the process from start to finish ourselves, as ordered. Oops!

Our yellow stickers were the catalyst for everything which followed. They set up a domino effect which caused havoc! By means of those pesky little yellow stickers, the Defence analysts found out what was being done and hit the roof because the responsibility which had long belonged to them, and legally belonged to them, had just been given to agency staff who didn't have any vetting qualifications.

They pointed out, and rightly so, analysts had been properly trained to identify fake documents, to recognise when extra data would be required, to know when they could legally forgo an official document, or when the information provided was 'of concern' and would need further follow up. Now, suddenly, they only needed to make phone calls if untrained agency staff told them to? I didn't blame them for being angry!

So, after just two weeks, those new 'you beaut' procedures were thrown out and replaced with another set. This time though the analysts were aware of what was happening, so they went over the changes with a fine tooth comb and continued to complain. With every complaint, the procedures changed again, with major changes being made every few weeks. This went on for months, causing great upheaval, discontent and confusion.

DSA management couldn't seem to get it right, and I began to wonder if they actually wanted to get it right. It seemed not! The rules kept changing despite the fact the original official procedures were still the only approved Federal standard ratified by Parliament and should have been followed as they were.

The physical reality for staff was that procedures were constantly changing yet nothing was written down. For me, that meant my memory was sorely tested and my flexibility was stretched to the limit. Nevertheless, I tried to keep up, we all did, but the place was in chaos and it seemed nobody knew what was going on. Everywhere I looked there was nothing but confusion, anger and misery.

How the hammer fell on Janice

Two weeks after Owen and I changed pods, Janice's worst suspicions were confirmed. She was still working on the considerable backlog of top-secret applications, entering the data, sending the complete reports to ASIO and handing those with missing data back to the team leader or an analyst. The trouble was she couldn't keep up. Applications for top-secret clearances were coming in faster than they were going out, so the backlog kept growing. And Janice was the only one working on entering them.

"What are all these files?" Helga demanded to know, pointing to the overflowing tubs of files in the passageway outside the pod where Janice was working. Helga was a short, dark-haired, officious woman in her early fifties with a thick European accent, who was always abrupt and could be counted on to be nasty. Everyone avoided her if they could. Her question to Janice was rhetorical. She already knew the files she was pointing to were top-secret files. Everyone did! It was written all over them – in thick red marker ink! This was not about the files, this was about Janice. This was the beginning of the 'firing process'.

Helga was holding a large pile of top-secret files with yellow stickers on them (Janice recognised them as the files she had given back to Francine and Betty) and was staring down at the three large plastic tubs of files on the floor in the aisle outside Janice's pod. "They need to be processed," she barked, stating the obvious.

Without waiting for an answer from Janice, Helga dumped the files she was carrying into one of the already overflowing tubs and hurried out the door. A few minutes later she was back with Paula, the second in command.

Paula always reminded me of the 'White Witch' from the Narnia Chronicles – sincere apologies to CS Lewis - she was young, tall, slim, blonde, beautiful in a pale sort of way, and cold as ice! We called her the 'Ice Queen'! Like Erik, she refused to look at agency staff and avoided speaking directly to us whenever possible. When she couldn't avoid speaking to us, she would still avoid our faces. Her eyes would always look past us, to something or someone else as she spoke.

I'll never forget the time she was addressing Defence personnel. They were having a meeting in the next pod to mine so I couldn't escape overhearing what was said. The analysts were being told about changes to their seating arrangements. Normally, they didn't get shuffled around every few days or weeks as we did, but now they were being ordered to move, yet were apparently being asked what they thought of the new arrangements. None of them held back. They all told Paula they wished to stay where they were, pointing out they were not agency staff, and expecting her to listen to their group consensus. When they'd finished, she gave her response.

"I've told you how it's going to be," she said, emphasising this as her final word by turning to leave the pod, "get used to it."

As she left, the analysts began to grumble.

"Why'd she bother asking us?"

"So she could report she 'consulted' with us."

"A waste of time..."

"They never listen..."

Paula couldn't be pleasant, even to the Defence personnel. The analysts knew there was no point arguing with her, or even trying to express an opinion, she would never act on their concerns. We knew that since Defence personnel were treated so badly, agency staff didn't stand a chance. We were simply sacked on the spot if we disagreed with her. And now poor Janice was about to get one of her tongue-lashings.

"Why are there so many applications?" She was standing outside the pod and looking down at the tubs. "How many are there?"

“Around fifty,” replied Janice, thinking it was easy to see how many there were.

“Why aren’t they done?”

Because I’m the only one doing them,” Janice’s tone was docile, “and I have to fit them in with my other work.”

Paula had picked up one of the ‘yellow stickered’ files and was flipping through it. “Why is this a problem?”

“I don’t have the correct dates...” Janice began.

“Work it out!”

“But if the dates aren’t there...”

“Put it through!” Paula threw the file back into the tub. “I want all of these processed today.”

“Many of them will not get through the ASIO database,” said Janice, oh-oh, she was arguing. This would not end well! No one could argue with the Ice Queen and get away with it! Nevertheless, though Janice knew she was not allowed to have an opinion, integrity was knocking and she had to answer the door, so she continued, “They’ll just bounce back as ‘errors’.”

Paula froze. “How could you possibly know that?” The words shot out of her mouth like frozen darts, and her tone was scathing as if Janice had stumbled onto some hidden mystery she had no right to discover.

“That’s what I’ve experienced...”

“Don’t you worry about the ‘errors’,” Paula warned. Then, pausing to compose herself, she said calmly and far too sweetly, “you won’t receive any blame for them.” And without another word she turned and left the room.

“Oh no,” Janice thought, “I’ve done it now.”

“Push them through,” Helga barked at Janice as she scurried after Paula, out the door and back up the stairs.

That day, against her better judgement, and knowing there would be a huge jump in ASIO errors, Janice obeyed her orders and put through fifty top-secret applications, complete with reports to ASIO.

She knew, as you know, when you know, when you know, that no matter how hard she worked the repercussions for her brazen attempt at confrontation were coming, and coming fast! No-one could argue with the Ice Queen and get away with it. The dye had been cast. Janice's fate had been sealed.

She was right, of course.

The next day, when the errors were counted, Janice was blamed for them as expected. DSA management was becoming so predictable! She was told she was being relieved of her data-entry duties because she was making too many errors. Of course! But, though she knew she would be punished somehow, she couldn't have guessed how degrading her punishment would be.

Her 'demotion' consisted of being made to carry large, heavy tubs of mail up and down the narrow stairs, out of the building, across the road and past the quadrant to the buildings on the other side of the next road, where the mail was delivered to and collected from.

Brian, a solid man in his mid-thirties, had been doing this lifting and carting since his humiliating first day and was often seen huffing, puffing and sweating as he transported the heavy tubs around the building. Now this job had been given to Janice. Unbelievable! This was a disgusting job to give to a slightly built woman just shy of sixty years old. This was way past bullying, way past harassment – this was abuse! But it didn't stop there...

She was also required to do the 'filing spreadsheet' and needed a computer to do the entries. The trouble with this was, she was not allocated a desk and therefore had no computer. Talk about stress! Were they trying to give her a heart attack?

From that time on until her final day with DSA, Janice wandered around looking for a spare desk and computer so she could complete her given tasks. I would often see her walking past my pod, holding a cardboard box filled with the office supplies she needed to do her job, looking for a place to sit, even for a few hours. Disgraceful!

Finally, she'd been forced into the dreadful self-defeating position of having to make a complaint, knowing that making a complaint would bring instant dismissal. But she contacted Dora nonetheless.

"I thought I'd be hearing from you," Dora said in a tone which didn't inspire confidence.

"Yes, I don't have a desk!" Janice began.

"Con told me you'd complained to him about it in front of the two new agency staff members."

Janice went cold. What a snake! Those two new staff were in the same small pod as Con. They couldn't help but overhear every conversation. Way to twist the truth, Con!

"I didn't complain, I was merely asking for a desk."

Dora wasn't listening. "You've also been complaining about the tasks you've been given to do."

"I've not complained," said Janice. It was like talking to a brick wall. "I just don't think it's appropriate or safe for someone of my age to be asked to cart heavy tubs of mail..."

"If Defence wants you to shred paper all day, or stand on your head, what is that to you?" interrupted Dora, "you should be willing and happy because you are, after all, still being paid the same as all the other contractors."

What? What did money have to do with it? Janice couldn't believe her ears. Where was the support?

"I'd like you to find me another position, outside Defence please, Dora," said Janice. "I took this job on the understanding my data entry skills would be used. If I'd known I would have to lump and load heavy boxes all day I'd have turned this position down."

"There's nothing available," Dora said sharply, "you would do well just to do the job you're paid to do."

It was obvious Dora would not be of any assistance. She was sold out to Defence and would do anything Erik wanted. But why was Janice being forced to stay when so many others were sacked over nothing? Did they just enjoy torturing her? It seemed so! She had now tried to quit, but her resignation had been refused. Why? She didn't know...

It was also obvious Con, the smiling assassin, was behind what was happening to Janice. When he reported someone to Dora, whether his report was true or false, it was taken as Gospel, and no questions were ever asked. In hindsight, it was easy for all of us to see that if Con hadn't been so nasty, more people would have kept their jobs. He was one of 'them'. So was Dora. We - all the other agency staff - had been thrown to the dogs.

Unbelievable brain-twisting mind games

A few days after Janice's demotion, the monthly Agency team meeting with Dora was due. I was told this one would be special, as Erik was putting in a rare - actually, a first - appearance. It was obvious he had something urgent to share with agency staff.

At the beginning of the meeting Erik introduced himself for the benefit of the new staff - there were always new agency contractors, at least four each month, but sometimes six - then bluntly said what he was there to say.

"Defence is a blame-oriented organisation," he actually said this with a hint of pride, "and there are certain expectations management have of all staff. There have been queries of late about weight limits."

He was looking at Janice now. I held my breath.

Janice had not been able to carry full tubs of mail and so had been lightening the load and making extra trips. Sometimes, Brian had been able to assist her by kindly offering to carry her excess mail in his tub to save her the extra trips. But now it seemed someone, probably Con, had reported her to Erik.

"The standard for everyone in Defence is 16 kilos." You could have heard a pin drop. "Defence expects its personnel to be able to carry a weight of up to 16 kilos over long distances if necessary."

What? I was horrified! I felt like screaming at him, 'that applies to strong, young men and women who are going through basic military training with backpacks on! It doesn't apply to sixty-year-old office workers!'

"So I expect all DSA staff to be prepared to carry loads of up to 16 kilos."

DSA staff? We were not DSA staff, we were agency staff. We didn't work under Defence rules but under civilian rules. He had forgotten that small detail and was applying Defence regulations to civilians. Was this even legal? Of course, it wasn't! Could we say so? No!

"There has been a sudden increase in errors lately, and so there needs to be more attention to detail," he continued.

Wonderful! Now he was making it sound like we were inefficient as well as stupid. Everyone in the room knew the errors he was referring to had nothing to do with 'attention to detail'. They were not typos. They were ASIO errors. They existed because there were no details to 'pay attention to'. Everyone knew this small fact except Dora, who didn't have a clue, and we weren't allowed to enlighten her.

Erik continued. "Formal training has been overlooked of late for reasons unknown..."

Honestly? How could the reasons be unknown to him, he was the boss for goodness sake! Another lie! Did he ever tell the truth?

"...however, I have introduced refresher training as a quality control measure." Then he concluded, "This training will commence tomorrow."

After Erik had left the room, Dora took up the issue of 'attention to detail'.

"I'm very disappointed there are so many errors being made by this team," she said. "Every one of you was personally referred by me because your skill-set testing results showed you have high visual accuracy, but the number of errors coming through shows you are not working to capacity."

Great! Now let's get lectured for something we're not doing wrong by someone who has no clue what we do. Typical! But we, sadly, were used to it. And we handled it the way we always did. We sat in a circle, listening to Pandora waffle on, saying nothing, and waiting for the meeting to finish.

Dora looked down at her list. "I'd like you to all provide me with your work phone numbers..."

"That's not possible, Dora," interjected Con. "I'm the only agency staff member authorised to take or make phone calls. The others have not been allocated a phone. When you need to speak to them, they use my phone."

How did she not know we had no phones? How long had she been sending people here? A year? Two years? No one said a word, we all kept our faces straight, but it wasn't easy. This woman didn't know how ridiculous she sounded. How could she possibly keep up the farce of being our boss? She didn't have any idea what the job entailed.

"Well, in that case, you'll all need to buy mobile phones and have them turned on, on silent, and sitting on your desk in case I wish to phone you during work hours."

Oh, please! Like DSA would let us do that! We get fired for talking! Speaking on a mobile would be suicide! *Come on!* She continued looking at Con for confirmation and Con nodded as if that was an okay idea.

What? I couldn't believe it - why was he keeping her in fantasy land?

Dora continued, "I've been trying to email some of you, and the emails just keep bouncing back, so I need to be able to contact you."

Oh! She had to be kidding! Didn't she know this was an intelligence organisation; that every email was monitored? Was she on another planet?

Suddenly Con looked up from his note taking wide-eyed and excited. "I'd like to announce that I'm now the new ASIO Interface Error Report Coordinator." He sounded like he wanted us to clap. In reality, his new role meant he would spend all day 'fixing errors', that is, making up fake information and sending it to ASIO as truth.

"Tomorrow's training will confirm which format the ASIO system needs you to use in order for information to pass through the system successfully," Con concluded.

"Oh, and congratulations on low absenteeism," interjected Dora, smiling her sweetest - most hideous - smile. "You're all showing your professionalism."

This woman was truly off with the pixies. Didn't she know we were under threat of job loss if we took time off? Oh, wait! Of course she did! She handed out the threats! Professional? Who was she trying to kid? There was nothing professional about any of this. My brain hurt. This was all too far from normal. Too twisted! Too insane!

Trained to outsmart the ASIO database

The next day, as promised by Erik, agency staff were ushered into the conference room for 'group training'. This was the first time I'd attended 'group training' within DSA. 'Refresher course'? No! This was a first! We were about to be trained, on masse, to outsmart the ASIO database. Although we didn't think of it that way at the time, that is precisely what we were being trained to do.

On the way to the training, a vague hope flashed through my mind. Maybe we were going to be given the list of sensitive database fields I'd previously requested of Jack? Of course, that hope didn't last long. Once the training began, it only took me a moment to realise I was being way too optimistic.

There were no lists. There were no procedures. There was nothing in writing. Of course, silly me! Training was by overhead projection. And nothing much was new. We were still required to enter everything we could from the applications, but when the information was missing it was implied, but never stated exactly, we had to be inventive. This is where it became vague and tricky.

- "Remove incomplete data..."
- "Alter dates...make them match..."
- "When mandatory data is missing...fill it in..."
- "Copy previous information...repeat it..."
- "Don't leave gaps..."

ASIO errors, it appeared, could only be fixed if we added information which wasn't written down; information which didn't actually exist. Ironic that while we were being openly lectured on 'paying attention to detail', we were being secretly taught that errors could only be fixed by doing the exact opposite; *not* 'paying attention to detail'.

There were no 'red flags' for ASIO to see!

There was never any mention of special sentences or code words which could be used to show ASIO the information was unreliable. We were not given special streets, like 'fake street', 'suspect street' or 'unknown street' to enter as red flags. There were no warnings at all! The word 'workarounds' didn't exist in DSA language as far as I knew, I never once heard it used. Neither was there any mention of adding comments to explain what we had added, deleted, copied or expanded.

What was impressed on us more clearly than anything else was that from now on no applications with missing information were to be given to analysts. "No more yellow stickers!" We could only give errant files to team leaders, but even then, the cases had to be extreme, that is, only when there was a lot of missing data. This instruction was another threat! We were not to hand applications back without very good reason – or else!

The rhetoric on how to 'fill in the gaps' was deliberately vague, but the threats which accompanied it were explicit. Anyone who didn't implement the vagaries would be out of a job. Oh, this place was a nightmare!

In short, it was made abundantly clear our job was to just 'fill in all the gaps' ourselves, by whatever means, and get the reports through to the ASIO database, no matter what. The strong implication was ASIO was aware of this arrangement and would pick up any inconsistencies at their end. How they would pick them up was not explained.

It took me quite a while to realise the information we were entering could never be picked up by ASIO. I later learned, to my shame, the false information we entered into the system had permanently contaminated the ASIO database with false information; information they could never find, and therefore never correct unless it was pointed out!

In hindsight, the harsh reality was, we were all being deliberately trained to falsify information and lie to ASIO in order to speed the processing of applications for the sake of money. We just didn't know it. I didn't know it!

Though I thought the information we were being given was vague and dodgy sounding, I reminded myself this was intelligence. It was probably supposed to sound vague and dodgy. The 'need-to-know' rule had been drummed into us; we would only ever be told what we needed to know, nothing more. But then I wondered, wasn't this one of those need-to-know times?

There were no answers to these questions. And I wasn't allowed to ask questions anyway. It was all a bit much, really. I had to let it go. Greater minds than mine had made this decision. Who was I to question anything?

Even though DSA's willingness to flout the rules and thumb their noses at established security procedures was staring me directly in the face, I couldn't see it. I didn't want to believe they would actually do anything opposed to Australia's best interest. That is, until my eyes started to open during the lunchtime conversation that same day.

A shocking revelation

As usual, Janice, Cassie, Jennifer, Owen, Jim and myself had gathered around the yellow cloth in our tranquil garden oasis, and Janice opened the conversation with an unusual question. "Have any of you received your secret-level clearance?"

"No," said Cassie.

"Nor me," I said.

Jennifer took a bite of her sandwich and shook her head.

"I have," said Owen. "It came through this week."

"So did mine," said Jim.

"I'm only asking because I haven't received mine yet," Janice explained, "and I was doing all those top-secret applications."

"At least you have a 'restricted'," said Owen. "I didn't even have a restricted clearance when I first started doing them."

"What?" I was shocked. "No clearance at all?"

"You could have been a terrorist..." Cassie joked.

"Maybe he is!" Janice laughed.

"How did you get onto the Base, Owen?" My mind flicked back to all those times I'd gone swimming at the Richmond RAAF Base when I was a child. I always had to ride my bike the three miles to the pool alone because my friends didn't have passes. It boggled my mind that Owen had been able to freely come and go onto one of our military bases daily without any form of clearance or pass. I was horrified.

"I was working here for a week before my restricted came through," Owen confirmed.

"Accessing top-secret data, with no clearance at all," said Jennifer, "that's intelligent!"

"How did you get through the gates?" I asked.

"The guards never asked me for my clearance," Owen explained, "I didn't think it was a big deal."

Again I was horrified. I'd grown up around military bases. No one was ever allowed in without a pass. The guards always checked. And now, here I was working in DSA, the centre responsible for those passes, and checking passes was irrelevant? Having them was irrelevant?

We were all required to have a secret-level clearance to do the work we were doing, and to gain one we all had to submit to a police check and a detailed investigation of the last ten years of our lives. None of us should have been doing this work without the proper clearance. My mind flashed back to the Army Officer who had given us our IT training. What would she think about all this I wondered?

I was dumbfounded, but my personal shock went unnoticed, and the conversation continued.

Janice was making light of it all. "The way I'm going, I'll probably be out of here before my secret clearance comes through."

"You and half the other agency staff," drawled Cassie, smiling.

"I wonder if that means all the work we've done is invalid?" Janice said, laughing.

The question was innocent. Janice was merely trying to make a joke, but the joke was ignored, and her thinking was taken seriously.

"That's a good question," said Owen without a smile.

Jennifer was nodding. "I wonder why they want short-term people without clearances entering this data?" she asked casually.

We all stopped eating.

I looked up at Jennifer, she was looking at me. She *had* noticed my shock and was on the ball as usual. Her question hit the nail right on the head.

The penny suddenly dropped for all of us with a 'kaboom' rather than a 'clink'. Yes! Why did they want short-term people without clearances entering this data?

No one said a word.

Things had suddenly gone from bad to worse. There was nothing specific; just a vague nagging that something was very wrong. I couldn't grasp the logic of it. It didn't make sense. Yet, I was suddenly aware of a strong but imprecise perception we were all party to something which shouldn't be happening; we were seeing things we shouldn't be seeing, and worse, we could all very well be real live pawns in a deceitful game of chess.

I began to imagine a nasty possibility:

- Question by an imaginary high-up official: *"Please explain this inconsistency..."*
- Response by a faceless DSA authority: *"That was done by an agency temp...didn't know what they were doing... fired for incompetence...a one-off..."*

My mind was going numb. There were just too many questions. What were they hiding? What were they getting us to do that we shouldn't be doing?

The silence continued. The possibilities were scary. We all knew it. Eventually, with unspoken consensus, we shook off our thoughts and began a new subject. After all, we truly didn't know if we were being bugged or not. Any further exploration of this topic would have to wait until we were in a safer place.

> *What does it say about the Department of Defence...? They were telling their bosses they were not comfortable with this and their bosses were saying, "Get on with your job."*
> (ABC 20 Sept. 2011)

**Did they really think
they would
get away with it?**

CHAPTER THREE

Personal threats? Of course!

Defence and the Recruitment Agency supplying temporary employees to DSA were jointly involved in the deception and mistreatment of agency staff. During the two years false information was being fed to ASIO, Defence called the shots, and the recruitment agency fired the gun.

The question had to be asked, why was a recruitment agency collaborating in this misconduct? Surely they had a duty of care to protect their employees. These employees were their responsibility. Surely they had the authority to point out to DSA any breaches of law and remove their employees until the breaches were addressed?

DSA management had a clear motive for their abuse and corruption of agency staff; they wanted to cover their deception, which was motivated by money. But what motive could the recruitment agency possibly have to subject its employees to such brutality?

The answer again was money. Always money!

The recruitment agency was not only receiving a portion of each of the twenty or so salaries every week as payment for supplying staff to Defence but were also receiving a commission for every single clearance application completed by the agency employees working in DSA. For them, this was where the money was.

This commission was so lucrative Dora called it the agency's 'bread and butter'. She made it clear to us individual employees didn't matter. Agency staff were temporary, not supposed to last. But the clearances? The clearances were everything! They were making the real money. They were keeping the agency in business. The great push from Dora was always 'more clearances'. What we had to do, or go through, to get them done was irrelevant.

A mountain view of the battleground is grand, but we didn't see things so clearly from the trenches. We were caught in a muddle of not knowing what was going on. We couldn't understand the cruelty, and we were constantly perplexed by Dora's hard-hearted, iron-fisted treatment of staff. Nevertheless, the light of understanding was beginning to break through. There was a glimpse here and a flicker there, just enough to let us know something else was going on, though at first, we couldn't quite work out what that something might be. That was about to change.

A sudden disaster for Owen

A few days after the penny dropped with a kaboom, revealing another little flicker of hidden reality, tragedy struck Owen's family. The events which followed changed the dynamic of our little group to the point where it would eventually be disbanded. The days of lunchtime camaraderie were all but over.

On September 29, 2009, Owen's family, as well as many people in Samoa, felt the effect of an earthquake which measured at 8.1, the most powerful earthquake recorded in 2009. About ten minutes later the sea rose up into four great tsunami waves, which raced towards the Islands of Samoa, American Samoa and Tonga with overwhelming speed. Samoa took the greatest hit. There was no time to prepare. Owen's family was caught in the giant wave.

"Oh, Owen," said Cassie putting a comforting hand on his arm.

"I'm so sorry," said Janice, with tears in her eyes.

"What can we do?" asked Jennifer, her tone was unusually soft.

It wasn't lunchtime. It was our morning tea break. We were standing outside in the shade of a nearby tree and only had a few minutes.

"Pray! Just pray..." Owen looked off into the distance like he was wondering whether or not to tell us something terrible. I'd never seen him without a smile, but now his face was full of pain. "We've lost thirteen..." his voice choked, "and there may be another one." He looked at us and his eyes filled with tears, "she's the one who needs prayer..."

"Of course we'll pray, Owen," I said, "and so will our friends."

"She's my cousin. We don't know if she's going to live or not."

"Is she injured?" Cassie asked as gently as possible.

Owen shook his head. "No."

We looked at each other. We were all wondering the same thing, "what was he doing here?"

Telling us his personal news was obviously difficult for Owen. He was never lost for words, but now he couldn't find them. We waited.

"She was holding her baby...nine months old...he was ripped out of her hands...she tried to reach him...she could see his head...but then a sheet of iron..."

I gasped. We all did. We knew what was coming.

"She saw him decapitated...in front of her eyes."

"Oh Owen..." said Jennifer.

"She's blaming herself...she doesn't want to live..."

None of us could say anything. We were horrified.

“My two other aunties are in hospital...there’s no family left to help her.”

Jim broke in, “what are you doing here, man?” Jim may have asked the question, but he spoke for all of us.

“You should be with your family,” Janice said gently.

“My mother’s distraught...there’s so much grief... she wants to go over there...try to help.”

“You need to go home, Owen,” Jennifer said quietly.

“We’ll pray for all of you, including your cousin, but you need to go,” I said.

“Come on, mate,” said Jim putting his hand on Owen’s shoulder, “let’s go and tell Con you’re leaving.”

As they turned to walk back inside the cement building block, our concern was for Owen.

“They won’t let him leave,” said Jennifer.

“Oh, they can’t be that callous,” said Cassie.

“I think they’ll let him leave...he’ll just pay for it later,” I said, wishing I didn’t have to think that way.

“Surely not!” said Cassie. Despite everything she’d heard and experienced, she still continued to hope for and expect the best.

“Well, all we can do is wait and see,” said Janice

They let Owen take leave that day, without firing him, but I had a nagging suspicion he would pay for it when he got back. They didn’t like us taking time off. They didn’t like their victims escaping their control. At this point in time, their hand had been forced, and they couldn’t say no. Saying no in a crisis would have been seen as way too un-Australian. Even DSA management wasn’t that stupid. Owen was, for the moment, untouchable.

Janice leaves on her own terms

While Owen was away, DSA management turned their attention to Janice. Erik had handed down a directive that anyone with downtime should ask their team leaders if they could assist in some other area. Janice found herself with time on her hands, and as the mail, filing and spreadsheets were all up to date, she took the initiative and spoke to Helga.

"I was wondering if anyone needed a hand with something, as I'm free," Janice explained.

"What are you talking about?" Helga barked back in her harsh, abrupt way.

Janice became flustered. "Erik said we should ask...if we'd done our work...if we could help out..."

"You need to speak to Con," Helga interrupted, and without hesitating waved Con over. "Janice is complaining!"

Now Janice was shocked. She tried to explain to Con she was merely asking if she could help out as she had finished her work. But it was no use. He wouldn't listen.

"Complaining is a sackable offence," Con said.

"She is just babbling, talking rubbish," confided Helga to Con. She spoke as if Janice was in another room or on another planet instead of standing right there, listening to everything being said.

Con turned to Janice, his eyes flashing, "you're wasting our time, Janice!" He was angry. "Three people are standing around not able to do their jobs because you are wasting our time."

With that Helga and Con exchanged knowing looks and Helga disappeared up the stairs. Con went back to his desk, and Janice was left wondering what she should do and since she still didn't have a desk, where she should go.

A few minutes later Con called Janice over to his desk. Dora was on the phone.

"I'm just touching base with you Janice to see how you're going." Dora always started her conversations with such calculated sweetness it set our teeth on edge.

"Nothing has changed," Janice replied half-heartedly, wondering if there was any point saying anything at all, "I still have no desk..."

"Well, that's a moot point now anyway," responded Dora. The sweetness was gone.

"I'm sorry, I don't follow," said Janice.

"Erik has asked you be removed."

Janice went cold. This was it. She was being fired. She felt disoriented, and her head began to swim.

Dora continued, "He said you've been complaining and wasting time."

Janice wondered how many times she would have to say it, "I was not compl..."

Dora wasn't listening either, as usual, and spoke over the top of her, "I want you to be professional and stay on until I can find a replacement."

What was that? Stay on? This was too confusing. "So, I'm not fired?" asked Janice perplexed.

"I will inform Erik of your professionalism," said Dora and hung up the phone.

Fired? Not fired? What? Janice couldn't get her head around it, it was too strange. All she could think was they wanted her to continue to work within a secure, secret organisation, even though she'd been fired. That was not intelligent, not even smart! It was absurd! Bizarre! What a twisted, psychotic mess! Janice knew then she needed to come to terms with this unprofessional behaviour and make a firm decision. She'd had enough.

Lunchtime came around, and we all gratefully escaped to the peace and tranquillity of the beautiful sunken garden. Janice wasted no time in telling us what had just happened.

"Why are you still here?" asked Jennifer setting off a rush of encouragement.

"Yes, why don't you just quit?" added Jim.

"You only have to give an hour's notice," said Cassie in her usual calming way.

"Yes, why don't you sack them?" I asked, hoping she would choose to resign because what they were doing to her was too terrible to watch.

"I don't know how you can put up with it another minute!" said Jennifer with compassion in her eyes.

"Well, Janice?" I asked.

Janice gave a wry smile and sighed. "If I'm going to leave Defence, I want to leave on my terms, not theirs. I don't want to be escorted off the base like a criminal, and I don't intend to be. But I have to sleep on it. I don't know exactly what I'm going to do yet."

That night, Janice couldn't sleep at all. She found herself awake for most of the night praying until it seemed clear not only that she should resign, but how and when she should give notice and the attitude she should display while leaving. It was not an easy decision.

The next day Janice resigned.

She didn't tell Dora straight away. Her mobile was nearly out of credit, and we weren't allowed to make calls from the Defence phones, so notifying Dora was not a real option. Besides, there were things Janice wanted to do before she faced that troll. She knew she would be screamed at, and she wanted to maintain her composure. Better to just do what she needed to do first.

She had decided to work her typical day and give notice an hour before knock-off time. Her first port of call was Doug. "Doug, I am giving my notice. I will not be returning tomorrow. Are there any papers I need to sign?"

Without saying a word, Doug reached over picked out the paperwork she needed and passed it to her, placing a pen on top of the papers.

Janice signed the paperwork and handed it back. "Goodbye," she said in the calmest voice she could muster.

Doug gave a sympathetic half smile and a nod but didn't say a word.

Janice visited each of her antagonists and personally said goodbye with a cheery smile and a note of genuine goodwill in her voice. This was who she was. A lady! A Christian! This terrible experience had not changed her nature or her convictions.

Erik wasn't in his office, so she knocked on Paula's door. "I wanted to let you know I'm leaving today. I just wanted to say goodbye."

Paula looked up. She was so stunned at Janice's effrontery she actually looked directly at Janice's face, her eyes glaring with anger. "You're leaving us in the lurch," she barked.

Janice sighed and replied, "The way I feel now, Paula, you wouldn't want me to stay." Then she turned and walked away.

Shortly after knock off time, as we were both walking toward the Roma Street station, Janice's mobile phone rang.

It was Dora. And she was angry! "I have just been informed by Con you've resigned. How could you! This is so unprofessional. I guarantee you this; I will not in the future seek any further work placements for you."

"Dora, you told me yesterday Erik wanted me replaced," said Janice

"That was not a certainty!" yelled Dora.

The penny dropped. Janice realised yesterday's tirade was just part of a game. The sacking wasn't real. It was cruel manipulation. Dora and Defence had only been playing with her, tormenting her, abusing and confusing her - for fun! Now she knew she'd made the right decision.

"Your actions will directly impact on your friends!" Pandora had no tricks left...and she was savage! "Because of you, management will be watching them carefully." The phone made a loud click. Dora had hung up.

Janice closed her mobile and put it in her coat pocket. Her hands were shaking. She wasn't saying anything. This was not good.

We reached the station and went upstairs for coffee. "What's going on, Janice?"

"She just threatened you all," Janice put her head down in her hands, "because of what I did today."

"What?" I was instantly livid! "She threatened *us*?" I asked. I felt a surge of rage. It was not anger. It was more powerful and more controlled. "How dare she threaten us!" I said quietly.

"It's my fault," said Janice, "I shouldn't have..."

"Your fault?" I interrupted. "How in the world can this possibly be your fault? You didn't threaten us!"

"But I resigned..."

"Yes, you did! And you did the right thing!" I knew Janice didn't deserve this final nasty blow.

Then suddenly, the reality of the situation struck me, my fury dissipated completely, and I couldn't help smiling. "You know Janice, you actually got the victory today, even Dora can see that, I think that's why she's so angry."

“But they’re going to be watching you...” Janice was clearly distressed and close to tears.

“Janice,” I said, covering her clasped hands with mine, “they’re already watching us. They watch everyone all the time. You know that.”

Janice nodded and looked up, still not convinced.

“It’s an empty threat,” I said as bluntly as I could. “You need to show her you couldn’t care less about her threats. What can she do to us, really? Fire us? Is that it?” So what’s new?”

Janice laughed. I laughed. The threat and its fake condemnation had just lost its power.

“As soon as I get home I’m going to email her; in my most ‘professional’ manner, of course,” Janice was still smiling, “and let her know I do not wish to remain on her books and I do not want to receive any further communication from her office.”

“Perfect!” I said, smiling back. “You’ve kept your integrity...and your dignity...you win!”

Seeing through the games

Despite my assurances to Janice, I knew they were not going to be merely watching us, they were going to be targeting us. That’s who they were. That’s what they did.

I was an experienced parent with two married children. I recognised childish games when I saw them. I’d been in DSA long enough now to be able to see through their games, and I was becoming more and more unimpressed by their immaturity.

Like spoilt children, everything had to be done their way. If they didn’t get their way, they would throw tantrums. Yet, as every child knows, tantrums are no fun if there is no one around to see them.

The DSA bullies made sure everyone saw what they were doing. It was their way of maintaining power. How stupid! It seems they didn't understand that employers have power anyway, or that they didn't have to demean their staff to get what was already theirs. Not intelligent at all!

DSA tantrums were nasty, childish, selfish, insane forms of punishment. Like a child sticking a pin into a captured bug to watch it struggle, the intention of the tantrum was to torture, not kill. That's what they'd been doing to Janice. Torturing her! Torture was more delicious than death to these people, and now we had been targeted there would be no instant sackings for us, just many threats of sackings. That was more fun!

I shouldn't have had to know this about them, but I did. I'd learned by experience.

Owen had been able to escape for a few days, on his own terms. Janice had been able to escape permanently, on her own terms. DSA had been thwarted. The next tantrum was coming. Like a cyclone at sea moving towards the coast, I knew it was coming, I just didn't know where it would land, or how much damage it would do.

Jack came up behind me, reached around and slapped three files on my desk. I jumped and turned around on my chair. "Jack," I said. "You startled me."

Jack laughed; a hearty, friendly laugh. My heart sank; this was bad - very bad.

"I've just been talkin' to Erik," he said, "and it seems y're makin multiple errors. He's sent a report to Dora informing her of his dissatisfaction." He pointed to two of the files. "These two have spelling errors in the names."

He was intimating again they were going to sack me, and that Erik had already put the process in motion. Now I began to wonder, was this a tantrum, one of their games, or the real thing? Hmmm - not sure!

I looked at the files. The names were printed by hand in thick black ink. I didn't recognise the handwriting or the names. "Jack, this is not my handwriting," I said simply.

Jack stopped smiling. He straightened up, picked up the files and opened them, scanning the interior for evidence of the names of the files' creators. He checked one and then the other. "Yes," he said, closing the files and looking sheepish, "These aren't your files." This was the first time I had seen him flustered.

Great! Now I'm being sacked for other people's mistakes! Fabulous! But I couldn't show what I thought on my face, any hint of criticism would bring instant dismissal. I put my head down and turned my attention to the third file. I remembered it. I had completed the application and filed it in the vault-window room just yesterday. "I remember this one, Jack," I admitted, keeping my tone casual.

"There's a problem with this one. I want y'to go downstairs, retrieve the application and bring it to me," Jack ordered, no longer flustered.

I nodded. This was unusual. I'd never been asked to retrieve a completed application. It's not what agency staff did! I sensed a setup, but I couldn't see what it might be; nevertheless, I still had to do as I was told.

With two of the files tucked under his arm, Jack went to the staircase and bounded up the stairs, taking them two at a time, almost running. That was odd. He never ran. It was obvious he was reporting back to Erik. And reporting straight away! But why? The penny dropped. Okay, so this is not a sacking, it's a game. A tantrum! How pathetic!

I went down to the vault-window room, which still always gave me the creeps, and opened the filing cabinet drawer. The application was not there. I searched again. Not there. I looked in all four drawers. Not there. Oh-oh! There were only two filing cabinets I ever accessed, in that room. I had just searched one; maybe I had filed it in the other cabinet by mistake. I searched each drawer. Not there. Oh no! Losing a file was definitely sackable. Yet I knew for certain I'd filed it. Well, maybe this wasn't a game after all. Without the file, I was gone.

I dragged myself back up the stairs to Jack's office. He was not there, so I supposed he must still be with Erik. I went back to my desk in Doug's pod again - I was seated there while Owen was away - and sat down, not sure what to do next. I turned my chair, so I could see the stairwell and catch Jack as he came back down the stairs, dreading the conversation I was going to have with him. Suddenly this application was everything. Nothing else mattered.

Doug swivelled his chair around to face me. "What's wrong?" he asked.

I nearly fell off my seat. Did I hear right? Was Doug actually speaking to me? He didn't talk to anyone. Not even to Defence staff if he could help it. He pretty much kept to himself. "Oh," I said, trying to cover my surprise, "um, I've lost an application. I know I filed it yesterday, but I can't find it today. I've searched both cabinets. It's not there."

Doug didn't seem surprised, but then Doug didn't seem to show any emotion - ever! "Come with me," he said, like someone who had a solution. So I followed him.

He led me back down to the vault-window room. "Show me the two cabinets you searched."

I pointed them out.

He looked at them, reading their paper descriptors and then looked around the room. "Over here," he said.

I was puzzled. I went to the cabinet Doug pointed out and opened the drawer. There was the file! I retrieved it and looked up at him amazed. "I didn't file it in here," I said.

"Yes, you did," he replied and pointed to the paper description.

The penny dropped again, so did my jaw. They moved the cabinet! They moved the whole cabinet across the floor to a completely different spot! What a setup! Various unsavoury names came to mind, but I didn't voice them. Christian's don't! I felt my anger begin to rise. They couldn't find anything to blame me for so now they were making it up. Unbelievable! I closed my mouth without saying a word, and my anger deepened. Then I went beyond anger and became very calm.

Doug remained silent. He had obviously seen this happen before. This game was not new to him. He knew exactly what to look for, and he'd chosen to save me. Suddenly I saw the real Doug. He was not like them. He didn't play their games. Now I could see he didn't even like their games. No wonder he kept himself aloof.

"Thank you, Doug," I said, looking into his eyes with heartfelt sincerity, "God bless you."

He met my gaze and smiled, a broad, genuine smile, accepting the blessing. Nothing else was said.

I turned and strode, with purpose, out of that ridiculous excuse for a room, around the vault door and up the stairs to Jack's office. He was there this time.

"Here's the application you wanted," I said, holding out the paperwork, meeting his gaze, almost challenging him to take it from me.

He looked genuinely surprised. "Oh, you found it," he said, taking it from my hand. It was obvious he didn't expect me to find the file for his face showed his puzzlement. It was my turn to watch his reaction, read his eyes and answer his unspoken question.

"Doug helped me," I said, knowing I was dropping a mini bomb - and that it would hit its mark. I didn't wait for Jack's response. After watching his eyes register their surprise, I turned and walked out of his office. There was no problem with that application. He knew it. Erik knew it. Doug knew it. And now they knew I knew it too.

I didn't hear another word about it. I'd been right. This was just another game. A stupid tantrum! Didn't they care about the psychological and emotional damage they were doing to people? Didn't they know how insane their behaviour was? They were playing with people's lives!

The greatest surprise for Jack that day was Doug. He was supposed to be one of 'them', but he'd shown his true colours. I guessed I wouldn't be sitting in Doug's area for much longer. They wouldn't allow that!

When I got back to the pod, Doug was waiting for me. "Have you ever wondered how many agency temps go through this place?" he asked in almost a whisper.

I shook my head. I still wasn't used to the new Doug.

"I've been running some numbers on the agency temps who have passed through here in the past eighteen months."

My, oh my, he was full of surprises today!

"Sixty," he whispered, "sixty in eighteen months."

"That's a lot of people," I said softly, making sure I wasn't overheard. "In any normal business, those figures would be a huge warning sign – 'management in crisis'."

He nodded. "Have you thought about the cost?" He was looking at me intently trying to see if I understood what he meant.

My eyebrows shot up. I indicated 'no' to him, and quickly did a mental calculation of the cost of the two clearances, restricted plus secret, which every new temp had to have, $1700 per head. I couldn't speak the amount out loud. This was dangerous ground.

He was watching me intently. "Now add those who are here at the moment."

I nodded in response. "And how long are we twenty going to last before we are replaced?"

"Around 100 in less than two years," he said and paused...people were coming up the stairs.

$170,000! The unspoken amount hung in the air. He had made his point. This was wasted money!

We turned our chairs back to our work positions, but the conversation continued in my mind. Who pays for this? The obvious answer was the Australian taxpayer. All these wasted clearances were nothing short of a huge, deliberate and indiscriminate abuse of taxpayer money. Why did he tell me this? Why did he want me to know this?

I was amazed at Doug. This was so unexpected. I felt warm all over. I had won a friend – an ally. In this horrible dark, dark place, there were still beautiful, flickering, shining lights. And they warmed the heart.

When the coast was clear, I turned my chair around and asked him why he was helping me.

"Which church do you go to?" he said in response and smiled a full, natural smile. His face was alight with life, and his eyes danced.

So...he was a Christian! That explained it!

It is was clear this quiet man, who barely spoke, wanted me to know he didn't like what he was seeing. As we chatted, he told me he was due to start his long-service leave and would be gone for three months. Ah, so that's why he was giving me this information now, he knew I wouldn't be here when he got back. What an unexpected blessing!

The dividing wall begins to fall

The next day I was moved out of Doug's cubicle and re-located, like a ping-pong ball, back to Crystal's pod. Whether it was because of my sudden friendship with Doug, because management was addicted to chaos or because agency temps were moved continuously to keep us aware we were only temporary and didn't belong, I will never know, but I wasn't surprised.

Since the last time I sat in Crystal's area I had worked in nearly every work station on the middle floor; a few days here, a week there, never longer than two weeks. But, I was happy to be working with Crystal again, for unlike some others Crystal and Linda didn't make me feel like the enemy.

This time I was seated in Cleo's old seat. It was still hers officially, and all her things remained in place, including her stained old coffee cup, but she was no longer using any of them and probably would not be using them again for quite some time. She'd been promoted. She was now a team leader. Did they only pick the nasty ones? This promotion happened just a few short weeks after she humiliated Brian. I guess she must have proven she was DSA management material! Thankfully, she was working in a different section.

"Hey Monica, come and join us," Crystal said.

I'd been absorbed in my work, minding my own business, shutting out the chit chat. I was good at that now, I didn't even hear the chatter anymore, but this time my name had been called, so I turned in my chair to give Crystal my attention. Crystal, Linda and a new trainee analyst, I'll call her Deb, had wheeled their chairs to the centre of the pod as if they were about to discuss something. They were all looking at me expectantly, waiting for me to join them.

This was strange. I wasn't allowed to enter into office things, like gossip, politics, work issues etc. to do so was a sackable offence, and I also wasn't allowed any unscheduled breaks, I'd seen what happened to people who took them. Not pretty! I wasn't even allowed to talk to Defence staff unless they spoke to me first, and so I was not sure what I should do about Crystal's request.

I smiled what I hoped was a rueful smile. "I'm not allowed...I'm sorry."

Crystal looked puzzled, "what do you mean you're not allowed?"

Didn't she know? How could she not know? "We're not allowed to talk to Defence staff. We get sacked if we do," I said, wondering how she would take my honesty.

The three of them lost their smiles. They were all silent for a while and then Crystal spoke up again. "We thought you were all snobs."

"You get fired if you talk to us?" asked Linda.

I nodded.

"But we talk to agency staff all the time," said Crystal.

I smiled. "Yes, I know, but we're only allowed to talk to you if you open the conversation."

"We didn't know that," said Linda.

Deb was shaking her head, showing she didn't know either.

"Well...we are opening this conversation with you now...so therefore you won't get the sack," said Crystal speaking with a logical kind of mock authority. "Come over here." She was waving me over, smiling.

I laughed. I liked this woman. But I still couldn't join them. "It's an unscheduled break from my work. I can get the sack for that too."

"Mad! What else can you be sacked for?" asked Linda.

I rattled off a short list.

They looked at each other and then at me. They were not smiling, and all three were shaking their heads.

"We didn't know," Deb said with genuine remorse.

"We wondered why no one stayed very long," Linda said, joining the dots.

"Why you kept to yourselves..." Crystal voice tapered off as the reality of my situation hit home.

"You know, Monica," said Linda, "this is not a break from your work. What we want to talk with you about is part of your job."

"Yes," said Crystal, "it concerns all of us."

"Including you," confirmed Deb.

"We have to discuss how we are going to decorate this pod for Christmas." Crystal sounded like she was presenting the perfect solution to all my objections.

"That is neither office gossip nor office politics," Linda confirmed.

"And you are part of this pod!" concluded Deb. They were all nodding and smiling.

I couldn't help laughing. Wow! This was not what I expected. These women were normal! But I had one last objection.

"I won't be in this area for Christmas," I said. "We're moved around all the time."

"Cleo's not coming back," said Linda.

"Well, not before Christmas anyway," said Deb.

"You'll be here!" smiled Crystal.

"Come on," said Deb, "join us!"

"It'll be fun," said Crystal, waving me over.

I was convinced. I wheeled my chair to the middle of the room. This was amazing! First Doug, and now this group. The strict walls of division between agency staff and analysts were beginning to disintegrate. I was starting to see the softer side of some DSA personnel, and I couldn't wait to tell the others.

Two down, four to go

It was Owen's first day back, and I was keen to find out how his family were doing. The sky was overcast, and the air felt moist like rain was imminent, but I headed for the garden anyway. So did the others. We laid out the yellow cloth and were putting our lunches on the table when we saw Owen and Jim coming down the path.

Immediately, we all smiled and waved.

"Welcome back, Owen," said Cassie, gently.

"Good to see your cheery smile," I said.

"How's your family?" asked Jennifer with genuine concern in her eyes.

"Coping," said Owen. "We've been overwhelmed with all the support. I spent most of my time running around gathering things people were donating to send over there. Truckloads!"

"I saw one of your aunts on the telly," said Cassie, "She did an interview - it all sounded so horrible."

"Mum's over there now," said Owen nodding, "she went over for the funerals. And she's going to stay for a while to help out."

"What about your Dad?" asked Jennifer.

"He didn't go over. He stayed back to look after the family...go to work...you know."

"And your cousin?" I wasn't sure if I should ask, so I tried to be as sensitive as I could.

"She's still not good. Mum's hoping she'll be able to give her some support. It'll just take time, lots of time."

We all nodded.

Owen looked around. "Where's Janice? Is she working through lunch?"

We looked at each other for a second to see who would tell him.

"She resigned," said Jim bluntly.

"Had enough," confirmed Jennifer.

"She said to say good-bye to you," drawled Cassie.

"When did this happen?" he asked, looking from one face to the next.

We filled him in on the details.

"I'm sorry she's not here anymore but to be honest, I'm glad she doesn't have to put up with this place one more day." He looked off into the distance, "The way they treated her," he shook his head, "disgusting!"

"Well, I have some news," said Jennifer. "I'm leaving too. This is my last day."

Suddenly our attention was on Jennifer. We didn't have to ask why she was leaving, the question hung in the air.

"I've been thrown a life-line by one of my old colleagues," she was smiling. "I'll be working with the State Government again in IT - my cup of tea."

"Oh, how wonderful," I gushed, secretly envious. The State Government was *so* much better than this.

"Congratulations," Jim bowed in a mock salute.

"I'm jealous," said Cassie, obviously recalling, as I was, the 'good times' we all shared in our previous State Government positions.

"Normal people!" said Owen, almost wistfully.

"Tomorrow I'll be contacting the Fair Work Ombudsman," Jennifer continued, "people outside need to know what's going on in here. This place is appalling."

"Let us know if we can help," I said.

"If they want confirmation they can contact me," said Owen.

"And me," agreed Cassie.

"There's another angle to this," I said. "Doug put me onto it."

"Doug?" Jennifer sounded as surprised as everyone else looked. Not only was he Defence personnel, everyone knew he was a man of few words who kept to himself.

I nodded. "Yes, Doug! He can be quite the chatterbox!"

I filled them in on the DSA filing cabinet game, how he'd helped me, what he told me about temp stats and how he'd made me think about the cost of clearances.

"Wow!" said Owen.

"That's amazing," said Jennifer.

I nodded. They were as incredulous as I'd been.

"That's another angle you can put to the Ombudsmen; the high turn-over," said Cassie.

"I don't know how either the Agency or Defence can justify it," said Jennifer. "Temps are supposed to work on temporary projects. This is not a temporary project, it's permanent. It deals with military intelligence material, and the workloads are increasing. Someone needs to investigate why temporary staff are being employed to do this work."

"We're going to miss you, Jennifer," I smiled, she was a sparky little fire-brand, yet logical and clear headed. She was doing the most sensible thing any of us could do, leave!

"We have to meet up for a visit sometime, Jennifer," said Cassie. "Don't be a stranger."

"I won't!" said Jennifer and gave us all a farewell hug.

"Our group is shrinking..." moaned Jim.

"It'll shrink even more if this rain gets us," laughed Jennifer as light raindrops started to sprinkle down.

We cleared the table, ran up the sandstone stairs and past the grassy quadrant reaching the cement building block just as the rain started to pour down in torrents.

The second of three significant events

Christmas was coming! The decorations were up, and the harsh, sterile atmosphere had lifted a little, but only a little. It seemed even Christmas was not able to penetrate the sombre atmosphere of this dark place.

"We have to do something to lighten the atmosphere a bit - bring in a little Christmas spirit," said Linda.

"Something bold!" I said

"Only two other pods are making any real effort. The rest are just giving token gestures," said Deb.

Crystal had a mischevious look on her face. "What about a great big naughty-n-nice list?"

We all laughed.

"That'll put the cat amongst the pigeons," said Linda. "Do you think it's wise?"

"*We* won't choose whose name goes on which list, *they* will," said Crystal. "It should be fun!"

"And it fits in with our "Santa's workshop theme," said Deb. "I'll make the fireplace."

"I'll bring in the tree and some music and nibblies," said Crystal.

"I'll make the presents to stick on the wall," said Linda. When we all looked at her, she said, "What? There's no room on the floor!"

"I'll make the naughty-n-nice lists if you want. Plus the absolutely fabulous list," I offered.

They all stared at me.

"Who's on the absolutely fabulous list?" asked Deb.

"We are, of course!" said Linda, smiling.

"No one outside our pod is eligible," I said.

"I love it," said Crystal, beaming. "That's a big job, are you sure you don't mind?"

"Mind?" I said, "You ladies are like life-savers to me. A ray of sunshine in a dark place. I'm happy to help out. Besides - it's Christmas!"

Over the next week, the filing cabinets along the back wall were transformed with plenty of paper and sticky tape into a large fireplace, a baubled tree was given pride of place on the 'mantle' above the fireplace, the wall behind was covered in large colourful cardboard cut-out 'presents', and containers of home-made Christmas goodies took pride of place under the tree.

The entrance to our pod, Santa's workshop, was flagged by two over-sized candy canes. And in the corridor, the outer surface of our pod dividers was wholly covered with three naughty-n-nice' scrolls; one for the naughty, one for the nice and one for the absolutely fabulous.

Of course, the absolutely fabulous list only had four places, and they were already filled with our names. The decision about who should be placed on the naughty-n-nice lists, though, was left to Defence personnel. Now, all we had to do is wait and see if people would take the bait and play our little Christmas game with us.

My clandestine role was to eavesdrop on the remarks made about the naughty-n-nice list by passers-by, covertly write them down onto yellow sticky-notes and form their quips into a 'comment tree' (a Christmas tree shaped yellow-sticker commentary) which we would display on the wall opposite the naughty-n-nice list. We had all agreed this unseen background role should protect me from blame.

Once the naughty-n-nice list was put up, it had a wonderful effect on everyone. The atmosphere finally began to lighten. People would come by to find out where they were on the list, or put their co-workers on the list. There were smiles and even laughter as comments were made.

"Why am I on the nice list? I'm naughty!"

"Where's the boss? Oh yes, that'd be right!"

"Don't tell Paula who put her on the naughty list!"

"Doug shouldn't be on the nice list...this is rigged!"

"I've got Santa fooled..."

Once the comment tree went up, there was even more laughter. Just about everyone who stopped to read the comments would walk away grinning. People I'd never seen smile, and those who had never looked me in the eye, were now looking into my face and smiling genuine smiles as they went past. Wow! What an amazing change!

About this time I was given a 'special' task. Giving me this task would turn out to be the second significant event which would lead to DSA's demise, for while doing this job I would discover what Defence was trying to hide. And that revelation, along with everything else which had happened and was about to happen, would lead to the uncovering of the broad-scale corruption which was rife, but unseen. This task would open my eyes - completely!

"Monica, I've something new for y'to do; a special job," Jack announced. He was smiling. His tone sounded to me like I had suddenly become his best friend.

Oh-oh! What now? I looked up from my work and raised my eyebrows, but didn't say anything. Was this Christmas spirit, or was he setting me up? This approach screamed 'set-up' so I wondered what was coming. He was just too friendly.

"We call these 'quickie applications'," he explained, handing me a sample application. "They're just simple upgrades from 'restricted' to 'confidential' so they won't take you very long at all."

"There's no file," I commented. Upgrades were only done on existing applications, which meant there was a file somewhere. We were not supposed to upgrade anything without checking the new information against the old information on file.

"We don't have to wait for the files for these, that's what makes them 'quickies'," Jack said. "There'll be thousands of them comin' in over the next few months, and we need to put them through as quickly as possible."

I wasn't convinced. Why was he still smiling? Jack was watching me carefully.

“Come with me,” he said and led me to his office area. “Take a look at this.” He opened a screen on his computer and showed me a long list of names, scrolling down through thousands of them.

This was a first! Why was he showing me this list?

“These applications are just for security guards who work on military bases,” he explained. “They all work for private security firms who’ve done thorough checks. All we need t’do is rubber-stamp the upgrade.”

That sounded reasonable to me. Jack knew what he was talking about. He’d been around a long time. He understood the system. Maybe there was nothing wrong. Maybe I was becoming paranoid. At that point, I didn’t realise he’d taken me away from the analysts to tell me this. He knew they would’ve jumped on this lie straight away.

“The hierarchy has ordered all these upgrades for security guards on bases, so it’s simply a matter of putting them through. Just paperwork! Once they’re done, they’ll be held until the files come in, then attached to the files and sent back to archives.”

He was obviously under orders. This is what smarter minds had decided. Okay, I was convinced. I think he could tell he’d convinced me.

“They haven’t started comin’ in yet,” he said, pointing to the application in my hand, “just do this one. See how y’go. Bring it t’me when y’done.”

Like a ship on the horizon, heading towards a field of submerged mines, disaster was imminent. The collision course was set. The explosion was inevitable. It was now only a matter of time.

It took a while for the special upgrades to start filtering through, and in the meantime, to my surprise, I stayed in Cleo’s seat. The girls had been right; I had not been moved and would probably not be moved now until after Christmas. Amazing! Six weeks in one spot!

As it turned out, keeping me in Crystal's pod was crucial to unlocking the chicanery. If I'd been moved on, I would never have seen the deception. If I'd not been able to build a rapport with analysts, I'd never have worked out I'd skilfully been trained to deceive and mislead.

I was now in the right place (with analysts) at the right time (Christmas tends to break down barriers), and doing the right job (these special upgrades) there was only one more piece which needed to fall into place before this whole sorry mess could be exposed.

Meeting up with old friends

Even though Jennifer and Janice were now gone from DSA, Cassie and I had a chance to meet with them again a few weeks later. We were part of the forty-strong ex-Home WaterWise employees Christmas party being held on the Kookaburra Queen, a paddleboat steamer which sailed the Brisbane river.

"So, what's happening at that dreadful 'D' place?" asked Jennifer. Defence had become a dirty word to us, so we now only used the letter 'D' when referring to Defence.

"So much to say, so little time," drawled Cassie.

"It's all still going off like fireworks," I said, not knowing where to begin. "There's just one explosion after another. It never stops."

We were at the back of the boat on the lower level, watching the river foam behind us as the massive paddle-wheel churned the water.

"One bloke only lasted a week," I said, "as soon as he was told he would need a secret clearance, and have the last ten years of his life examined, he was out the door. Absolutely refused to have his privacy invaded! And then there was George..."

"Oh, George," said Cassie. "He exploded!"

"You would've loved it!" I laughed.

"Everyone else did," said Cassie.

"What happened?" asked Janice

"He was an older man...late forties...so I guess he just wouldn't take the garbage," said Cassie.

"He blew his stack and told them they were the most disorganised bunch of people he's ever worked with - told them they had no people skills and didn't have any idea how to time manage workflow efficiently. He told them he was doing his work and would appreciate it if they didn't pile his desk with more until he'd completed the tasks he'd already been set," I said.

"Really?" said Jennifer smiling.

"That was brave," said Janice.

"What happened to him?" asked Jennifer, knowing no-one ever gets away with that kind of behaviour at DSA.

"Nothing!" I said, watching the amazement spread over my friend's faces. "They had meetings at the highest level, thanked him for his input, then appeared to back-off."

"As they do," said Janice referring to her encounter with the Ice Queen.

"I can't figure them out," said Cassie

"No point trying," said Jennifer.

"Meanwhile all the others downstairs cheered and clapped and congratulated him for speaking up, that is, when the bosses weren't looking, of course. Then a few days later he was gone," I said.

"We don't know if he was sacked or left of his own accord," said Cassie.

"What a crazy mindless place to work," said Jennifer.

"Yes, well, it gets better," I said. "You know how Owen used to get gout in his knee sometimes?" Cassie continued.

Janice and Jennifer nodded.

"Well, it just suddenly flared up again. His knee was twice its normal size. It was huge," said Cassie, using her hands to show the size of his poor knee. "He said the pain was excruciating."

"He was using crutches to walk," I said.

"His doctor gave him a certificate for two days off, but Dora said he couldn't have any time off, even with a doctor's certificate," said Cassie, "and threatened him with the sack if he took time off work."

"But he had a doctor's certificate," said Jennifer.

I nodded. "Yes, he did!"

"Anyway, he came to work, and by lunchtime he couldn't bend his leg at all," said Cassie, "he was in agony."

"Oh, they're so cruel," said Janice.

"He rang Dora again and told her how bad things were and that he needed to go home," I said, "and do you know what she told him?"

They shook their heads.

"She said she didn't know why he came to work that day since he was so unwell." I watched their faces. The concept was so twisted, so abnormal, it took them a moment to adjust their thinking and remember how utterly absurd conversations with Dora actually were.

"What?" said Jennifer. "Oh, she's just mad!"

"Poor Owen," said Janice.

"It gets worse," I said. "Then Pandora told him he could have a day off if he got a doctor's certificate!"

"Didn't you say he already had one?" asked Jennifer.

"Yes!" I said, unable to hide my disgust. I couldn't help feeling angry about this horrible twisted mess, and it showed in my voice. "Owen was threatened with the sack if he didn't go to work, and then berated for working."

"That place is insane!" said Jennifer.

"What did he do?" asked Janice.

"The sensible thing. He took a couple of days off," said Cassie. "His knee went down, and he is walking normally again."

"But who knows how long it will be before this rises up to bite him," sighed Janice. "You know what they're like. It'll come back at him for sure."

"It already has!" I said. "He has a bung knee, so now they've given him a job that requires him to climb two flights of stairs several times a day."

"Why am I not surprised?" said Jennifer.

"How low can they go?" asked Janice.

"This week they moved him up to the top floor with me," said Cassie. "Well, not with me," she laughed, "on the same floor. He's now doing top-secret positive vetting."

"Oh, he's joined the elite group, has he?" Jennifer asked.

"Who left?" enquired Janice. "The pregnant girl, what was her name - Jill?"

Cassie and I nodded.

"Do you still meet in the garden?" Janice asked.

Cassie glanced at me, "no," she said gently.

"It's not safe anymore," I said. "My job is being threatened every week. And Owen feels the hammer is sitting just over his head. He doesn't want it to fall. He has a family to support. They have to come first."

"It's just not the same without you two," Cassie drawled with a rueful smile.

Jennifer and Janice grinned.

"So Dora's threat was real," said Janice.

Yes," I said, "they're watching us, but it's not your fault. They were watching us anyway."

"I'm glad I'm out of that horrible place," said Janice.

"What happened with the Fair Work Ombudsman?" I asked Jennifer.

"I lodged the complaint," said Jennifer, "but I wasn't given a reference number. They told me to speak to DSA management first. The fellow who rang me obviously didn't read anything I wrote. He also didn't appear to understand the problem. He told me that after I'd spoken to management, I'd be able to phone a different number. Useless! There's no point speaking to management if I no longer work there, and if I no longer work there, it seems there is nothing they can do. The whole thing is stupid! There has to be a better way."

"Are you talking about that place again?" The question came from the stairwell behind us. It was Graham, our good-natured old boss, now retired. We all missed working with him. He was descending on us with a small army.

"Skulking around in the shadows, talking about secret things," Sharyn was full of fun and mischief, always smiling, and as bright as a button.

"Fess up," said Greg, not expecting to be taken seriously, "what's this all about?"

"They can't tell us," said Graham, "cause then they'd have to kill us."

We all laughed. It was such a ridiculous line. But everyone used it.

"They haven't got drinks," said Maria, "what's a party without a drink?"

"Come on, girls," said Denise linking arms with Jennifer and Cassie, "food's getting cold."

Sharyn linked arms with Janice and me and purposefully directed us up the stairs behind the others. Our friends were wonderful. We'd just been rescued.

The third of three significant events

Christmas was lovely, but the New Year didn't go as well as I'd hoped. Though Christmas was filled with family and laughter, the New Year became a nightmare.

On New Year's Eve, I was phoned and told a good friend of twelve years, Peg, had died suddenly after a short illness. The funeral would be near Newcastle, NSW, a two-day round trip, and I couldn't miss her funeral. But would attending cost me my job?

The next day, New Years Day, my daughter-in-law Kristy came rushing through my front door holding my eighteen-month-old grandson.

"Can you watch Jaylan?" she was distraught, "my brother is missing."

I took JJ out of her arms as the story gushed out of her. "We were all at Tallebudgera, swimming in the river - mum and dad, Stephen, my sisters - he was swimming with us. He disappeared! We can't find him."

The Tallebudgera River, on the Gold Coast in Queensland, is a saltwater tidal river and though a favourite swimming spot for local families because of its calm surface, it is notorious for its undertow in king tides. Kristy's seventeen-year-old brother was an epileptic, and they were afraid he may have had a fit while swimming, and been washed out to sea.

"Police rescue has been called in. I have to go!"

"Where's Stephen?" I asked, concerned, wondering what my son, her husband, was doing.

"He's terribly upset - blaming himself. Heath was right behind him when he disappeared. Stephen's been diving down trying to find him for hours." Poor Kristy, her heart was being pulled in so many directions.

"JJ and I will be fine; you go and be with your family. Do what you've got to do," I said.

"Thank you," she replied as the tears started to roll.

"I'll phone around and get everyone praying."

"Thank you," she said, dabbing at her tears.

"Are you alright to drive?" I asked, ready to drive her back to the Gold Coast if she needed.

Kristy took a deep breath, wiped away the tears and straightened up. "Yes, I'm fine." She started to move toward the door. "I don't know when I'll be back."

"Don't worry," I said, and waved her away, "go!"

Police Rescue and Surf Lifesavers searched all day but couldn't find him. It wasn't until the following day after a rescue helicopter was brought in, that his body was found wedged against a large sand dune at the bottom of the river.

Kristy's parents were devastated. This was their only son and the youngest of their four children. They couldn't face going back to their home, with the Christmas decorations still up, his shoes at the front door, and his Christmas gifts unused. They couldn't face going into his room. They moved in with Kristy and Stephen.

I was glad Kristy had a large supportive family and that she and my son went to a caring church. Even though the weight of her parent's grief and the responsibility for organising the funeral had fallen onto this lovely young couple, the overwhelming support they were receiving meant I could return to my restrictive work routine knowing they did not have to cope alone.

As for me, I was facing a personal dilemma. Two funerals! There was no way I would be given three days off. It would be hard enough getting time off for one! I would have to choose which funeral to go to. The stark reality was I couldn't go to both funerals and keep my job. I had to make a choice. I chose family over friend and found myself in the awkward position of having to tell Peg's children I would not be able to attend her funeral. That was the hardest phone call I'd ever had to make.

I knew DSA management wouldn't let me go on a two day personal trip to NSW, but would they allow me to go to Heath's funeral? I didn't know.

The first thing I did on my return to work was advise Dora of Heath's death and request permission to go to his funeral. The exact day had not been set and would depend on when his body would be released by the Coroner's Office. I told her I would keep her informed. Meanwhile, I started on a new pile of the special 'quickie' applications, which were now coming in thick and fast.

I put them through as directed. No checks or balances. I had no file to check the information against, so I just accepted what Jack said, that the information had been approved before we received it. Even when the names didn't match, for example, if Linus Starlinus (fictitious name) had become Joe Star and there was no change of name certificate, I would assume one had been provided before the pack was sent to us and enter the new details anyway. Likewise, if there were any gaps in information, I would re-use information which already existed, like a previous address or employer, adding them into the gaps and stretching the dates around them to make them fit the missing timeframes, as we had been trained to do.

I'd been told the accuracy of this information was not vital to the clearance process. It was made clear to me my responsibility was simply to get them through the ASIO database without triggering an error report.

This grated against everything I'd ever been taught about applications. All my previous training in Parliamentary service, State Government and private enterprise, had emphasised accuracy and the importance of legal proofs for personal information. In the Queensland State Government, people couldn't even get a rebate for a purchased garden hose if they hadn't provided original documents to prove who they were, where they lived and their purchase price. But hey, this was intelligence. They did things differently. I just had to do as I was told. After all, I was at the bottom of the pile, the lowest rung on the ladder, what did I know?

Still, I couldn't shake the nagging feeling something was wrong, even though I was being congratulated for the number of applications I was doing. I was getting through eighteen 'quickie' packs a day, not bad when I considered I was usually only able to do ten normal packs. Not having to check information at all almost doubled my output. One thing I knew for sure was these 'quickies' made my stats look good! Real good! Dora and Defence were thrilled.

"You need to provide us with all your previous addresses," Crystal was speaking on the phone to an applicant, "if you can't provide details of your previous addresses we will not be able to approve your clearance."

What? Did I just hear right?

Linda was also on the phone, "You need to tell us where you were employed at the time, sir, and the name of your employer. We need exact dates."

Wait a minute! What were they saying? Accurate details? Exact dates? That's not what I was doing! That's not what I'd been told! Alarm bells began ringing loudly in my head. Why were the analysts telling the applicants they had to provide these details when I'd been told these details were not necessary or even important?

Deb was requesting a change of name certificate, "You need to supply the original. Until you do, your clearance cannot continue to be processed."

I wasn't allowed to ask questions, especially not of analysts, and it seemed I'd been lied to by the team leader, but I wasn't sure. I had to work this out! I kept listening, maybe they were working on higher level clearances. I looked at the files on their desks. No, the same level as I was working on. I'd been told my applications were 'special', maybe that was true, maybe not. Why hadn't I noticed this before? I searched my mind to understand, then I realised.

Until I was invited to get involved in everything Christmas, I'd taught myself to shut out all the conversation around me. Being given the job of eavesdropping on every naughty-n-nice conversation while I did my work changed that. When I became involved in their Christmas games, my ears had opened and now, despite the fact Christmas was over, my ears were still open. I was alert - and hearing everything. And, I was now suddenly aware I'd been lied to.

But what was I going to do about it? I didn't know.

Heath's funeral had been set. So I emailed Dora requesting the day off, expecting her to get back to me promptly. She didn't. The afternoon before the funeral she had still not responded. My stomach was in a knot. I wasn't going to get tomorrow off. Still, nothing was going to stop me from attending Heath's funeral, so I made a firm decision. I was going! Even if it cost me my job!

The moment I made that decision the knot left my stomach and peace entered like a balm. Good-bye job! I decided to say goodbye to my new friends.

"Well, it looks like it's my last day today," I'd turned my chair around and was speaking to everyone in general.

Crystal, Linda and Deb turned around to face me. "What do you mean?" asked Crystal.

"I still haven't got permission to go to the funeral tomorrow," I said.

"Just go! You won't get the sack," Deb said lightly like I was worrying over nothing.

I smiled and shook my head. They just didn't understand. "It's been wonderful working with you...getting to know you. I want to say good-bye while I have the chance."

"But you're a good worker," said Linda.

"You know the job," said Crystal.

I shook my head again. How could I explain it to them? They didn't have a clue.

"Hello ladies," Con was standing outside the pod with his usual fake expression in place. I wondered how long he'd been standing there and what he may have heard.

"Just letting you know, Monica, that Erik has given approval for you to go to the funeral tomorrow."

I raised my eyebrows, wondering why I hadn't heard from Dora earlier. "Is Dora away?"

"Oh no," said Con using his hand to brush my comment away. He looked like he was waving to a friend somewhere off in the distance. "It's just that I wanted to make sure you got the message before you went home, in case you didn't check your emails and decided to come in tomorrow."

Emails? I suddenly saw the game. They had decided to give the permission via email so late in the day I wouldn't see the email before knock off time. Then when I came in to work tomorrow, I would see the email and spend all day upset knowing it was my fault I was not at the funeral. Nasty, nasty, nasty! With difficulty, I stifled the urge to expose their motives. Could these people sink any lower?

"Thank you for letting me know, Con," I said, controlling my tone and my words. He was acting like my friend, but I knew he was the enemy, so why the good deed? Had he overheard my conversation about leaving? He must have, why else would he tell me about the email?

Then the light of understanding dawned.

Of course! He did overhear! And now he was covering their tracks. How sly! How sneaky! When he found out I would not be coming in tomorrow, the torturous game they were playing was over, and he had no choice but to make sure I got the message today. What a snake! These people were unbelievable.

"No problem, see you when you get back," Con said cheerfully and turned to leave, but I wasn't going to let him off that lightly. I was angry now, and I wanted him to know I understood the game being played.

"Con, can you let Dora know I've been checking my emails regularly, for days, waiting for this news, as everyone here knows." I turned to the analysts – they nodded.

I continued, "And also that I had no intention of coming in tomorrow, permission or no permission." The fake smile started to leave his face. "There was no way I was going to miss Heath's funeral, Con, even if it cost me this job. My family comes first."

"Rightly so," he said, but he wasn't smiling. His intention was written on his face. He was going to run back to his computer and write a report on my attitude. What a ridiculous bunch of people.

At this point, I couldn't have cared less what kind of report he would send back to Pandora and her puppet master. Something had changed in me and was not going to change back. I had already decided to walk away from this pathetic excuse for a job. When I made that decision, I lost my fear. They no longer had any power over me.

I'd heard somewhere that when evil goes too far, pushes too hard, goes beyond the limit of what people will bear, it's at that point fear is broken. That's when victims rise up and fight back. Historically, that's supposed to be why wars are kept short; because people can only be pushed so far before they turn on those pushing them. Somewhere deep inside I knew that Erik, Dora and Con had just gone too far.

I was now not only in the right place, at the right time, doing the right job, but my mindset had been tweaked, giving me the right mental attitude to be able to handle what I needed to do next.

I had lost my fear.

I was no longer afraid of losing my job.

I didn't know what was about to happen. I was just being led, step by step, and prepared by God, to do what he had placed me in this job to do. I could've quit like Janice and Jennifer, but I stayed because of the miraculous beginning. My faith was in God and his unseen will. I had asked God every day to show me why he wanted me in this place, but I hadn't received an answer. So I stayed. And now I suddenly felt strong, bold and ready. For what? I didn't know...

The day the truth exposed the lie

Heath's funeral was beautiful, if one can say that about a funeral. The chapel was packed. Every pew was filled, and the walls were lined with people standing at sombre attention. Yet there were twice as many people outside the chapel as there were inside, standing quietly, giving the service their full attention.

For a young man, Heath had made a lot of friends. He had just finished high school, so his classmates formed a choir and sang his favourite songs and his closest friends shared their favourite memories. Many of his football mates were Maori, so they performed their traditional funeral haka for him on the lawns outside the chapel after the service. The Surf Lifesavers and Police Rescue members who had been involved in finding him attended and then there were the people from his church and those from Kristy and Stephen's church, as well as large numbers of family and other friends. He was only seventeen, but he was loved in life and honoured in death.

I returned to work the following day to be greeted with gentle queries about the funeral. Despite the no talking rule, these wonderful women had found a way around it and always spoke first. They made me feel like a human being instead of a bug which needed to be squashed.

"How was the funeral?" Crystal's eyes were filled with compassion, yet I could see she didn't want to pry. The others had turned and were waiting for my answer, so I quietly gave them a very brief overview.

"But how are you?" asked Linda.

I smiled. How had we become such good friends? They genuinely cared. "I'm fine!" I said, "Honestly! "Ready to get back to work." I hoped this was all the reassurance they would need.

It was. They all nodded their agreement, and we settled into our normal routine.

"I'm phoning about your clearance application, I need a few more details." Deb's words reminded me of what I had been thinking before the funeral.

Crystal had answered an incoming call, "Oh, you have that information for me? Great! Let me write it down."

"No, not enough detail," said Linda, "we need specifics."

That did it! I couldn't continue putting these applications through unless I checked with Jack that I was doing the right thing. The trouble was - that was a dangerous thing to do. If I questioned him about anything, I would be sacked. If I told him my reasons for questioning, I would be sacked. If I didn't put the questionable ones through, I would be sacked. Yet if I continued to put them through as I had been directed, I may be doing the wrong thing.

I chuckled to myself, 'doomed if you do and doomed if you don't'. It was time to bite the bullet.

The thing which amazed me was how bold I felt. I was now more interested in hearing what reasons or excuses they would give than in their reaction to me. These people had literally lost their power to make me afraid.

Over the next two days, I put aside the most outstanding problems. One application had no birth certificate - a birth certificate was mandatory information. Another had only three years of employment information - five was mandatory. Still another had a change of name with no proof the person on the application matched the person on our system - a change of name certificate was mandatory.

I had plenty of examples to choose from for about forty per cent of applications had some kind of missing information, but on this occasion, I wanted to take just a few of the worst back to Jack.

Now that I knew the analysts, who were highly trained in vetting, required this information up front before any clearance could be granted, and what they were doing was correct procedure, it therefore followed that what I had been told to do was not correct.

The ramifications were ugly, and I didn't want to think about them. Could it be that I'd been trained to enter data illegally? No! That couldn't be...could it? I must have misunderstood. The blame must be mine.

But had I made a mistake? Had I misunderstood? Had I been doing things the wrong way all this time? I had no written procedures. Nothing was ever written down. So I had to know. Was this my misunderstanding, or something worse? Had I been deliberately trained to do the wrong thing? Horrible! Horrible! Horrible!

I couldn't continue entering data, not knowing...

I decided to lay these applications before Jack and see what he said. His answer would tell me, once and for all, if this was my mistake or worse...that it wasn't!

If he told me to pass them to an analyst so they could have their facts checked, I would know I had completely misunderstood the process, and the fault would be mine entirely. But, if he told me to put them through anyway, I would know, without a doubt, I had been deliberately trained to falsify data and pass that falsified data on to ASIO.

I took a deep breath and set off towards Jacks' office, files in hand. Jack was at his desk.

"Jack, I have a few problems here." I placed the three files on the desk in front of him.

He didn't look at the files; he looked up at me instead. Oh-oh! This was not good.

"One has missing data, one has no birth certificate, and the other has a completely different name to the name on the system with no change of name certificate."

Jack slowly stood up and picked up the files. Turning to face me, he opened the first and scanned the contents.

I'd carefully avoided asking a question, so why did he stand up? Had he read my approach as a challenge?

Looking up from the files, he stared directly, piercingly, into my eyes. Then suddenly, without flinching, he snap-closed the files and handed them back to me, "Be creative!" he said. His eyes never blinked, never left my face. He was watching me intently.

I held his gaze. So! It is deception! The worst of all possible scenarios. I'd been tricked into falsifying data! Lied to! No wonder they didn't want us talking to analysts!

I tried not to show my newfound knowledge on my face, but I guess I failed because his eyes changed and I could tell he knew I had worked out what was going on.

You could have cut the tension in the air with a knife.

His eyes were speaking volumes. Though the expression on his face was inscrutable, his eyes were telling me loud and clear I had just lost my job.

Neither of us said another word. I turned and left the pod. The lie was exposed. The truth had broken through.

A nasty, unnecessary fallout

I didn't tell Crystal or anyone else what had just happened. But I had no doubt Jack had gone straight up to the puppet master. Bad news travelled like lightning in that dark place.

"Hello ladies," said a familiar voice. The smiling assassin! Of course! Right on time! I knew I couldn't be getting the sack, it was already knock-off time, and they were required to give an hour's notice. So why was he here?

"Monica, I want to ask a favour," Con said like we were best friends. "I need to get home quickly this afternoon for an appointment, so I need to use the T2 express lane."

Con lived in the same general area as I did so his reason was feasible, but I didn't think for a minute he was telling the truth. What was he up to now? Best to face it head-on. "Not a problem, Con," I said pleasantly. "I could do with a lift home."

I said goodbye to the others and followed Con out to his car, a sporty red and black two-seater, reminiscent of a red-backed spider, which I thought suited him to a tee.

As we headed into traffic, his reason for wanting to get me alone became obvious. "Have you heard the news?" he asked. He sounded so innocent.

So this was it. "What news would that be?" I asked.

"About Jim and Owen."

I turned my head to search his face, but he had no intention of looking at me. His head was fixed in the forward position, feigning attention to driving.

"What about them?"

"They were both let go this afternoon."

"Both of them?" I was shocked. I couldn't breathe.

"Yes, both of them."

"But why?" I felt numb. "They are good workers."

"It wasn't about their work, their work was good..."

"Then why? Why get rid of good employees? It doesn't make sense."

"Well, Jim was going back to university anyway..."

"Yes, but not for another month."

"And Owen was going to America."

What? Did I hear right? Was that their reason? Couldn't they think of anything better than that? "This is January, Con. He's not going to America until March!"

"True, but that was not the only reason."

"What do you mean?"

"Erik wasn't happy Owen had taken so many days off. It's not acceptable."

So, it had come back to bite him. He had dared take a couple of days to grieve when he lost thirteen members of his family in one day. He had dared to take time off to rest his swollen knee under doctor's orders. What a terrible person he was!

"That was three months ago." I reminded Con.

"It's still not a good attendance record."

"What about Jim? He didn't take any time off."

"Well, he was going to be going back to uni anyway."

Dora's words to Janice pounded in my ears, "*your actions will directly impact on your friends*."

I wondered if this could be regarded as a direct impact. Was this my fault? Was this because of what happened in Jack's office today? Questions tumbled around in my head, but I had no answers.

Why Owen and Jim? Why together? Why this afternoon? It seemed they were sacked so suddenly Defence didn't have time to work out a decent excuse for sacking them. Or maybe it was all just a coincidence.

Was it a coincidence two of my friends were quickly dismissed the very day DSA management realised I'd worked out what was going on? Was it a coincidence they were bustled out the door before I had a chance to tell them what I knew? Did I believe in coincidences? Not this time. There were just too many.

The saddest thing for me was I didn't get a chance to say good-bye. In the space of a just a few weeks, I had lost four people I'd been close to without being able to say good-bye to any of them, a friend of many years, a family member and now two close work colleagues, and my poor heart was finding it hard to cope.

If I had known at that moment things were about to get a whole lot worse, I don't know that I'd have found the courage to continue. The ship had struck the mine, but the explosion and its fallout had only just begun.

> *The Inspector-General of Intelligence and Security stated, "there was a wide variation in the use of incorrect data and little by way of documentation. Further, except in limited circumstances, the use of the modified data had not been agreed by ASIO."* (IGIS Report, page 4)

Did they think

their threats

would keep us quiet?

CHAPTER FOUR

Witnesses? Shut them down!

Defence personnel were not free from the sadistic cruelty which permeated DSA. Public humiliation was standard practice, and it was not unusual for Defence analysts to be loudly berated for minor incidents, like requesting clarification of vetting procedure or asking applicants too many questions. It was not uncommon for female Defence staff to be set upon by multiple team leaders until they were reduced to tears.

Everything was monitored closely and consistently micromanaged. Any mistakes in data input, poorly worded sentences in emails or unnecessary questions to applicants during phone calls were picked up within minutes of being done. Then, within a few more minutes, everyone around the person who made the 'mistake' would hear them being loudly berated.

Stress leave was out of the question, but several Defence personnel were forced to use their long-service leave as stress leave, because the pressure placed on them by DSA management was intense, yet there was nowhere for them to go to complain about the treatment they were receiving. Official complaints were always reported back to DSA management, who savagely punished the complainant. In the eyes of permanent DSA staff, complaining only made things worse. DSA had all the exits covered. Or so they thought!

Agency temps and Defence analysts alike were generally unaware of the way each group was being treated. The enforced segregation of the two groups was powerfully effective and supported by physical separation as most temps worked on the top floor or in the basement while Defence analysts occupied the middle floor. It wasn't until Owen and I were seated on the middle floor with the analysts that each group began to witness what was happening to the other, and the dividing wall began to crack.

When the dividing wall of segregation developed a crack, it was the beginning of the end. Like the proverbial finger in the dam, nothing was going to prevent the truth from pushing through. Though DSA management did everything in their power to prevent the dam from breaking, their efforts weren't enough. The truth was too powerful. The only option left to them was to shut down the witnesses. After all, they had worked extremely hard at developing a financially lucrative, though illegal, system of streamlining applications which had so far been undetected by ASIO. They'd been so clever. They were not about to let anyone spoil it. Agency temps were easy to get rid of, but Defence witnesses were not an option.

Eavesdropping and spack attacks

After the revelations, stress and repercussions of the previous Friday, and not knowing what would be facing me on my arrival at work on Monday, it was nice to be greeted with kindness.

"How was your weekend?" asked Crystal with a friendly smile. "You look a little flustered this morning."

"Oh, it's probably because I've lost four people in the last few weeks and it's a bit much to take." I smiled. "Don't worry about me, I'll be fine."

"What do you mean by four people? I thought there was only your friend and Heath?"

"And Jim and Owen," I said, expecting Crystal would know they had been dismissed.

"They were fired?"

"On Friday...I'm sorry, I thought you knew."

Crystal looked shocked and so sad I wanted to go over and hug her, but of course, that kind of emotional display was out of the question. Nevertheless, I felt for her. She had a soft heart.

"I'm going to miss them," Crystal said with genuine affection, "especially Owen."

"Me too!" I could feel myself getting hot. I didn't want to get upset, but there was a prickle at the back of my eyes, and I knew I had to change the subject.

I started using my hands as fans to try and cool my face, and as I did, Jack walked past, stopped and stared at me.

I smiled up at him. "It's a bit hot this morning."

He was not amused. He could see my face was flushed and my eyes were too moist, but he didn't say anything. After a few seconds, he continued walking.

It was nearly time to commence work, so I turned my chair around and started my computer. I had only been working a short time when Con arrived.

"Good morning, ladies!"

Oh, I was so over his fake-ness!

"Monica, can I see you for a moment?" He pointed to the front entrance, "In the foyer?"

He called me by my name - not 'sweetie'. Oh-oh! Not good! Okay, so this was it. I was sure I was going to be fired this time. I knew it was coming. It could no longer be avoided - not after last Friday's revelations.

Jack hadn't wasted any time! I wasn't even officially at work when Jack walked past, but he'd obviously gone straight to Erik and then Con. I was on the mat! I just wasn't sure how it was all going to play out.

"Jack has just reported to me you are 'falling about crying'." He said, using his hands to make elaborate quote/ unquote marks in the air.

I looked him square in the eyes. "Do I look like I am 'falling about crying'?" I asked. It was blatantly obvious that was not the case.

He looked at me unconvinced. I was amazed. How could he possibly be unconvinced?

"Is my makeup washed away?" I leaned towards him so he could get a closer look. "Look at my face, Con, can you see any sign of tears?"

"There doesn't appear to be..."

"Why would he say something like that to you when you can see it's completely untrue!"

"I think I'm going to have to call Dora."

This was totally unreasonable but nevertheless typical, "why would you need to call Dora?" I asked.

"Because you got upset when you learned Jim and Owen had been dismissed!"

What? How absurd! "Con, you told me yourself on Friday afternoon, in your car, that Jim and Owen had been dismissed, are you saying that I fell about crying then?"

"No...but I still have to call Dora."

So, I was going to be sacked for being upset about Owen and Jim's dismissal. For goodness sake! I couldn't fathom how anyone could deny logic the way logic was being denied at that moment.

I tried again. "I don't understand this, Con. Isn't it obvious to you I am not showing any signs of distress?"

He looked down at his notes, “Why don’t I call Jack?”

“Good idea!” I responded and waited while Con disappeared to return a few minutes later with Jack.

This new ‘set-up’ was not very smart or well thought out. And I was becoming annoyed. So when Jack arrived I didn’t wait for him to speak, I opened the dialogue. “Con tells me you told him I was ‘falling about crying’,” I said, being careful to not ask a question. “I don’t understand why you would say that.”

“I thought y’were...”

“I think it is plain I am not.”

“And I think it is plain y’re upset because Owen and Jim were replaced,” Jack stated firmly.

There it was again. My suspicions had just been confirmed. Jack was making an issue of me being upset over Owen and Jim’s dismissal...but why?

“And what if I was upset?” I was beginning to feel justifiably angry.“I’ve lost four people whom I was close to in the last few weeks, Jack, and I didn’t get a chance to say good-bye to any of them. Crystal was just asking how I was coping...is that a crime?”

“Emotional displays’re unprofessional...” Jack’s words faded as he spoke them.

I shook my head in disbelief and tried again. “I didn’t just learn about Owen and Jim’s dismissal today, Jack. Con told me about it, in his car on the way home on Friday afternoon. I’ve known about it for days!”

Jack’s eyes narrowed. My guess was he didn’t know that rather important little fact. He glared at Con.

Con looked embarrassed.

“Well, I must’ve been mistaken,” Jack said and turned and left the room.

“I’ll still have to contact Dora,” insisted Con, who was now suddenly angry as well.

“What?” I said. “Why?” I was surprised by Con’s manner. “Jack has just said he was mistaken. Surely there’s no issue here.”

“Dora needs to be kept informed of everything.” He stood up, looking uncomfortable. “She’ll be contacting you.” The meeting was over.

If these two wanted to sack me for last Friday’s revelation, they’d well and truly messed it up. I guessed it was now up to Dora to finish the job for them.

When I arrived back at the pod, Crystal looked up at me with red eyes and tears flowing down her face.

I was shocked, but not game to speak out loud, because Jack was in his pod only a few feet away, so I wrote her a note, “What’s wrong?”

She picked up her pen and wrote me a return note, “I got grilled by Jack while you were away.”

I looked up from her note and mouthed, “Why?”

Crystal scribbled some more, put the note in a file and placed it on my desk. “He wanted to know every word we had exchanged. Every word! He is reporting me to Erik.”

“What can he report you for?” I scribbled and returned the file to Crystal’s desk.

“I don’t know,” Crystal scribbled back, “something about the Code of Conduct.”

“I’m so sorry,” I mouthed, then scribbled, “how can someone be in trouble for caring about another person?”

She looked at me with sad, sad eyes, shrugged her shoulders, and went back to work.

This place was hell! Nothing good was allowed to live here.

Grilled to perfection

Dora contacted me by phone that same morning. Con arrived at about 11am and escorted me to the conference room where I was 'grilled' mercilessly by Dora for more than an hour.

She had already been informed by Erik of the conversation I'd had with Crystal, courtesy of Jack's interrogation, and was convinced our innocent, caring, and very short, conversation had sinister motives.

"You've broken the 'office politics' rule," Dora began.

"I don't understand, how have I broken it?" I asked.

"You had no right to discuss any DSA business with any DSA staff member. This breach brings instant dismissal."

Okay. So it's happening. This is my official dismissal. Good! At least this horror will be over soon...

"You've broken the 'office gossip' rule," Dora continued.

Oh, there's a list...

"In informing a DSA staff member about the dismissal of agency staff, you've entered into 'office gossip'. This breach brings instant dismissal."

And she doesn't want me to interrupt.

"You've broken the 'criticism of management rule'."

I don't remember criticising the management...

"By being upset, you showed you disapprove of Defence's decision to sack Owen and Jim, thereby entering into criticism of management. This breach brings instant dismissal.

Oh! Surely that has to be a contorted stretch of the facts in anyone's book. I'd had enough. It was time to take the bull by the horns. "Dora, am I being dismissed?"

Dora wouldn't give me a straight answer, which was a bit puzzling considering I seemed to be in breach of every rule possible, so I decided to try to reason with her, though I wasn't about to hold my breath since reason seemed to be in short supply.

"Dora, when soldiers die in battle and their mates take time out to grieve, their grief doesn't show disapproval of the army, it shows empathy with the fallen, and neither does talking about their fallen mates constitute 'gossip', 'politics' or 'criticism of management'. So I don't believe I'm in breach of any of these rules."

"You've broken them all, and they bring instant dismissal."

"So am I sacked, Dora?" I couldn't believe I could not get a straight answer out of her. Did she want me to beg her for my job? That was definitely *not* going to happen! This job was no longer important to me. Begging was out of the question. The sooner I left, the better.

"No one is sacked from Defence, you're merely being replaced."

How lame! Another side-step. Did she want me to quit? Well, that was not going to happen either! I wasn't going to throw in the towel. This ridiculous scenario was going to run its full course. After all, God had put me here, and I firmly believed by now I would only leave when he was ready for me to leave. Besides that, I still didn't have any idea why he put me here in the first place, or what he wanted me to do.

I tried again, "so, am I being replaced?"

While I waited for Dora to finish her ranting and make a decision, I tried to remember how many times I'd had my job directly threatened in the last seven months, my goodness; it must have been at least twenty times, maybe more, not counting the daily indirect threats. It was all becoming a bit of a yawn really.

Then suddenly, Dora backed down. “You still have a job, Monica.”

I was incredulous, God had done it again! Against all odds, and all threats, I was still here. Amazing! But why was I still here?

Then her tone became extremely menacing. “If I hear, even one more thing, Monica, just one more, you will not have a job, and I will not consider you a good candidate for any other position.” The phone clicked. Dora had hung up.

Talk about making a mountain out of a molehill...

My highest priority now was to find out what God wanted me to do, and just do it so I could get out of this place. It was painfully obvious to me I wasn’t going anywhere until I found out why I was here.

“What happened?” asked Crystal gently when I returned to the pod.

“Are you fired?” asked Linda. They were both concerned and prepared for the worst.

I shook my head and smiled. “I can’t believe it myself, but no, I’m not fired, incredible!”

What was it about?” asked Crystal.

Aware of listening ears, I decided not to answer her question directly. “I’m going to write down what was said so I don’t forget,” I said, and I let Crystal know with my eyes I’d show her what I wrote.

“Well, something’s going on,” said Deb, “Con has gone home - taken a few days sick leave...”

I spun around and looked at Deb. I was surprised Con not only had suddenly taken time off but that he seemed to be the only agency staff member who could take ‘a few days off’ and not be fired!

"...and Jack has just announced he is taking seven weeks leave starting immediately...something about stress," Deb concluded.

I raised my eyebrows. Stress? I'd just been through the same events as these two men, and they were putting the pressure on me not the other way around, yet, they, it appeared, were the ones who couldn't cope. Interesting! Was this God's protection? It certainly seemed so!

"We thought for sure you must have been fired," said Crystal, "you were gone so long."

I shook my head again, stunned at the news about Con and Jack. "Con was with me in the conference room," I muttered, more as a thought than a comment, "he didn't seem to be sick..."

"Well, I for one am glad you're still here," said Linda with an encouraging smile.

"So am I," said Deb from across the room.

Crystal came up close to me and spoke very softly into my ear. "Defence personnel have a meeting tomorrow, something to do with whether we should be speaking to agency staff or not."

I looked at her aghast, and my mouth dropped open. So much horror had happened in such a short space of time. I was dumbfounded! Could things actually be getting worse? Apparently, they could!

Ordered not to talk to agency staff!

The meeting Crystal told me about was held early and was over by mid-morning. At morning tea Crystal did something she'd never done before, she came outside to find me while I was having my morning tea break.

"Would you like to go for a walk?" Crystal asked, wanting to lead me away from prying ears.

"Love to," I smiled, knowing this unusual behaviour signalled bad news.

We put some distance between the other agency staff and us. We didn't have to worry about Defence staff overhearing us as they rarely had morning tea outside. When we reached the middle of the manicured quadrant, Crystal opened up. She was speaking softly, and her voice was shaking with emotion, but she was maintaining control. "I can't believe what they've just done."

"What happened?" I asked quietly, following her lead.

"We've been ordered not to talk with agency staff." As she spoke, tears began to well in her eyes. "I can't talk to you anymore." She looked at me with pain on her face and then looked up at the sky, trying to control her tears.

"Ordered?" I asked. "You can't talk to us at all?" I looked down at the ground and shook my head. Management was unmistakably desperate now. The walls between Defence and agency had begun to crack. They were frantically trying to shore them up before they broke completely.

"We've been told if we talk to any agency staff member, the person we talk to will be fired."

I looked up again. I couldn't respond. I couldn't tell Crystal what I knew. I just stood there shaking my head.

Crystal's voice was full of emotion, "They're going to fire you, Monica, and they're going to blame me when it happens because I can't help talking to you." She looked at me with soft, moist eyes, "you're my friend."

I was horrified! So that was the new tactic. I didn't think they could sink any lower. I didn't think this could get any worse. I was so, so wrong!

I double checked what she'd just said. "They're making you think their firing of me is going to be your fault?"

She nodded, wiping away the single tear which rolled uncontrolled down her cheek.

I looked firmly into her sad eyes. "That can never be your fault!" She wasn't convinced. "They're going to fire me anyway, Crystal, it's just a matter of when. This is just another one of their low tactics; a way of punishing you. I'm so sorry you're involved."

I was strongly tempted to tell her the real reason they would be firing me, and all my friends, was because I'd found out what was going on, but she was in enough strife already, telling her would only make things worse for her.

After all, that was why she'd been interrogated so ruthlessly by Jack; he wanted to know if I'd told her what agency staff had been trained to do. That's also why they'd ordered the ban on communication. They'd been 'found out', and they were trying to contain the damage.

"Well, I'm not sorry we're friends. I'm glad we're friends. This is wrong!" She wiped the tears from her eyes and looked at me with a new resolve, "I'm going to do something about it."

I smiled at her. I loved her fighting spirit. "What're you going to do?"

"I don't know yet, I'm going to talk it over with my husband tonight and see what he thinks, but there must be something we can do."

"Yes, there has to be something..."

"Meanwhile, I'm not going to be able to talk to you, and that's going to be really hard." Crystal started to get teary again.

"Only at work," I said. "They can't stop us from talking outside work."

Crystal laughed; a genuine happy laugh. "You're right," she said, "they can't stop our friendship."

"No," I said, "they can't!"

Crystal checked her watch. "I think I should go back first. I'll see you inside."

As I watched her walk away, I wondered how on earth anyone in Australia thought they had the right to order people not to talk to others, or care about them. This was outrageous. Sure we worked in 'intelligence', but this had nothing to do with security.

Everyone, all analysts and agency staff working on clearances, had the same security level. We were accessing the same files, using the same programs and data. There was no 'security' reason for this atrocity. This was a cover-up. Pure and simple!

DSA management was working hard and fast to cover their deliberate and illegal breach of National Security and their blatant deception of ASIO. The truth had been discovered, now they had to stop the truth from spreading.

Choose this day whom you will serve

That afternoon I was moved out of Crystal's pod and back to Doug's pod. Doug was no longer there, he'd taken long-service leave, so I was alone. I no longer had to do 'special' applications; that task had been passed to others... funny about that! So I was back to doing regular secret and top-secret applications, selecting only those with complete information. I would never 'fill in' an empty field again.

Though I couldn't have imagined things getting worse than they'd become, amazingly, they did get worse, and the next change happened suddenly that afternoon.

All the lingering camaraderie from Christmas dissipated as if it had never existed. Since Christmas, Defence personnel had been making eye contact with agency staff, saying hello in corridors and generally exuding a pleasant demeanour. Now suddenly, that was all gone. There were no more nods, no greetings, there was not even any eye contact. Agency staff had become like lepers; avoided like the plague. And except for spurts of expletive-filled conversations between Defence personnel, the building was as quiet as a morgue.

What a nightmare! This place was hell on earth! An infernal vortex spinning out of control, getting blacker every day. The only thing I knew for sure was that I did *not* want to come back tomorrow. DSA management was on a diabolical power trip, with no end in sight.

"How can they do this to people, God? How can they do it?" There was nothing else I could do now but pray. This whole situation was insane.

That evening during a prayer meeting with my friends, while I was privately talking to God about it, telling him I couldn't face another day, I began to see everything from a completely different angle. And I saw clearly! Suddenly I knew I could handle whatever I had to face, for as long as it took. I finally understood why God had brought me here.

I remembered Christ's Commandment was that we love our neighbour as ourselves. That's what I'd been doing, but now care and concern for others had been outlawed. Human kindness had been outlawed. Common decency had been outlawed. Friendship had been outlawed. In effect, the law of Christ had been outlawed. This meant my faith was on the line. This was crunch time, and I now had to make a choice. Who was I going to obey, God or man? It was clear I could no longer do both.

This latest situation had put me in the position of having to choose between the law of God and the law of man. It was no competition, really. I had stood with God for a long time, and I wasn't about to change now. I also knew anyone who ordered me to disobey God's law would find they had God, Christ, the Holy Spirit and all the angels of heaven against them. Not a winning position!

I understood the military needed to teach people to kill, and killing to defend your country had never been regarded as immoral, not even in the Old Testament. But this was not military. There was no nobility in any of this brutality. This was not about war. This was about money.

Only a few weeks earlier the head of DSA, Frank Roberts had travelled up from Canberra to announce the new Australian Government Security Vetting Authority (AGSVA) would be located in Queensland. This decision was apparently made because DSA Queensland had shown they were able to process applications faster than any other vetting office in Australia.

It didn't seem to matter that those applications were only half done; that information was made up and entered as if it was correct just to get the applications through quickly. It didn't seem to matter that National Security was being compromised or lives were being put at risk. It didn't seem to matter that so many Australian laws were being flouted or that God's law was being flouted. Not a bit!

What did God's law have to do with all this? Only everything! The whole fabric of our society was based on people caring for others. Without care and concern for others our society would only disintegrate into lawless chaos, but these disgusting, small-minded, bureaucrats had outlawed 'loving your neighbour' and all human decency.

The only thing which mattered to them, it seemed, was that this new deal would save over $5 million in vetting expenses and produce $45 million+ per year in revenue.

Christ's words, "*you can't serve both God and money,*" were never truer than in DSA Brisbane.

DSA management were not only happy to ditch their humanity, they had no qualms about introducing the same torture tactics used on military prisoners, like those in Guantanamo Bay, into an Australian Government workplace. Under their authority staff were isolated, forbidden to speak to one another, continually threatened and kept in a constant state of confusion and disorientation - essential torture tactics. We could not rely on the protection of Australian law, for it didn't apply to anything done within DSA, and so we literally become people without a country.

An extreme over-exaggeration? No! This was our reality! Nevertheless, despite the pressure of the constant psychological torture being used to force compliance to illegal activity for the sake of money, my choice was to stand for God's law and continue loving my neighbour.

That meant I had to be prepared to be openly friendly and speak to whoever wanted to speak to me, no matter what the cost. I found strength in the hope God would one day lead me out from this place with joy and peace as his sure and true word promised he would do.

I finally understood why I was in such a wretched place. What a relief! This is what I had to see; people were being ordered to disobey God's law. Ordered! This was not his will at all - and never would be. All God needed was someone to be his witness, that is, to witness what was happening and ask him to act. So that's what I did.

Every day from that day till the day I walked out the gates for the last time, I prayed God would tear down the evil which had raised its ugly head in that place.

Every time I needed to get up from my desk and walk around the building, I would claim the victory as I walked. My prayer was simple, "Go, get'em, Lord! Uphold your law! Uphold the victory of your Son!" I had full confidence that is precisely what God would do. That's why I was here; to witness what was going on and hand it over to him, so he, himself, could act.

From that time on, I felt the victory of God. I chose to live by God's law, and so I would smile and say hello to all my co-workers, including Crystal, each morning and greet them cheerfully when I passed them in the hallways. They may have been ordered not to say hello to me, but I could still greet them. I was no longer offended by their unwillingness to speak to me or even look at me. I saw their rejection as an act of kindness. They didn't want me to be sacked! I could only thank God for them.

Liberation! Finally! Hallelujah!

My day of liberation came two weeks later. It started out like every other day, but then the unexpected happened - always a good sign. And the unexpected came from Crystal. Once again, she did something out of the ordinary. She walked past my pod and motioned me to follow her, indicating she wanted to talk. Wow! She knew the consequences for me and was still prepared to ask me to take the risk, so I gathered this was important news.

I followed her down the corridor and into the long, narrow filing alcove next to the kitchen. There was no room to manoeuvre, it was hard just turning around in there, impossible for anyone to squeeze past. And we were alone.

I entered first, and as I turned to face Crystal, I was almost blinded by the brightness of her smile. She was beaming. I hadn't seen her smile for weeks.

"I have good news," she mouthed, not quite game to even whisper.

I smiled back at her, followed her lead and used hand gestures as well, "I can see that! I need sunglasses!"

"I've just arranged a meeting with Erik, Paula and a few others to talk about the treatment of agency staff," she said, and her eyes were dancing with excitement.

"When?"

"In a few days, would you like to be there?"

"Why would you want *me* there?" I wasn't sure how I could help.

"To back up what I'm saying...be my witness."

I nodded and smiled. "Happy to!"

Crystal almost jumped for joy, but then looked concerned. "You know going to that meeting could cost you your job."

I laughed, silently, "What doesn't?"

We both laughed, almost uncontrollably, not out loud, of course, but in a muffled, hands over mouths, shoulders shaking, let's not make any noise, kind of way.

"So, you'll come?" Crystal asked when we regained control of ourselves.

"I would be honoured."

Crystal turned to leave, I tapped her on the shoulder and she turned back. "Thank you," I said, looking directly into her eyes so she would know I meant it with all my heart.

She tilted her head to the side with an unspoken question and raised her eyebrows.

I smiled. "For sticking your neck out for agency staff." I put my hand on her arm. "You don't have to do this!"

"I know," her manner was matter-of-fact, "but it's the right thing to do."

I was humbled. This woman was not only kind, she was also brave. No wonder I liked her.

"I'm going up to see him now," she grabbed both my hands, "wish me luck."

"I'll do better than that," I gave her hands a squeeze, "I'll pray for you."

Crystal left the alcove first, and a few minutes later I returned to my pod.

About an hour later, Crystal came down the stairs with a huge smile on her face and gave me the thumbs up sign as she went past. Erik had agreed I could be Crystal's witness at their meeting. Wow! That was good news! Well, so we thought...

Neither of us had any idea that within the next hour Erik would betray his word to Crystal and give the order for me to be sacked.

Just after lunch, Con came mincing into my pod. I hadn't seen him at all since our last conversation in the foyer, which seemed so long ago now, nearly three weeks. He was the agency team leader, but he had been skilfully avoiding me, so I knew this sudden appearance could not be good. This time, there was no smile - no greeting - no fake excitement - he was all business.

"This afternoon you're going to be moved back into your original seat upstairs," Con said. He looked like he wanted to be somewhere else...and I knew why.

The scenario was easy to read; they wanted me to resign. I wasn't going to do it! They would have to fire me.

The seat he was referring to was the 'arctic blast' seat, where I'd been positioned for the first three weeks of my employment; the seat where I'd had to wear a heavy woollen coat, scarf and gloves just to do my job. The air was so cold I'd eventually been forced into the untenable position of having to make a complaint. Even though at that time I'd fully expected to be sacked for complaining, God had intervened, and instead of being sacked I was moved down to the middle floor with the analysts and Jack; a move which they now obviously regretted.

It didn't take a genius to figure out what DSA management was doing. Their actions were immature, childish and totally predictable; as predictable as those of a spoilt child throwing a tantrum. Pathetic! Someone would have to step up and be the adult here, and it looked like that someone would have to be me.

The reality was the air conditioning had still not been fixed, and everyone knew, including Con, that I couldn't physically tolerate the cold in that position and so would need to make a complaint. Even blind Freddy could see I was being set up again. If I sat in that seat, I would become ill. If I said I couldn't tolerate the cold, I would be sacked for complaining. I laughed to myself and shook my head. Didn't they know how transparent they were?

My decision was easy, no point dragging it out. "You know I can't sit in that seat Con, the air is too cold for me."

Con didn't say a word. He turned on his heel, sprinted out of the pod and up the stairs as fast as he could, taking them two at a time.

I watched him with detachment. Run! Con! Run! Places to go! People to see! He was obviously reporting back I'd complained about the air conditioning.

He returned a few minutes later, "I informed Paula of your complaint, and she told me to tell you to wear a jacket."

Why wouldn't they sack me? Did they just want to torture me? Of course they did! This time I wasn't going to give them the chance. I was over their games. I had no intention of moving upstairs. It was time to finish this. "It's a health and safety issue Con. You know it is! I know it is." I was totally relaxed.

Con didn't say another word to me. He turned and left the pod.

At 3.15pm that afternoon, I swivelled around to find Dora standing behind my chair.

"Oh, Dora!" I was a little surprised she didn't announce her arrival. "You startled me; I didn't hear you come in."

There was only one reason Dora ever turned up at this time of day. Russian roulette! Today was my day! Yay! She was late, though. I was supposed to receive an hour's notice. She was supposed to be here at 3pm, so this sacking would now be illegal. But I decided to let that go. I couldn't wait to be fired.

"May I see you in the foyer?"

The foyer was not a very private place for a sacking, we would've been better staying where we were; nevertheless, I stood up and followed her to the foyer.

"You are being dismissed," said Dora in her usual blunt manner once we were seated.

"The air conditioning?" I asked.

"Yes, you complained."

"It's a health and safety issue, Dora."

She ignored me.

"I want to make it clear this is not about your work. From all accounts, your work has been exemplary."

Yes, let's not make the work we do here the issue – too dangerous. To my knowledge, no one had ever been sacked for 'work-related' issues. It was always personal. Always trumped up. Fabricated! Like everything else DSA management did.

This was their third attempt at sacking me in the three weeks since the actual 'work-related issue' took place in Jack's pod, and this was the most feeble excuse of all, but I didn't care. I knew now why I had been placed in DSA by God, and I knew I'd done what he wanted. Thankfully, it was time to go.

"It's not your work ethic either," Dora continued. "You've been conscientious and maintained the high expectations Defence requires."

How hollow were her platitudes! I knew she didn't mean a word she was saying, yet she sat there, going through the motions, speaking politely to me in sickly sweet tones as if our previous conversations had not taken place. Diabolic! Meanwhile, people began leaving work for the day.

No one had to be told why Dora was there, there was only ever one reason. They obviously felt as uncomfortable interrupting 'the sacking' as I felt having this personal moment exposed to prying eyes. It was frankly humiliating.

The door opened again, and Crystal stepped in. She summed up the situation in an instant and froze on the spot. All the hope and joy she had felt that morning had just been thrown to the ground and brutally crushed underfoot.

Erik had betrayed her! He had lied to her! He had assured her I could be her witness in the meeting next week, and in the next breath, he'd had me fired, leaving Crystal exposed and vulnerable.

Erik had killed two birds with one stone, so to speak. By sacking me, he had killed the meeting next week. If Crystal went through with the meeting now, it would be to her detriment. She would be squashed like a bug, and she knew it. It was written on her face.

I stood up and went over to give her a farewell hug. The air was thick with emotion, but neither of us was free to say what we wanted to say.

"Are you surprised?" I whispered into her ear.

She was too emotional to speak for a moment, and then her simple response said it all. "No."

"You have my email address..."

Crystal nodded and left the room. She couldn't speak. She was devastated. We both were.

There was nothing left now but to gather my things, tidy my desk and leave the premises. I wouldn't have the chance to let Cassie know I was leaving; I'd become a non-person. I would be escorted off the Base, by Dora, as if I were a dangerous criminal or saboteur.

We went back inside to my desk.

Paula came downstairs to collect my Base pass from me herself, which I thought was odd as they were generally given to the team leader. Had Con gone home sick again? Paula still couldn't look me in the eye. When I gave her the pass she took it and walked out of the pod, no thank you, no farewell, no sorry-to-see-you-go, not even a nod, nothing!

"Good-bye, Paula," I said, to the back of her head.

"Do you have everything?" asked Dora.

“I have my coffee mug and yellow table cloth,” I said as I looked through the bits and pieces in my drawers, “nothing else is important enough to keep.”

It felt strange leaving my work half done on the desk, as if I would be back to finish it later, I guessed someone else would finish what I’d started. With a final glance to check I hadn’t left anything of mine behind, I turned and walked away from the worst job I’d ever had.

“You know you stayed on longer than most,” said Dora as we walked past the vivid green, white edged quadrant. “CML doesn’t like people staying longer than five months,”

“CML?” I asked, “who is CML?”

“They’re the recruitment group who holds the contract with Defence to supply staff,” Dora explained. “Our agency works for CareersMultiList, and you work for us.”

“So there’s a ‘middle-man’ involved here?” I asked, “Or middle company, should I say?”

Dora nodded. “Yes, they work out all the minute details with Defence.”

I was puzzled. I was no longer an employee. She didn’t have to say anything. “Why are you telling me this?”

“They told us they don’t want anyone working longer than five months and you’ve been here for seven.”

Another lie! I couldn’t believe anything this woman told me. Did she know how to tell the truth? I was beginning to wonder if she even knew the concept existed.

“You told me when I took this job that I was replacing someone who had been here eighteen months. Some agency staff still working here, at least two, have been here for years Dora, and if what you’re saying is true then why weren’t we offered a five-month contract? At least that way we wouldn’t have had to face this terrible, sudden death, one hours’ notice thing.”

"One hours' notice is the law."

"Rubbish, Dora! It's an abuse of the law. One hours notice is the minimum required to be given in exceptional circumstances, like when somebody is caught stealing or doing something they shouldn't be doing. It is not a general rule, and it's not supposed to replace common decency."

"CML insists...our hands are tied."

"Is CML an Australian company?" I asked. "It doesn't sound like it. This is not the way Australian employment works. It doesn't match the rest of Australian workplace law."

"CML tells us how many staff to supply and they tell Defence how many applications need to be processed to pay for the staff. That's why there is such a great emphasis on clearances," Dora continued.

"Do CML pay for the clearances for all those throwaway agency staff, Dora, or does Defence pay?" I asked.

"I don't know," said Dora rather sheepishly, "all I know is they pay the bills."

"What I can't understand Dora is why Defence is bowing to these people instead of putting Australia's security first."

"Oh well, I don't know if that's what they are doing."

"I do, Dora! That's exactly what they're doing - with your help! You have no clue what's going on behind those doors. It's not about processing certain numbers to pay for staff, it's far more serious than that!"

I had no idea why Dora had decided to 'leak' this information to me, probably just shifting the blame for my dismissal from herself to 'them', and I had no idea if what she'd said about a middle man was true. What I did know was Dora was vicious and nasty and couldn't be trusted. I would be glad to see the last of her.

When we reached the boom-gate, I turned to say my final farewell and walk away, when Dora caught my arm.

"I would be happy to recommend you for another position," she said.

Cringing at her touch, I stepped back out of her reach until she removed her hand from my arm. After this experience, there was no way I would ever work for this woman again, not in a million lifetimes.

"Have you been able to find work for Owen yet?" I asked. "You remember Owen, good worker, family man, you fired him a few weeks ago, for no reason. Have you found work for him?"

"Oh, I don't think he's back from America," Dora sounded so sweet and innocent, "I'll find him something when he gets back." She obviously didn't know Owen and I had stayed in contact after he left Defence.

"Owen hasn't left for America yet, Dora," I was trying to keep my tone professional even though Pandora had just been caught out telling another whopping great lie. "He won't be leaving for another five weeks; meanwhile, he's using up his holiday money to feed his family. If he doesn't get work soon, his holiday will be ruined. Why don't you find *him* a job?"

Dora didn't even try to respond this time. Another lie just wouldn't cover it.

"I'll find my own employment Dora, and I'll send you an email to confirm my wishes. Goodbye."

I turned to leave and suddenly felt as light as air. It was like a great burden, or heavy weight, had been lifted off me. A huge smile broke out on my face, and I felt like singing. I was happy! Happier than I'd been for months. Had I truly forgotten how good it felt to be happy?

I took a long, deep breath of fresh air and spun around on the spot. "What a beautiful day!" I said out loud.

Dora was watching me, so I gave her a great big smile and a cheerful wave and hurried off down the street. I was free!

I couldn't believe how good I felt. I wanted to dance, I wanted to skip and run like a child. I had an overwhelming sense of joy and was so elated I could hardly breathe. All I could think was I was free, free, free! And it felt great!

I wanted to shout it to the skies and tell everyone I passed on the street, "I never have to work in that awful place again!" I felt like I was going to burst with joy. And finally, I did!

When I arrived at Roma Street Station, I took the escalator to the mezzanine for a celebration coffee. Except for two trapped pigeons flapping around the ceiling, looking for a way out, the place was all but deserted, and suddenly I could contain myself no longer. Those two trapped pigeons, desperately seeking a way out, triggered a profound appreciation in me of my new found freedom. Without any concern for the opinions of others, I threw my hands into the air and cried out loud, "Hallelujah!" Then as I brought my hands down, I found myself thanking God for bringing me out of that place, not just with joy, but with exceeding joy, as his word promised he would.

The joy didn't go away. The intense feeling of freedom I felt on leaving that dreadful D place stayed with me for nearly two months. And my sincere daily hope was that I would never have to experience anything like that workplace again for the rest of my days.

> *The Inspector-General of Intelligence and Security stated, "staff expressed a belief that they were, at the very least, pressured into ignoring security concerns, and in extreme cases, coerced into approving clearances about which they held serious doubts."* (IGIS Report, 2012 page 61)

Did they hope
we would
just go away?

CHAPTER FIVE

Personal threats? Of course!

The problem of National Security and the harsh work environment endured by those working within DSA could not be ignored. So in March 2010, two weeks after I was dismissed, seven people, both current and ex-DSA employees, banded together to begin the process of bringing what was hidden into the light.

By the end of March, complaints about the treatment of staff within DSA had been hand delivered to Craig Emerson MP in his capacity as Minister for Independent Contractors, Brett Raguse MP, our local member of Parliament, with a request they be forwarded to the Minister for Defence. Emails had been sent to Frank Roberts, the head of DSA, Mike Quinn, within the Defence's Directorate of Fairness and Resolution, and to the agency for breaches of the APS Code of Conduct.

These complaints were forwarded to the Minister for Defence Personnel, Mr Alan Griffin MP, who immediately ordered three simultaneous investigations, two of which were to be done by an independent party, albeit under the guidance and monitoring of DSA. The two miss-named 'independent' investigations were set up to separately address the complaints of agency staff and the complaints of Defence personnel while the third was to be conducted by DSA into the management practices of DSA Queensland.

Strange things began to happen at DSA. Crystal became an outcast, bullied continuously while being accused of bullying and being in breach of one thing after another. Instead of being able to stand up for what was right, she found herself in the recurrent position of having to defend herself against untrue accusations. Dora lost her position, and the agency suddenly ceased supplying new personnel to fill positions within DSA. There were usually new staff every week, but for nearly two months there were no new staff at all. On top of that, Defence personnel began resigning or being removed.

The explosion of truth had produced fallout, but the ship of corruption was still sailing. Some things had changed, but the bullying of Defence staff had increased, and the illegal vetting practices continued as if nothing had happened, nevertheless the truth had exposed many problems, the wreckage now had to be addressed, and the rest of the corruption could no longer be easily hidden.

Crystal is targeted, as predicted

Around two weeks after my joyful release, I began to have a nagging feeling my involvement with DSA was not finished, and I was also concerned about the outcome of Crystal's meeting with Erik. I hated to think she could be targeted because she had tried to stand up for me, and other agency staff, so I phoned her at home.

"How are you?"

"Not doing so well," Crystal sounded defeated. "I spend my time caring about others, and they just come along and squash me."

Oh, this was not good, "What happened?" I asked, feeling like I was being drawn back into a horror story. A difficult adjustment, since I was now chronically happy.

"They accused me of bullying." Her tone was matter-of-fact like this was old news. "They said I'm in breach of the Code of Conduct."

"What? How could they accuse you of bullying?"

"Cleo was in the meeting, and she said you had dobbed me in." I so admired Crystal's honesty...she was always direct...but I wasn't expecting to suddenly be the enemy.

My mouth dropped open. What did she think I'd done? That place never ceased to amaze me! "How...um...how...?"

"Do you remember the time when we sticky-taped all your stuff?"

Though puzzled as to why she would bring this up, I nevertheless chuckled as I recalled the day. I had come back from lunch to find the keys on my keyboard had changed places, my files had been stuck together, my ruler had been taped to the desk and my drink bottle had been doctored with glad wrap. It was hilarious! I loved that they felt they could muck around with me. It made me feel like I was one of them. Like I belonged...

"Yes, I remember that day," I said, smiling into the phone. "One of the better memories I have of that horrible place. You made me feel welcome."

"Do you remember the email you sent to Cassie telling her about it?"

"Yes..." Suddenly, my heart started to sink, and I didn't feel like smiling. "What about it?"

"They said it was proof I was bullying you."

"What?" I yelled through the phone in shock. I was horrified. "How could that email...possibly...? I was telling another friend how accepted I was by you. Not a small thing in that place! Being accepted was big news!"

"They said it was a complaint." Crystal sounded like she needed reassurance. "They said when they 'read between the lines' it showed you were making a complaint about my behaviour. They said I was being mean."

"Oh, Crystal," I could hear the uncertainty in her voice. She was wondering if I'd betrayed her. Those people were so ugly! "You? Mean? You're one of the only nice people in that hell hole. You were never mean to me, and I loved what you did that day. I thought it was wonderful. It made me feel like I belonged. I certainly wasn't being bullied."

"Well, they're making it official." Crystal said sadly. "It's going on my personal file."

Now I was mad. How dare they! But I knew what to do. It was no mistake I had spent the last few days going over the Public Service Code of Conduct. I was suddenly in awe of God again, and the way he equips us for battles we don't even know we are about to fight. "They can't make it official if I don't agree with their assessment," I said.

"That's all well and good, but you're not here," Crystal snapped. "There's nothing you can do." Poor Crystal, she was on the verge of crying.

"Oh, yes there is," I said firmly, speaking confidently, so she would understand I knew what I was talking about. "I've been reading over the Code of Conduct for the last few days Crystal, and I know this; for a breach to be formalised there has to be an official complaint against you - and I haven't made one!"

"But they're going to use your email..."

"They won't be able to use it if I write a Stat Dec stating you've never bullied me." What a pack of monsters! Good thing bullies aren't too bright!

"Can you do that?" I could hear the hope in her voice.

"I sure can!" I said, "I'll get it done and witnessed and email it to you in a few days. You can use it or not, that will be up to you."

Crystal began to cry with relief. "Thank you, Monica. I'm so glad you're out of here, but I miss you heaps. You know they put me in the naughty corner when you left."

"Naughty corner?"

"Your old seat in Doug's pod," she giggled as she sniffed, "didn't you know that was called the naughty corner?"

I laughed long and hard, remembering all the times I'd been seated there. "I had no idea, Crystal." I said when I could contain myself, "and I was there quite a bit!"

We laughed our way through various memories, and it was good to hear Crystal laughing with me. She could do with a good laugh.

"I like the solitude," Crystal continued when the laughter died down, "I don't have to worry about all the stupid games." She was trying to be cheerful, but the sadness in her voice was unmistakable. She was obviously having a tough time. "You know Con hasn't spoken a single word to me since that dreadful day in January."

"No great loss, surely..."

She laughed again, "I sure do miss you..."

"Hang in there, girl. It's only a workplace, not the whole world, and the way they see things in there is not the way the rest of the world sees things. I'm going to look into what can be done."

"Well, I won't hold my breath. Nothing ever changes around here."

Poor Crystal! They were trying to use me against her. How typical! How diabolical!

That conversation confirmed to me something had to be done. And logically, if something had to be done, then I was the one who had to do it. There was no point expecting other people to carry the load. If I wanted something done about the breaches of the Code of Conduct and the lies to ASIO, I had to be prepared to volunteer. The big question now was, 'how do I go about making an official complaint?'

Choosing the road less travelled

I wrote out the Stat Dec and arranged for it to be witnessed. One of my friends was a Justice of the Peace, so I made an appointment with him, and we met at a small, discrete coffee shop in Daisy Hill.

"Done!" Barry said and began putting his JP stamps back into their box. "You said you needed to talk about something else…"

"Yes, I need your advice," I said, folding the Stat Dec and putting it back in its envelope. "I have a problem, and I'm not sure which way to approach it."

"Is it to do with the Stat Dec?"

"Yes," I smiled. He was on the ball, as usual, "bullying at Defence."

"Well, Defence is Federal, not State; so you might want to talk to Craig."

He was referring to Craig Emerson MP, Federal Member for Rankin. We both knew Craig well. I had previously been Vice President of one of the local Labor Party Branches for two years, and Barry was a Life Member of the Labor Party. We were not only on a first name basis with him, but Craig had shown he was willing to discuss with me any issue I wanted raised by handing me his private mobile number, which I still carried.

"Hmm, not sure about Craig. I was thinking maybe Brett," I said.

"Well, yes, he's Federal too..."

"I like the way he thinks Barry. He's analytical. He'll look for a solution."

I knew Brett Raguse MP, Federal Member for Forde better than I knew Craig. I had previously worked with Brett in the office of Barbara Stone MP, State Member for Springwood. Brett was the Electorate Officer then, and I was Ms Stone's secretary. He was easy to work with, efficient, intelligent, tackled problems by looking at them from various angles and always greeted me with a hug. Yes, that was what I needed – a friend with brains and clout!

Barry looked at his watch, "24th February, Parliament is sitting."

"Oh!" I felt a little disappointed, "so they're both in Canberra."

"Stuart Fenech is Brett's Liaison Officer," Barry was a mine of information, he always knew who was who in the zoo, "run it past him, see what he says."

"Yes, thanks Barry, that's exactly what I'll do."

I relaxed into the high backed leather chair. Suddenly everything was starting to come together. I could see a way through, but I wasn't sure I should begin the journey.

When I got home, I did what I normally do when I'm uncertain, I turned to God. I knew a miracle had put me into DSA, and the hand of God had kept me there against all odds until I eventually saw what I was supposed to see and was finally, gratefully, led out in joy; a joy in which I was still living. So despite the fact I thought my involvement had finished, doors were beginning to open in front of me, and I couldn't ignore them.

When I opened the Scriptures that afternoon, one verse stood out, almost in flashing neon lights, and I not only knew I should begin the journey but how I should begin and what would happen when I did.

> *Write the vision down, make it plain on paper, so that he who reads it will run with it.* (Habakkuk 2:2)

From that moment on, I was confident this was something I was supposed to do. I also knew deep down where faith lives that at the end there would be victory.

I had absolutely no doubt there would be victory because I knew from past experience that when God tells his people to do something, victory is always the end result.

All I had to do was make a complaint on paper so that anyone reading it would be compelled to act on what was written. I believed God's word, and felt absolutely confident that after I'd done my part, God would do the rest.

"Hi, Janice," I said into the phone, "how are you?"

"Still looking for jobs, nothing new to report. What about you?"

"No job, but busy as a bee!"

"Well, that sounds interesting." The curiosity behind her words made them sound like a question.

I decided to get straight to the point. "I'm putting in an official complaint, want to join me?"

"Jennifer already tried the Ombudsmen's Office, they're not interested." She was under-enthusiastic, to put it mildly.

I wanted to blurt out all my good news, but couldn't, I would have to explain step by step what I'd done. "I'm going through political channels."

"Can you do that?" Janice sounded doubtful, but curious again.

"Sure can! I used to work for a Member of Parliament, remember? I know how the system works."

"What do you mean?" Now she was fully curious.

"Well, when a complaint is received by a local Member, it's forwarded to the relevant Minister's office for action. When the Minister, or his Liaison Officer, investigates the complaint and makes a decision about it, they send their findings back to the local Member, who passes on the Minister's response to the person who made the complaint."

"So?"

"So it means that putting a complaint through a local Member is the quickest way to get it seen by a Minister."

"Oh!" I could hear the proverbial penny dropping, "So you mean we should complain to the Minister for Defence?"

"That's exactly what I mean!" Whoo-hoo! She got it! But would she be interested?

There was a pause. I could almost hear Janice thinking. Then suddenly, she spoke. "I'm in! Who else can we get?" Her response was sharp, definite and carried a hint of excitement.

"I'm going to email Owen and Jennifer." No turning back now.

"I could email Cassie," offered Janice.

"Are you sure about Cassie? She's still there..."

"Yes, this would get her sacked," said Janice, "and I wouldn't like to feel I was the cause."

"No, neither would I, let's leave her out of this loop."

"Good idea," said Janice. "Who else is there?"

"I don't have anyone else's contact details," I said. When people disappeared from Defence it was usually so sudden there was no time for good-byes, let alone phone and email exchanges.

"Well, three or four might be enough," said Janice vaguely, clearly still trying to think of others who may be interested.

Of course! How Scriptural! I chuckled into the phone, "You're right, Janice! Three will be plenty! Our complaints only need to be based on the *'evidence of two or three witnesses'*," I said, knowing Janice would recognise the Scripture I was referring to immediately.

"How are we going to start this?" asked Janice, curious to know our next move.

"I already have," I said. "You know I used to work in the office of the Member for Springwood."

"Yes,"

"Your current local member, Brett Raguse, was working in the same office at the same time. I shared a workspace with him for nearly a year. I know him really well."

"I didn't know that," Janice interjected, "but do go on."

"Today I phoned his office and spoke to his Liaison Officer about the situation in Defence. Stuart took some details and said he would talk to Brett about it when he returned."

"Oh, that's good!"

"It gets better! He didn't actually wait until Brett returned, he emailed him while he was sitting in Parliament and told him our story straight away!"

"While he was actually sitting in Parliament? Wow!"

"Yes, wow! Then, to my great surprise, less than an hour after I first spoke to Stuart, he phoned me back! I just finished speaking with him and called you straight away."

"What did he say?"

"He said Brett is happy to take our complaints to the Minister for Defence. All we need to do is get our letters together."

"Oh, fantastic!" Janice was now gushing with excitement. "Oh, this is the best news I've heard for a long time! Ooooh," she squeaked, "who would've thought working at DSA could lead to such fun!"

I couldn't help laughing. Janice's enthusiasm was refreshing after our arduous ordeal. I was so pleased she was onboard. Things were definitely falling into place.

Our group gets back together

Over the next few days, Owen, Jennifer, Donna, Janice and myself all began drafting letters which could go through Brett's office to the Minister for Defence. Now there were five of us. Our weakness was we were all agency staff, it would be better if we could have our stories confirmed by Defence personnel. It was time to tell Crystal what we were doing, so I phoned her.

"That's where we're up to. Owen, Janice and I have completed our letters. Donna emailed me tonight and said hers will be finished tomorrow, and Jennifer is drafting hers."

"I can't believe you're doing this." Crystal's voice was shaking with emotion.

"The five of us alone have complaints so serious the Minister will have to act. We've used words like, discrimination, bullying, intimidation, abuse, segregation, isolation and humiliation – not one of these practices is legal. We're all using testimony rather than accusation. It's more effective," I said. I didn't tell her it was a Scriptural principle. Crystal wasn't a Christian.

"If ever there was a cause, I believe this is a good one." Her voice was a bit too thick. Was she crying?

"Are you okay?"

"Sorry, there's just so much pent up emotion," she sniffed.

"We don't have to talk about this."

"No, I want to, but I get physically sick from things like this, and that scares me," Crystal blew her nose, "don't get me wrong, this is really important to me."

"Do you want me to continue?"

"Yes, please do," she sounded a little stronger. "I'm okay now."

"In our letters, we've named Erik, Paula, Con and Dora as the main sources of abuse."

"What about Jack and Cleo...and Helga?"

"Yes, and the rest, Crystal! We can't name them all... well, not yet anyway."

"So, you think it actually might get somewhere?"

"Yes, I do! With five eye-witnesses, this is already a very strong complaint. The trouble is, it doesn't address your situation."

"No, it doesn't! You are all agency staff."

"Exactly! The final nail in the coffin would come if a Defence permanent backed our claims."

"It would also show the problem is widespread and entrenched," Crystal confirmed.

"Yes, it would! Would you be game?" I knew this was a big ask. I knew how much it could cost Crystal to be involved. I didn't expect an answer straight away.

"Hmm, not sure, I'd need some kind of protection." Crystal wasn't sniffing anymore, she was still cautious, but I could hear in her voice there was a ray of hope, a very small one, flickering ever so faintly, "I still have to work there."

"I might have a solution."

"It'd better be a dammed good one," Crystal snapped. Her tone was sharp, and she immediately pulled herself up, "Sorry, not belittling you, but you're not here anymore. You know what they're like and the way they work. They can quite easily make my life a living hell for a long time. This'll be something that'll never be forgotten as far as they're concerned."

"Yes, I understand," I spoke as gently as I could. "But what if you could meet with the Minister for Defence face to face and tell him your story. Would you be interested?"

Crystal laughed in derision, "you can't arrange that!"

"No, but I know people who can."

An intense silence filled the phone line. Not even the sound of breathing could be heard. Crystal was all ears.

"Let me tell you what I mean," I said, speaking into the silence. "I went to the office of Craig Emerson, Minister for Independent Contractors and told his office manager I needed some advice on how to make a complaint about Defence. She immediately phoned his Ministerial Advisor. I was on the phone with her for about twenty minutes. The short of it is, his Advisor told me, and the office manager, that as soon as I brought in the letters of complaint and any supporting documents, she would organise a meeting between Brett Raguse, Craig Emerson, the Minister for Defence, herself and us. Now, that is heavy duty in anyone's language, Crystal!"

"No way! When did this happen?" Crystal was almost breathless.

"Just a few days ago."

"I can't believe this!"

"So I figure, if you had the courage to come along we could verify each other's stories and our combined complaint from both sides, permanent and agency, would present an impossible situation for DSA."

Crystal began to laugh. And kept on laughing.

I laughed with her. It was so good just thinking about the possibility of a solution.

"I know you're going through hell, Crystal, and I know what I am asking you. However, this is an open door which goes straight to the top. These MPs want to know what's going on. They're all ears. And they have the power to stop the rot in a way which doesn't cause you any harm. Please think about it."

"I would like to think about it." Crystal had become cautious again. "And I'd also like to talk it over with my husband."

"Of course!" I was smiling, but Crystal couldn't see it.

"I can't believe how much you've done, in such a short time."

"Nothing's been done yet, but if we turn on this spotlight together, DSA won't have the power to turn it off."

"The fight will be outside their control."

"Exactly!" Now she was getting it, but would she join with us. I held my breath.

"Look, why don't we get together - my place. Are you free next weekend?"

Wooo-hoo! I jumped for joy and threw a joyful victory fist into the air, though Crystal couldn't see me. Yes! She was in! I was ecstatic!

When I spoke my voice was calm, "I'm free!" I said.

"Come for dinner!"

"I'd love to Crystal." I was beaming; grinning from ear to ear. Another door had just opened. Awesome!

"I'll get back to you with the details."

When I got off the phone, I sat down in my armchair dumbstruck with awe. So much had happened in such a short time, it was incredible, but it had also been effortless. I felt like I was sitting in the back seat of a long limo. Someone else was steering this huge, luxury vehicle through unfamiliar territory, and all I had to do was sit back, relax and enjoy the ride.

Defence's goose was being cooked

"You made it." Crystal was smiling her broadest smile as she welcomed me into her home. "I wasn't sure if you would be able to follow my directions."

"I'm normally hopeless with directions," I said as we hugged, "but I didn't have a problem today."

I presented her with a large box of my favourite after-dinner mints and followed her through the house into her spacious dining room. The table had papers spread all over it, and someone was standing near the window, looking out at the lush tropical backyard garden.

"Linda!"

When I called her name, Linda turned to greet me, and the smile on her face was as bright as the sunlit window behind her. "Surprise!" she beamed.

I looked from Linda to Crystal. They were both smiling like children with a secret. This could only mean one thing. I looked back to Linda. "Does this mean you're in?"

Linda nodded and came over to greet me with a hug. "I think you're both incredibly brave. I don't know how much I can do, but I support you all the way."

I was overwhelmed. All I could do was laugh. We were now seven, five agency and two Defence. This was going to work!

We spent hours going over events, listing incidents, making notes, discussing the best way forward.

"These are the same vetting issues I told Erik about over two years ago when I thought he might actually care." Linda twisted her face into a grimace. "Wrong!"

"So all this has been going on for two years?" I asked.

"Round and round the not so merry-go-round," agreed Crystal and Linda nodded.

"It started slowly, but now everything keeps changing, and no one knows what's supposed to be happening from one day to the next," said Linda.

"Every supervisor has a different version." As she spoke, Crystal went over to the kitchen and filled the jug with water for coffee.

Linda was angry. "That is exactly the problem with putting people into management roles who don't have the background knowledge required, and who focus only on stats and impressing upper management bullies rather than being accountable for the integrity of vetting, solid procedures and their team's morale."

"Erik and Paula don't want people in management who think about those last three points," said Crystal. "Good people get in the way of their management methods!"

"We can't disclose these things," Linda was stating the obvious, "we'll be prosecuted if we say anything."

"Drawn and quartered," said Crystal.

"We can say what we want about the bullying," I said, "just not the security issues."

"The Official Secrets Act forbids it," said Crystal.

"Well, maybe - why don't we take a look at the Act?" suggested Linda.

"It would be simpler just to ask someone who knows," I said.

"We can be prosecuted for talking to a lawyer," said Crystal. She was dead right. Saying anything at all about procedures could land us all in jail.

"We can't be prosecuted for talking to a Member of Parliament," I said, knowing I was dropping a bombshell.

Linda and Crystal stopped talking and looked up from their lists.

"Go on," said Crystal.

"Parliamentary privilege - totally secure," I said.

Linda was nodding, "Of course! We can say anything." she said.

I continued, "you can lay it all on the table, the whole lot, everything we've discussed...and more."

"And it can't come back to bite us." Linda smiled. She was on the same page, but Crystal still had doubts.

"I want to see what Jeff thinks." Crystal left the table and went to find her husband. When they came back, we told him our thoughts and asked his opinion.

"I think you need a few approaches," he said, "agency complaints about bullying," he turned to his wife, "your complaints about bullying," he looked back at our group, "and a combined complaint about security issues."

"A three-pronged attack," said Crystal.

"We start with one, and while they're looking at that, we send the second from a different direction. Then while they're busy with those two, we hit them with our main complaint," I said.

We sat back in our chairs. This made absolute sense. We all nodded in agreement.

"We need to organise our complaints," said Linda.

"The agency complaints are organised," I said. "We can limit the first five letters to bullying if necessary."

"I'll help you make your bullying complaints honey," Jeff suggested, "they can come through my official channels, that way they'll by-pass DSA, but still reach the right people." Jeff worked in Defence as well and understood the system.

"So those two areas are covered," said Linda smiling. "How do we go about the vetting side?"

"I'll make an appointment for the three of us to see Brett Raguse," I said. "I know him as well as I know you girls. I worked with him. He'll give us good, accurate advice about threats to National Security. If there is a way through, he'll find it for us."

"What about seeing the Minister for Defence?" asked Crystal.

"Our main complaint will go to him. We need to be organised before we see him," I said, "best to see Brett first."

"How soon can you make an appointment with him?" asked Linda.

I shrugged my shoulders, I didn't have a clue. "Parliament's sitting - he'll only be in the office a few days this month. I'll see what I can do."

Finally, we had a plan.

At the office of Brett Raguse, MP

I arranged the meeting with Brett by phone and wrote a letter to confirm the reason. Three days later, when the first two agency letters were completed, I hand delivered them to the offices of both Brett Raguse MP and Craig Emerson MP. The other three agency complaint letters had not arrived in the mail, so I planned to take them with me to the meeting with Brett, which had been set for the 23rd of March.

As the day of the meeting drew nearer, Crystal became increasingly nervous.

"I'm really scared!" Crystal said as we sipped our coffees. "If DSA finds out, there'll be hell to pay."

We had chosen to meet at McDonald's so Crystal and I could travel to Brett's office together. Crystal couldn't sit still; she kept looking around, expecting to be 'caught' talking to me.

"It's okay, Crystal, we are allowed to associate, we're not in DSA." I tried to reassure her, but it didn't work.

"What if they see us together, they'll know." She was so nervous her knuckles were white. "Do you think I'm being paranoid?"

I shook my head at her and smiled, "You're displaying more courage than any of us. You have to face those bullies every day. To be honest, Crystal, if you hadn't tried to stand up for agency staff and been shut down so harshly, I wouldn't be taking this action now. I'm doing this because of you."

"I wish I could be stronger." Poor Crystal, she was now so nervous I began to think she might not be able to go through with the meeting.

I had to do something to help her. But what?

"Why don't we go over the points for today again... make sure we've covered everything." I offered.

"Okay!"

As we went over the points and discussed possible outcomes, Crystal became calmer, and when we finished our coffees, we walked out to my car and started the ninety minute trip to Beenleigh. Linda would be waiting for us in the car park opposite Brett's Office complex.

"I don't know if Brett will be able to answer all of our questions," said Linda, as we walked from the car park to Brett's office, "but he should be able to let us know how the official complaint system works and what steps to take."

"And whether he thinks our concerns will be taken seriously, or not," concluded Crystal.

"Do you think we'll be able to remain anonymous?" asked Linda, unusually nervous, "I mean, even in the meeting?" These women were so brave. They were trusting me completely, knowing that if I was wrong about Brett, they would be in serious trouble.

"He will act according to your wishes," I said as gently as I was able."That's definite! This will be completely confidential unless you say otherwise."

I never got tired of reassuring them. To my way of thinking they were hero's who could be, figuratively speaking, shot down any minute, yet they were still willing to go into battle.

We entered Brett's office and were immediately escorted into his small, comfortable, tastefully decorated meeting room. As I sank into one of the soft lounge chairs, I smiled. This room was obviously designed to put people at ease; make them feel at home. So like Brett to care about the little things.

The door opened, and Brett walked in. The three of us stood up, and Brett came to me first and welcomed me with a hug. "It's been a while," he said, "good to see you, Monica."

He turned to the girls and held out his hand, "Hi, I'm Brett."

The girls followed his lead - first names only. I knew I could count on him. As they each shook his hand, I could see them begin to relax.

"I'm Linda."

"I'm Crystal."

"Thank you for seeing us, Brett," said Linda, "but before we say anything, I just need reassurance about one thing." She was coming straight to the point. "Is it true what we say here is covered by Parliamentary privilege?"

"We don't want to be prosecuted," added Crystal with a nervous smile.

"Yes, that's right," said Brett, "well, that is, as long as you don't want to give me super-secret satellite codes."

We all laughed. His well-placed joke had put the girls completely at ease, and we spent the next ninety minutes laying everything before him.

“Bullying is being used to enforce practices which are putting Australia’s National Security at risk,” I started the ball rolling, with a bit of background. “The five letters of complaint from agency staff concentrate on that aspect, but we are here to find out how to go about officially exposing breaches of security within an intelligence organisation, without being prosecuted.”

“We want to know if the Official Secrets Act prevents us from speaking out about things which are causing harm to Australia,” said Crystal.

“We need protection,” I said.

“We know the Act says we would be in breach if we revealed things which could potentially harm Australia,” said Linda, “but what about when we want to protect Australia, does the Act prevent us from speaking up?”

I wouldn’t think so, but I’m not a lawyer,” Brett responded. “What kind of things are we talking about?”

We told Brett about the way clearances were being doctored, the manipulation and outright manufacture of data, the deceit of ASIO and the determination of management to ensure those practices continued. We gave specific examples and all the while Brett listened intently.

“Have any of you been personally bullied?” Brett asked, concerned.

“All of us,” I said. The others were nodding in agreement. “It’s routine at DSA.”

“You know bullying is completely against Australian law,” said Brett. “No one ever has to put up with it!”

Crystal burst into tears. She was shaking her head. “The law doesn’t apply within DSA! They do what they want and get away with it.”

Linda went over and sat beside Crystal, putting her hand on her arm for support. “You’ve no idea Brett, I’m currently on long service leave because my health can’t take the strain of that place anymore.”

"There's been investigation after investigation," I said, "all internal. Nothing ever changes. DSA believe they're above the law."

"They're not above the law," said Brett, sitting forward on his seat. "I think you've identified some serious issues here, but you're going to need proof."

"What do we need to do?" asked Linda.

"I'm prepared to take this to Alan Griffin, Minister for Defence Personnel." Brett turned to me, "do you remember him, Monica? He was the one I contacted over the F111 de-sealer issue."

Brett was referring to the previous time he'd assisted me with a complaint. My sister, Kathleen was secretary to a group called the 'goop troupe', which had been fighting for justice for the 900 plus RAAF service men and women who were dying because of their contact with the deadly chemicals they had to use while sealing and de-sealing the fuel tanks of the F111s.

For ten years Kathleen had taken the group complaints to Defence without success. Then, with the assistance of Minister Griffin things began to change, and after some to-ing and fro-ing, Kathleen had been invited to address the Senate and present the de-sealers plight.

Though it was too late for many, including Kathleen's husband, who died at the young age of 49, the plight of the remaining de-sealers was recognised and some small and grudging assistance was given by Defence.

"I remember Minister Griffin," I said nodding, "he acted promptly."

"Tell you what I'll do," Brett said. "I'll send these first complaints off to Alan Griffin while you gather your evidence for the security breaches. It doesn't have to be a lot, just something for each allegation. Concentrate on what you can prove." He leant forward. "Get the evidence to me as soon as you can, and I'll pass it on."

"What about the meeting with Craig Emerson and the Minister for Defence?" I asked.

"I haven't heard anything from Craig's office yet." Brett looked over at Jason, his electorate officer, seated inconspicuously at the other end of the room, taking minutes all through the meeting. Jason shook his head, confirming there was no message. Brett looked back at us. "I'll let you know when I hear something."

We all stood up. The meeting was over. The girls were happy and genuinely grateful to Brett. We gushed our farewells and headed back to the car park.

"Let's have coffee," suggested Linda.

We found a tiny place tucked away in a back street and spent an hour re-hashing the meeting and writing notes. Brett's advice and offer of assistance had been invaluable.

The hammer falls on Crystal

A few weeks after the meeting with Brett, my home phone rang. "I hope you're not busy," I recognised Crystal's voice straight away.

"Never too busy for you, m'dear."

"I have ze good news, and I have ze bad news." Crystal's tone reminded me of the old 1970's 'Laugh-in' good news/bad news skits, and I laughed.

"Bad news first, please."

"Okay! Two days after the meeting with Brett, I was ordered into Paula's office and 'grilled' for three and a half hours," Crystal said. "I think they must've got a whiff of what we're doing."

"Oh, no!" I said. It was obvious Crystal thought Brett had betrayed her. I held my breath.

"Paula was out for blood. She threatened me and let me know well and truly how many people I would be up against if I continue with whatever I am doing, assuming I am doing anything and assuming I am continuing. She was covering all bases." Crystal said.

"It sounds like they know."

"It does, doesn't it?" her voice had an edge to it, and I had to put her mind at ease, somehow...

"If they do, I can assure you, Crystal, it didn't come from Brett's office." I was convinced I was speaking the truth. "Maybe they've heard about our bullying complaints."

"Well, it seems I'm the bully. Apparently, I am a terrible bully, and I bully everyone all the time, especially Cleo, can you believe it?" Crystal said. "They're literally gunning for me - and for anyone who tries to support me."

"Ah! So they *have* heard about the bullying complaints," I said. "Are you all right?"

"No." Crystal had gone into matter-of-fact mode again. "I'm as sick as a dog, vomiting all the time, crying, and it's just stress. I can't handle it at the moment."

"Can you take any time off?"

"The doctor gave me a couple of weeks off, but Jeff arranged for us both to meet with someone from Defence's Department of Fairness and Resolution in the middle of my leave. That meeting was at DSA, and it was a waste of time."

The penny dropped, "Oh! So that's how Paula found out you made a complaint, the meeting was held at DSA!" I shook my head, there was nothing 'fair' about their choice of venue! "Paula obviously didn't know what the meeting would be about and was fishing for information, like Jack did, to try and get you to spill the beans," I said. "What happened in the meeting?"

"It was in Erik's office, and I told this HR guy what had been happening, and Jeff pointed out all the laws being broken, but it didn't mean anything to either of them."

"Not even Fairness and Resolution?"

"No!"

"Well, I suppose that was an obvious outcome, seeing they were prepared to expose you by holding the meeting in Erik's office," I said. "It show's whose side they're on!"

"Jeff's really angry," said Crystal. "He'd only heard what I've told him about the bullying; just second-hand information, but now he's seen it happen first hand, for himself. With that and the grilling I got from Paula, he wants to put in an official complaint tonight. That's why I called. That's the good news!"

"Oh, fantastic!" I said, "That *is* good news, but I'm so sorry it's taking such a toll on you."

"So am I, but at least now Jeff can see what I have been up against and I don't have to fight on my own."

"Good on Jeff! What a champion!"

"I think they've gone too far, Monica." Crystal's tone had become very calm and matter-of-fact again. "I don't have any choice anymore. I have to fight for what is right, no matter how it makes me feel."

"You need protection!"

"I have five weeks leave owing. I'm going to take it."

"Good! Just try and catch your breath, my friend, and get lots and lots of rest."

What a relief! This would mean a total of seven weeks leave for her, a welcome break from that horrible place, and it would give her the time and space to think clearly about what she wanted to do next.

It was the end of March, just six weeks beyond my Departure from Defence. We now had two arms of complaint in place, and Crystal was taking herself out of the line of fire. Things were looking up.

Heads begin to roll

A lot happened over the next two months both inside and outside DSA, and we seven remained in constant email contact, with all of us copied in on every email:

- "Did you know? No new agency staff have been hired since Monica left in mid-February? Not one! People are still leaving, but no one is being replaced." Cassie.
- "I was told by my team leader there were no more agency staff coming in because there were not enough qualified people to do the job." Crystal.
- "Rubbish! Another lie! We're in the middle of a recession! I personally know at least twenty people qualified and available to do that job, but now I know what I know, I wouldn't offer DSA to my worst enemy." Monica.
- "Maybe that's the problem. Maybe they're not game to supply any more staff to DSA until this mess is sorted out." Janice.
- "Hey, guys! Did you know that in the Saturday career's guide, March 27, the employment agency was advertising their Operations Manager position? Wasn't that Dora's position? Heads rolling - people jumping ship maybe?" Linda.
- "It's good for me. I told Erik I was resigning and he offered me part-time instead. I guess they can't replace me if I leave and there's hardly anyone there now." Cassie.
- "Speaking of jobs, my old boss contacted me about an opening. I put in my resume, did the interview and am now employed again. Back with normal people! Wooo-hoo!" Monica.

- "I received my ADF service medal at a little ceremony this morning presented by an MP. I mentioned a couple of things to him about DSA, he was interested and is going to get back to me. Can't hurt to have a couple of MP's sniffing around, huh?" Linda.

- "DSA has begun their internal investigation. I had my interview today. Very shocked at some things I revealed. They didn't like your Stat Dec, Monica. Too bad!" Crystal.

- "Not sure if Crystal has let you know yet, but big news. The complaints you put through the Minister's Office have finally reached DSA and have resulted in a fantastic response! Just in the sweetest of time too. The internal investigation seemed to just be on it's wrap up - well so they thought - and then bammo - your complaints were obviously received. Unreal!!" Linda.

- "The heads of DSA came up from Canberra, called a meeting, wanted to know if what was in your five letters was true. Everyone was nodding, even APS staff. No one objected." Cassie.

- "Whatever the outcome, it's been an awesome ride! I'll leave it in God's hands. *Bring down your large hard hand, Lord and start smacking some butts. Amen!*" Owen.

- "Dora came in today and announced she is resigning - said someone had complained about her being a bully - said she couldn't understand how anyone could accuse her of such a thing!" Cassie.

- "Smack! There goes one!" Owen.

- "Ooooh! They must be feeling it now! Would love to be a fly on the wall in Erik's office - as long as I'm protected by anti-Erik spray and can have a very long and thoroughly cleansing shower afterwards." Linda.

- "It will be interesting to see how the D culprits are handled. Somehow, I don't think they'll be sacked, just moved on. Such is the joy of being a permanent government employee." Jennifer.
- "Just letting you know, Jack was called to Canberra, came back and surprised us all by resigning. He didn't say why." Crystal.
- "Smack! There goes another one!" Owen.
- "It's all very vague. There seem to be two investigations being run - one for contractors and one for APS. But they are not being explained or communicated. Nobody actually knows what's going on." Linda.

It was all happening! After receiving Crystal's complaints through Jeff, and our complaints through Brett Raguse MP, Alan Griffin, Minister for Defence Personnel, had ordered two simultaneous investigations, the first into the treatment of Defence personnel at DSA and the second into the treatment of agency contractors working within DSA.

Though these two investigations were called 'independent', they were not even close to being independent. They were still controlled by DSA management, and in typical DSA fashion, Erik and Paula were keeping all staff, both Defence and agency, in the dark about the purpose of the multiple investigations being conducted right under their noses. Nevertheless, it seemed our complaints were having an effect. Heads were already rolling, and this was just the beginning. We hadn't even been interviewed.

Haphazard, half-baked investigations

On the first of July 2010, I received a letter from DSA by express mail, dated 23 June, telling me I would be contacted shortly by an investigator seeking to set up an interview time.

I thought it was odd this notice should be delivered by express mail until I received a letter from Alan Griffin MP dated 28 June, five days later, stating the investigation had been extended because DSA told him they couldn't find some of us.

I was astounded! Had DSA just lied to the Minister? Our information hadn't changed. They had every detail of our lives for the last ten years at their fingertips, on their database; our phone numbers, addresses, our next of kin, siblings and parents and their phone numbers and addresses. To say they couldn't find any of us was an outright lie.

The express letter was the first contact they'd made with any of us. There'd been no previous attempts! It was painfully clear that yes, they had lied to the Minister about us before they even tried to contact us!

Why? What was the point of this lie? Covering their uncontrolled disorganisation? Or deliberately putting us in a bad light? Or both? Did this mean the outcome of the investigation had already been decided? We were told it was supposed to be an 'independent' investigation, but now I began to wonder if that was actually true. This was not looking good.

The day after I received my 'overnight' notification from DSA that we would be contacted by an investigator, I was phoned at work.

"Hello, Monica, I am Julie from Robert Brennan and Associates, and I'd like to set up a meeting with you for next Monday or Tuesday."

"Hello, Julie. Today is Friday. Monday or Tuesday is short notice. Are there any other times available?"

"Didn't you receive notification I would be contacting you?" She was sounding pushy.

"Yes, it arrived yesterday, and it said you would be contacting us sometime in the next few weeks."

"I am flying up from Canberra on Sunday. I only have Monday and Tuesday for interviews."

"Robert Brennan and Associates, is that a legal firm?"

"We are management consultants."

Management consultants? Not lawyers? So they had no intention of looking at the breaches of the law. I sighed. "Okay, well as it turns out, I have already arranged with my employer to take Monday off for a dental appointment, so Monday morning would be good for me," I said.

"Are you in contact with Donna and Jennifer?"

Whoa! Red lights started flashing! She was fishing! Why did she want to know if we were in contact with each other? Where was this going?

"Why?" I asked.

"It's just I don't have contact details for them."

Really? Defence intelligence had told the Minister they had trouble finding some of us, but now, here was the truth – DSA didn't give the investigators our contact details! No wonder we couldn't be located! I shook my head. Would the games never cease?

"I know how to contact them," I said.

"Can you give me their details? I need to speak with them as soon as possible."

You've got to be kidding me! Was this investigator asking me to breach the Privacy Act? Definitely not a lawyer! Unbelievable!

"What if I pass your contact details along to them so they can phone you?" I was starting to get a little annoyed at this woman. Rushed, disorganised, pushy and now wanting me to do her work for her. Some management consultant! No, not looking good at all!

"I've booked you in for Monday. I will confirm the time via email," Julie concluded.

The following Monday, the interview was conducted in Julie's private hotel room. Another disappointment! I would have expected to be interviewed in a conference room or an office, not a bedroom. It wasn't professional, and I felt uncomfortable being there.

"I'm just going to go over what you've written in your letter of complaint," Julie said. "You used the word 'collaborate'. That's a very strong word. What did you mean?"

She's checking grammar? What about the serious issues? Strong word? Not strong enough! Did she think the word was a random choice? I took a deep breath. "I meant in the strongest possible terms, that Defence and the employment agency jointly worked together to bully, harass, intimidate and psychologically torture employees."

"Oh!" she looked back down at her notes, "Can you give me an example of how they collaborated?"

Was this it? Were these the kind of simplistic questions we were going to be asked? "Examples are all through my letter, Julie. Let me refer you to the day of my dismissal." I pointed out the example on the paperwork in front of her. "Basically, Erik said jump and Dora said how high?"

The interview continued along those veins. It seemed the only thing this investigator wanted to do was check that what I'd written in the letter was grammatically accurate. In our meeting, I used strong words like bullying, harassment and psychological torture and yet not one of those words, or their implications, was picked up or discussed. After two and a half hours of explaining 'what I meant by' I was exhausted. It was like sitting for an English exam.

"In conclusion, is there anything about the management style in DSA that you would like to see changed?" Julie asked.

What? I nearly fell off my chair! Didn't she know how unreasonable her question was? The concept wasn't even relevant! How could I possibly give her an answer? It was like she was reading a list of 'management consultant' questions she'd found on the internet. Her questions didn't fit our complaints. I felt like knocking on her forehead and saying 'Hello! Is anybody home?'

As quickly as my frustration came, it went. What the heck, Julie was only a management consultant, and not a very good one at that! It was obvious she didn't have the legal qualifications to investigate our bullying allegations, and she probably didn't have the security clearance to investigate intelligence issues. That meant all she could report on was management style. How disappointing! How pathetic! How typical of Defence! Some investigation - carefully organised to avoid the issues.

"It's not about management style, Julie," I said quietly, hoping she would listen and try to understand. "They all need to be sacked! All of them!"

She looked up, dubious and paused her record taking.

How could I explain this to her? "They don't have a management problem, they have a morality problem! They are very good managers. They have successfully managed, over a long period of time, to break the law, deceive ASIO, destroy Australia's National Security and manipulate any investigation which comes along. They know what they are doing. It's deliberate! What they need is to be sacked! I believe they need to be replaced by the military – people who actually care about this country."

Julie was looking at me stunned. She put down her pen, so I guessed she wasn't going to write what I'd just said in her report. "Well, we are out of time," she said. "I have another appointment to go to over at Victoria Barracks."

Of course we were out of time! We were just getting to the good part! It was clear to me she was out of her depth. I sat back in my chair. I had so much more to say and no way of saying it.

“If you think of anything else, please let me know... email me...and I will include your comments in my report.” Julie was standing now and packing her paperwork away.

“Thank you,” I said, a little taken aback by my sudden and somewhat informal dismissal, “I might just take you up on that offer.” I stood up, gathered my things, said goodbye and left the room.

I wanted to talk to the others but I couldn’t. My interview was first, so I had to wait until they’d all been interviewed before we could communicate again. Bummer! Oh, well, the dentist was waiting with his needle and drill. I chuckled to myself. Saving the best for last! What a day!

Defence manipulates the outcome

A few weeks after our interviews, we arranged to meet for pancakes at a converted convict-built church in the inner city. The place was packed and oozing medieval atmosphere. The original ornate stained glass windows were still intact, and between them, shields and swords adorned the red brick walls. Neat ribs of dark brown woodwork covered the high arched roof from which hung two imposing, hand-crafted, wood candelabra chandeliers.

With the low buzz of chatter, intermittent laughter, the clink of glasses and lively Gaelic music filling the air, we felt assured no one would overhear our conversation. Every padded pew was filled, so we found ourselves seated around a long refectory table on hard wooden backless benches, and despite the crowds around us, entered into our own little world.

“You know, you picture security and intelligence, and you think they’ve got it all,” said Owen, “James Bond! A well-oiled machine!”

“Yes, that’s right,” laughed Jennifer, “efficient...well planned...well thought out...”

"Trim! Taut! Terrific!" added Donna, "and, of course, well dressed!"

"Obeying the rules," said Cassie.

"Ready to die for Queen and country," I said.

"Those were my expectations," laughed Owen. "What a letdown!"

"It turned out to be more like 'Maxwell Smart' fighting 'Kaos'," said Janice.

"And we didn't even have to leave the building," Jennifer rejoined.

We were all on the same page - all laughing. It was good to be together again. We were a team. And we had passed an important milestone, no matter what the outcome.

"I think we can all be proud of what we have done," I said, and I meant it.

"Three simultaneous investigations is quite an achievement," agreed Janice.

"It's a shame we all had to lose our jobs for this to happen," said Donna.

Owen made his 'sorry-I'm-saying-this' face, "I hope it hasn't been a waste of time."

"How can it be a waste of time?" asked Janice.

Jennifer was nodding, "I'm not overly confident with the process," she said.

"I question the process too," Owen agreed, "Julie was only a consultant, and her company is so small, or new, it doesn't even have a website."

"So, you think this is a whitewash?" I asked.

"Possibly," said Jennifer as Owen nodded in agreement.

"Well, I have to admit, I thought meeting in her hotel room was highly unprofessional," said Janice.

"It was extremely uncomfortable for me," Owen raised his eyebrows and looked indignant.

I had never seen this look, he was always so easy going, but not this time.

His tone was serious as he continued, "A man alone with a woman in a hotel room...?" He broke off, shaking his head in disgust.

"Of course! I hadn't thought of that," said Janice.

"She could've cried rape," I said, realising how uncomfortable it must have been for a Godly man, who would never consider cheating on his wife, to be placed in such an unseemly position.

"*You* could've cried rape, Owen," added Donna, lightening the mood.

We all fell about laughing again. Ridiculous was normal when we tried to think like DSA.

"Very compromising, Owen," said Jennifer when the laughter died down, "they should never have put you in that position."

"At least I was interviewed over the phone," said Donna.

Jennifer nodded, "so was I."

"And the questions were pathetic," I added, "like a surprise English exam."

"I was hoping for something more substantial," said Owen, "like some legal discussion about breaches of the Code of Conduct."

"She wasn't interested in the security issues either," Janice agreed.

"I sent her an email about all that," I said, "I don't know whether she will put it in the report or not."

"So did I," Janice giggled, "I sent her copious notes, pages of them. She'll have lots of choice for her report."

"At the end of the day, she works for Defence," said Owen, "she'll report what they want reported."

"They're independent investigators," said Janice.

Jennifer chuckled. "Really? Who pays the bills?"

Jennifer and Owen were right! If DSA had chosen the investigators, Defence was paying them, and they were reporting back to DSA, then this investigation was nothing more than a covert DSA investigation. A cover-up!

"Yes," nodded Donna, "they want to be hired again next time. They'll say what needs to be said!"

"A professional organisation wouldn't have let it come to this," said Jennifer.

We all nodded in agreement.

"Well," said Donna, raising her glass in a toast, "I would do it all again in a heartbeat!"

"Yes," said Janice, raising her glass, "it's not about us, it's about all those who still have to work there!"

"Set my people free!" quoted Owen with his broad grin set firmly in place.

We clinked our glasses in total agreement. It was worth the try.

What we didn't know, at that stage, was though Minister Griffin had said he wanted the investigation wound up by 30 July 2010, it had hit a snag. It was being delayed by the sudden absence of one vital witness. Erik! Erik had taken leave! And had done so just two weeks before the end of the investigation.

This meant the findings would not be given to Minister Griffin. A Federal election had been called for the 21st of August 2010, which meant a possible change of Government, with a possible change of Minister.

Had Erik not taken leave, the investigation would have been completed on time and Minister Griffin would have been able to review the report and comment on its content prior to leaving his portfolio. That was no longer an option.

When we found out the end date for the investigation had been delayed, and why, I couldn't help but wonder at the devious nature of the DSA hierarchy. An interview only took a couple of hours, and could be done over the phone, if necessary, so why was taking leave being used as an excuse to delay the finalisation of this investigation? I was convinced it had been delayed to take advantage of a possible change of Government.

My cynicism might have been called into question if Erik had returned to DSA the following week and completed his part of the investigation so it could be wound up according to the Minister's request. Instead, my suspicions were confirmed.

When Erik left, he left for good. He never returned to his position within DSA. In effect, he abandoned his post suddenly, just two weeks prior to the winding up of an investigation into his personal 'management style' at DSA Brisbane.

Our suspicions are confirmed

Our suspicions that the three investigations would only result in a whitewash grew steadily over the next few months, and it was difficult to live with the possibility that all our efforts could come to nothing. We had no confidence in DSA or Defence, or in their investigation process. Everywhere we looked we could only see gross incompetence, trickery and manipulation; so it came as no surprise that our suspicions were finally confirmed in early December when the original four met up again at our favourite Italian restaurant, just prior to Christmas.

“Any news on anything?” asked Jennifer

“I don’t know why you’re still waiting for news,” said Cassie, who was the only one of us still working at DSA. We had never pressed Cassie for information. We knew she could lose her job. We didn’t tell her everything either, for the same reason. But when she volunteered snippets of information we were grateful.

“Wait ‘till you hear this,” added Janice, who obviously already knew what Cassie was about to say.

“Oh?” I asked, not sure what to expect. There was no such thing as ‘good’ DSA news.

“A while back, agency staff were told the investigation was over, and nothing had changed, so it was business as usual,” drawled Cassie in her own unflustered way.

“When was this?” I asked.

“The end of September,” Cassie answered.

“September!” said Jennifer, more shocked than angry, “three months ago?” She was shaking her head in disbelief, “and we haven’t been informed?”

“I guess they don’t consider us important enough to notify,” said Janice.

“And nothing has been changed?” I asked Cassie, finding it hard to grasp what I was hearing.

“No!” she shook her head as she looked at each of us one at a time, “everything is the same.” Her eyes were filled with apology for being the bearer of such bad news. Cassie was so kind. She didn’t belong in such a dreadful place.

“You’re still entering data the same way?” I asked.

Cassie nodded, shrugging her shoulders in apology.

“DSA has obviously been told the outcome,” said Jennifer in her logical, matter-of-fact manner, “and the agency has been told the outcome, and yet we five are being kept in the dark!”

“So it looks like it’s a cover-up after all,” said Janice, saying what we were all thinking.

“If the bullying is rubber-stamped at high levels, it’ll get even worse!” I said. “Don’t they know that?”

“I don’t think they care,” said Janice.

“I wonder if that D place will ever get its act together,” said Jennifer, shaking her head.

“I think it’s bigger than the D place, Jenn,” I said trying not to sound too pessimistic, “I think it goes beyond Defence - all the way to the top!”

It was time to face the obvious. We all knew it. And a fog of disappointment descended upon us.

“Three investigations to nowhere!” said Janice, summing it all up.

All we could do was nod in agreement.

We eventually did get our letters of notification, but they didn’t arrive until the following week; the week before Christmas - after all the public service offices had closed for the holidays - which meant an immediate response was out of the question. Was this planned? Of course it was!

The federal election had been run in August and as a result Minister Griffin, who had originally ordered the investigations, had been replaced by Warren Snowdon MP. By the end of September, our investigation had been brought to a close, and everyone had been notified of the outcome except us; the people who had made the complaints.

Even though our five original complaint letters about bullying were accompanied by a strongly worded covering letter which emphasised in four dot points our concerns about breaches of National Security, Minister Snowdon’s response showed no indication any of our concerns had ever been queried by him, let alone taken seriously. It seemed his response was merely a ‘rubber-stamp’ after all. Erik’s ploy had worked! Defence was off the hook!

On around the 15th of December 2010, five long, nail-biting months after our interviews in July, and three months after the completion of the investigation, each of us finally received this short message from Warren Snowdon MP. It was dated 26 October, yet it had taken nearly six weeks to get to us. Was Australia Post that slow? No! The date had been manipulated - another lie - typical!

> *With regard to the complaints made by Monica Bennett-Ryan, Janice Weightman, Owen Laikum, Donna (surname removed) and Jennifer (surname removed) the investigator was unable to find any evidence of bullying or harassment.* (Warren Snowdon MP - 26 Oct. 2010)

So much for ministerial integrity. It appeared Defence had acquired the Minister they wanted. It was now as clear as day to us that Defence corruption was not limited to DSA but went all the way to the top.

Where to now? Where do you go when even your elected Ministers willingly support corruption? There was only one place I could think of - the media!

Now things were starting to get interesting!

CHAPTER SIX

ABC Lateline Story? Not true!

In April 2011 three of the original group of seven contacted ABC *Lateline* investigative reporter and producer, John Stewart, outlining our situation. He acted immediately, and in May 2011 the story of the abuse of DSA staff, the corruption of data, the deceit of ASIO and the danger to Australia's National Security was aired on ABC's *Lateline*.

The most immediate response from Defence was silence. When queried about the silence Defence Minister, Stephen Smith, said we hadn't given him anything 'specific' to comment on.

The next day, he revised his statement by saying he would be taking our allegations seriously. We knew what he meant. The problems would remain. It would only be our allegations about the problems which would be taken seriously. In other words, they would be targeting us.

That same day, before any of our claims could be investigated, the outright denials began. The office of Stephen Smith officially reported there was no evidence to support our allegations. ASIO publicly stated they also took our allegations seriously and would work with Defence as required. Federal Labor Member for Gordon, Brendan O'Connor, announced to the world through the Sky News network that our allegations were 'not true'.

That was a strange reaction, considering the heightened security warnings being given regularly to the general public. Three people had just openly confessed on television to breaching National Security, and Defence, instead of condemning our behaviour, told the media and all Australia, prior to any investigation of our claims, that we had definitely *not* breached National Security. Their response was unplanned and ridiculous! We had caught them off-guard!

Within a few days of the *Lateline* story, many current and ex-DSA personnel contacted the ABC to confirm our story was true, albeit requesting anonymity, which the ABC was happy to provide. Meanwhile, Defence continued to publicly deny the problems, while at the same time, much to everyone's confusion, the Minister for Defence confirmed the veracity of our claims by announcing that a costly, high-level investigation into our allegations would be led by the Inspector-General of Defence.

We had no physical proof for our allegations. Unlike most whistleblowers, we weren't able to provide any evidence to back up our claims, for all the proof was digital; held in secure Defence files and inaccessible to anyone without the proper clearance. All any investigator had to do was check the digital records. But would they? Or would Defence only be interested in coming after us? Was this investigation just a trap in disguise? Was it their intention to use it to gather evidence so they could prosecute us?

As it turned out, it was a trap. All we wanted to do was tell the truth. All they wanted to do was prosecute us and send us to jail.

The media was our only option

Even though I knew the only avenue of complaint left to us was the media, that option suddenly became impossible, and it seemed the door to the media had been firmly closed.

In January 2011, massive flooding devastated Queensland, parts of NSW, Victoria and Tasmania. It was recorded as the biggest natural disaster in Australian history with an estimated recovery cost to Australians of upwards of $30billion. The flooding was followed closely by a record category five cyclone, 300 kilometres wide, which cut a devastating path across Queensland and finally died down in the Northern Territory three days later, becoming a low-pressure system which caused more severe and widespread flooding across inland Australia.

The army was deployed to rescue disaster victims and hunt for bodies in the most devastated areas, and they worked tirelessly as they always did in such circumstances. Now was not the time to make any complaints about Defence to the media.

Our military were our heroes!

In early January 2011, before the flooding began, Janice and I put our heads together and wrote a letter to Minister Snowdon stating our objections to the findings, or lack of them, in the Brennan report and asking him to reconsider the evidence of bullying within DSA along with the serious breaches to our National Security. We received his response at the end of March, and it confirmed his earlier apathy; he just wasn't interested.

The big question now was what to do next? The media was out of the question. The Minister wasn't interested. DSA was becoming old news, yet the problem was still continuing. According to our insiders, bullying was still rife within DSA, and Australia's National Security was still being compromised. Yet, though it appeared nothing had changed, and no doors were open, I continued to have a deep assurance that God was in control, had heard our prayers, and that things were about to change. Who can explain deep-rooted belief? I can't!

A week later, the change came.

In late March 2011, the Australian Defence Force Acadamy *Skype Sex Scandal* hit the media. It was a horrible thing to happen, but it opened the doors again. And this time the doors were open so wide nothing could close them. A young female officer cadet had taken her complaints about sexual abuse to the media, and suddenly there were complaints of Defence brutality coming out of the woodwork. This was our opportunity, and I was going to take it!

I gathered the paperwork to review what I could tell the media, and as I re-read Minister Snowdon's letter I saw something I hadn't noticed before. Ah! So that was why we'd been asked so many questions about management style and none about the breaches of the Code of Conduct or National Security; the investigation had never been about our complaints. I suddenly saw the game - hijack a taxpayer-funded investigation approved for National Security issues and use it to pad out the pet project.

> *The firm contracted to investigate the allegations was asked to separately review the management arrangements of the National Coordination Centre (DSA) given its central role in the security vetting process and the imminent move to undertaking vetting for the majority of Commonwealth Departments.* (Warren Snowdon MP March 20, 2011)

No wonder the investigators were '*unable to find any evidence'* of bullying, and National Security issues were only '*mentioned in-passing*', the investigators did exactly what they had been ordered to do; advise on management arrangements! They had used our complaints as a cover while they advised on an entirely different subject. This meant the investigators were corrupt as well! Great!

Minister Snowdon had inadvertently revealed the truth. Management arrangements were supposed to be a 'separate' investigation to our allegations. But we were only involved in one investigation, and it was about 'management styles'. Our strongly worded complaints about bullying and coercion were *never* investigated!

Shortly after recognising Minister Snowdon's bombshell I arranged to meet with Crystal and Linda in an out-of-the-way bar for a drink after work one afternoon. I showed them the telling letter and brought them up to date.

Crystal was hopping mad. "Can someone tell me why they don't just put down their fighting tools and say 'okay, we stuffed up, and we've been found out, now let's move forward and make sure this doesn't happen again'?"

"That's too easy," said Linda.

"Call me green, but honestly, what are they gaining from all of this?" snapped Crystal.

"What is Australia gaining?" asked Linda. She looked at us without a smile "or losing?"

"There are too many people in high places who don't seem to care about Australia," said Crystal, "they're only interested in their own personal success."

"I think there could be quite a few red faces when the truth comes out," I said

Linda was on to me straight away. "What do you mean, 'comes out'?" she asked.

I smiled and let the question hang in the air for a moment. The girls could see I was teasing them, and I had their attention. "I'm tossing up going to the media," I said.

"No!" said Linda and her eyes were suddenly dancing with fun, "really?"

Crystal started giggling. I guessed it was a happy kind of shock response.

"There's nowhere else to go anymore," I continued. "I just need to talk to the others and see if any of them want to do this with me."

"And if they don't?" asked Linda

"Then I'll do it myself," I said. "Want to join me?"

Linda sat back in her chair, ready to listen, "go on," she said, taking a sip of her chardonnay.

Crystal was on the edge of her seat, fidgeting with the stem of her wine glass, gazing absently into the golden liquid, deep in thought.

"I don't want to put myself out on a limb," I said, "but someone has to say something, and I can't see anyone else with their hand up."

"If you go to the media, then so will I," said Crystal. She had stopped fidgeting and sounded calm, almost too calm. Did she know what she was saying?

"Crystal, are you sure?" I asked. She was still working at DSA; she had more to lose than any of us. I hadn't expected her to volunteer and I wondered if she should.

"I'm sure!" she replied emphatically, looking up and smiling at each of us. She was totally confident. "I can remain anonymous and give supportive evidence behind the scenes," she explained.

"We both can," said Linda, suddenly sitting forward. "Give them my name too."

Now it was my turn to chuckle. We poured some more wine, clinked our glasses to seal the deal and settled back in our seats to nut out the next step.

"Who are you going to contact?" asked Crystal. "One of the current affairs shows, I suppose?"

"I don't know yet," I said, shrugging my shoulders, "probably all of them."

"Well, now is a good time," said Linda, "with all the allegations of abuse coming through the media since the ADFA story broke."

"Oh, that's right," agreed Crystal. "There are so many bullying complaints coming in Minister Smith announced he would be setting up an external review because there were too many to handle." She turned to Linda, "what was that review called?'

"'The DLA Piper Review', I think," said Linda. "They already have over 700 complaints, and they're going to be looking at all the allegations of abuse given to the media between April and June this year."

"Great!" I said, bouncing forward on my chair again, "That's just perfect!" It was about time we got some good news. "So, let me get this right. If we act now, we will be in that timeframe, which means whatever we allege will be further investigated. Is that right?"

Crystal and Linda both nodded.

"Yep," said Linda, "any complaints to the media..."

"Oh, it would be so good to have this investigated again," I said.

"And this time by lawyers, not some small-time management consultants," said Linda.

"What a rort that was!" said Crystal.

We seemed to be all in agreement. "So is this what we want?" I asked.

Crystal and Linda looked at each other and then back to me. "Yes!" they chorused.

We flopped back in our chairs again and laughed. Wow! We were we actually doing this!

Becoming whistleblowers

Over the next few days, I wrote my 'story' letter and researched the news media. Where was I going to send it? This was not a flash-in-the-pan news item. It had the potential to be explosive. It needed to be handled with care. Could the media be trusted not to exploit the situation for immediate ratings? In the end, I chose to limit my contact to four major current affairs shows via their own websites and waited to see what would happen.

Days went past. Nothing! No response!

"I guess they're sick of stories about Defence," said Janice, who was aware of what I was doing. We often met for a Saturday morning 'browse and coffee' at the local Christian Book Store, and this was one of those meetings.

"I suppose," I agreed.

"The military was wonderful during the floods, maybe no one wants them criticised," Janice continued.

"Except we are not criticising the military," I said.

"We know that," said Janice, "but most people don't make a distinction between military and civilian in Defence. They're all just Defence.

She was right. How could any true-blue Australian tolerate criticism of Defence when the Army was doing such a great job helping Australians?

"I guess it's one thing to contact the media," I said, feeling a little disheartened, "but quite another to have them accept the story."

"Yes, well, I don't think there is anything wrong with the story," Janice said, rather sharply for Janice. "In fact, I think it is an exceptional story, and I would think any reporter worth his salt would see that."

I smiled. Just when I needed some encouragement, there it was. Janice to the rescue!

"We complained about several serious breaches of our rights under Federal, Queensland and even International laws, and an investigation was ordered into management practices of all things. Management practices! Which have nothing to do with breaches of law! This is the exact reason they didn't find any 'evidence' because they weren't looking for breaches of law, they were looking to improve their management style. The whole thing was a whitewash."

"Bravo Janice," I said. She was on a roll. Talking so forcefully all I could do was smile and nod.

Janice laughed, a quiet lady-like giggle, "I knew this wasn't over," she said in a more demure tone, "and I am glad we're taking it further. I just hope a few of the others feel the same way."

"Crystal and Linda are on board, and I've spoken with Jennifer and Donna." Then I had to tell Janice the bad news, "but they are both sitting this one out."

"Oh? Why is that?" asked Janice, with concern for our friends in her eyes.

"As you know Jennifer's house went under in the floods and she's still homeless. She's living with relatives and spending all her free time renovating and trying to get her home back to a liveable condition.

Janice nodded."The cleanup is taking a lot longer than people thought."

"Well, it could take another three months for Jennifer," I explained. "She said she doesn't need any extra pressure at the moment."

"That's reasonable," said Janice, "I don't think I'd like to be living in temporary accommodation for six months, spending all my spare time cleaning and renovating."

I shook my head. "Neither would I. I told her we would keep her in the loop."

"And Donna?"

"Donna wants to remain anonymous," I said, "which is fair enough."

Janice nodded. "This one is a little bit more public. Oh, by the way, do you think you would want to show your face? Or will you be interviewed 'blacked out' or behind a screen or a big potted plant or something?"

I chuckled; next, she would have me in a trench-coat with a fedora pulled down over my eyes, "I actually hadn't thought about it," I grinned, "what are you going to do?"

"Me?" Janice seemed surprised by my question. "Why would I need to be interviewed?"

"Why not?" I asked, more as a challenge than a question.

"Oh, well," said Janice recovering quickly, "I guess it would give me a chance to have my say."

I nodded, "yes, it would! And from what I've just heard you have plenty to say."

Janice giggled again. "Apparently, I do!"

"And it will add more weight to the story if more than one person is being interviewed," I continued.

"What about Crystal and Linda?" asked Janice, knowing I had spoken to them.

"Background information only at this stage," I said. "We will need Defence or ex-Defence personnel to confirm what we are saying is true."

Janice nodded, "Have you contacted Owen?"

"Yes," I smiled, "he's in!"

"Oh, wonderful!" Janice gushed, almost jumping off her seat, "so there are three of us!"

I nodded, smiling at Janice's reaction. "Owen's super keen. When I told him what I was thinking all he said was, 'let's do this!'"

"Wow!" Janice said, "so we're ready to go, all we need is for someone from the media to get back to you."

"That's all," I said, "if they ever do."

"There was some talk recently about Defence hiring current affairs journalists to help them with their PR," said Janice, "I know I read it somewhere..."

“Is that so?” I said, again amazed at Defence’s subtle manipulation. I shook my head at their mind games. So, now they were employing television journalists, but not just any television journalists, only ‘current affairs’ journalists. How deceptive! Did that mean they were now buying off the media so they could control what would be reported about Defence? It sure seemed so! “Well, then, Janice,” I said, “we should pray only the right person will answer. After all, we don’t know who we can trust, but God does.”

“It’s a shame Owen’s not here,” said Janice. “He’s a strong believer in prayer.”

I was suddenly struck by our unique situation. “How amazing is this, Janice,” I said, still musing on what I had just realised, “The three people going into this particular lion’s den are dedicated Christians.”

Janice rose to the challenge and spoke what we were both thinking, “Who would have thought the three of us would somehow end up working together in DSA ‘*for such a time as this*’.”

Contacted by ABC producer, John Stewart

In mid-April, three weeks after we received Minister Snowdon’s bombshell, we were contacted by John Stewart, producer and investigative reporter for ABC’s *Lateline*.

John turned out to be our answer to prayer. In all our dealings with him over the next year and to the current day, he never once broke his word to us or betrayed our trust. Here, at last, was a man of integrity.

His first contact was by email, to confirm a few details, and then he phoned.

“From what you have given me, I think this is an important story,” said John. “Is there anyone else who may want to come forward?”

"There are three of us who are willing to speak with you openly," I explained, "but there are others who will have to remain anonymous."

"Are you all Defence personnel?"

"No!" I took a deep breath. It was hard to go back to square one and explain from the beginning. So much had happened. I had to remind myself this reporter knew nothing about our situation, and it was up to me to educate him. He would need to know the basic set up of agency versus Defence, the treatment of staff and the gist of the multiple fake investigations before he could understand what this story was actually about. Yes, this was going to take some time.

"The Defence personnel wish to remain in the background, we three are ex-agency staff, who were contracted to the Defence Intelligence and Security Authority known as DSA."

"Can I speak with them?"

"That won't be a problem, John. I will email your details to them, and they will contact you directly. There are another two agency staff who were involved in the initial investigation who don't wish to be involved in this. They are happy for you to see their letters to confirm what we are saying, but at this point, they also wish to remain anonymous." I said.

"So when did the falsifying of documents start, do you know?" asked John, his questions were blunt, but delivered with courtesy.

"In 2009, I believe, but it could have been earlier. I was employed in 2009, and three weeks after I started in July, the processes suddenly changed. The changes didn't make sense."

"What do you think may have been the motivation for Defence to abort the proper checks and push the clearances through?"

What a question! I was astonished at how quickly John was piecing everything together. I was obviously dealing with a very intelligent man.

"The new AGSVA contract," I said, I knew I would have to explain what I meant, I just hoped I would get it right. "Defence wanted to set up a centralised vetting agency for the whole of Australia, but were not sure where it would be located…in which State…so they sort of pitted the DSA offices in each State against each other, and the one which showed they could work most efficiently would win the contract for their State.

"Queensland won?"

"Yes," I confirmed. "It was announced by the head of DSA Canberra at the end of 2009 that the new AGSVA would be located in Queensland and all the DSA Queensland staff would be running it."

"So in order to win, they had to cut corners?"

I laughed. "You've got it in one, John," I said. His questions were so 'to-the-point'!

"When did they start charging money for clearances?"

Another bold question! "I can't answer exactly, that's one of the things which will need to be confirmed by the analysts, but I believe it was just before I started, around the same time the idea of the new AGSVA was being developed."

"How many clearances do you think have been compromised?"

"Thousands," I said, "maybe tens of thousands. I don't know."

"Have any terrorists slipped through the net, do you know?" John's voice was calm and matter-of-fact.

Another bold question! I couldn't help thinking that these were the kinds of questions we should have been asked by the investigators. But they weren't interested!

"No one has slipped through as far as anyone knows, but it's only a matter of time. It only takes one. I think the most risky are security guards working on military bases," I said. "They're often recent arrivals, new Australians, who may still have overseas associations which may compromise them."

"They were not checked properly?"

"No!" I said and paused, was I actually saying all this? "When information was missing, it was just made up and entered into the database as if it was factual."

"How do you know this?"

"It was my job. That's what I was ordered to do!"

"You made up information about security guards on Australian military bases?" John asked.

When the question came out of his mouth it sounded so very, very bad, yet that was the point…it *was* bad!

"Yes!"

"How many others entered false information?"

"More than a hundred people that I know of. Just about everyone," I said, "certainly all the agency staff. We were all lied to, given false procedures, and told certain fields on the database had to be filled in, but the information we put in them didn't matter."

"Was this only for low-level clearances?"

"No, the same applied to secret and even top-secret."

"Why are you coming to the media?"

"There's nowhere else to go, John," I said. "We've been everywhere else. The Ombudsmen's office didn't want to know. A Cabinet Minister didn't want to know. We sent our complaints through the correct complaint channels, both inside Defence and outside. No one wanted to know! When our complaints could no longer be brushed aside and they had to have an investigation, it was a paper tiger, set up to ignore the facts. What amazes me John is that you have asked me more relevant questions in this short interview than I have ever been asked by anyone. No one in authority in Australia, even at the highest levels, wants to know anything about what is going on at DSA."

"Would you be prepared to come on television and say all of this publicly?"

Ouch! This was crunch time! And it was more terrifying than I thought it would be. It was one thing to tell John in private what had been going on, but going public meant possible prosecution for breaching the Official Secrets Act. Once I was 'out there' there was no turning back. I wasn't sure if I was ready. I took a deep breath before answering. "That's a very scary thought, John," I said.

"We could film you blacked out, and leave your names out of it, but it would be better if your faces were shown and we could use your real names. It would make the story more credible."

I knew from his gentle tone he would not force us to go beyond our comfort zones, but I understood the logic of being completely open, and it made absolute sense. Nevertheless, I couldn't make this decision alone. I would have to talk to the others and see what they wanted to do.

"Do you mind if I get back to you on that one, John?" I asked. "I need to talk this over with Owen and Janice and see what they think."

"Sure," John responded. "You know it's highly unusual to find three people who are willing to speak out. That says to me that things in DSA were very bad."

"It's a shame there are not more than three," I said. "I know so many more would love to speak up, but they're afraid, and with good reason. Here's hoping we three stay out of jail."

"If you come forward, the others might also come forward," said John.

"I suppose we should contact a lawyer to find out what we can and can't say," I said. "Prosecution is a reality, so we have to be careful."

"I think you should contact a lawyer," John said, "but I also think there would be so much bad publicity from Defence prosecuting you it would just not be worth it for them. It would look terrible for the Defence Minister... for his department...to be going after someone who had the moral courage to speak up about failed processes and security risks to Australia. That's my view, but I'll talk to the lawyers at the ABC and see what they say as well."

"Thanks, John," I said. As I hung up the phone, I felt encouraged. Finally, a good interview!

John was refreshingly professional, but this story wasn't about him, or even us. It was about some pretty serious issues affecting Australia's National Security.

I remembered the rash of 'security' advertising run on television telling people to alert authorities about anything they thought might be suspicious. Signs were placed on walls in public places and inside trains and buses telling people to report any unclaimed luggage; presumably in case of terrorist attacks.

In the light of the farce I'd just lived through, which showed no one in authority actually cared about Australia's security, those warnings were a total waste of taxpayer money. An absolute joke!

A miracle of provision - free legal advice

It was difficult for Janice, Owen and I to find a time and a place to meet. Owen and I were working full-time, Janice was working part-time, and Owen's Saturday's were tied up with church and family. So it seemed, other than evenings, Sunday was the only day of the week the three of us could get together for a face to face chat. There was so much we needed to discuss we decided on a leisurely Sunday brunch at a coffee house in Springwood.

After the waiter took our orders and the social chit chat was out of the way, we settled down to discuss the reason for our gathering.

"John wants to interview us as quickly as possible," I said. "We need to give him a date."

"Look how hard it was for us to find this little bit of time," Janice responded, "it seems we can only meet on Sundays."

"Does he do interviews on Sundays?" asked Owen.

I nodded. "Yes, he told us he would be available anytime."

"I'm going to Western Australia to visit my daughter and her husband in two weeks," said Janice, "so the best Sunday for me is next Sunday. The problem is that's Mother's Day."

"Oh, it is too," I said. I had forgotten completely about Mother's Day. "So that's out."

"Not necessarily," said Owen, "How long do you think the interviews will take?"

"A couple of hours," I said, shrugging my shoulders to show I didn't have a clue. My guess was as good as theirs.

"My family can work around that," said Owen. "We have our big celebration at church on Saturday anyway." He chuckled. "The kids give all the mothers a flower and the men take over the kitchen, so I should be able to disappear for a few hours on Sunday."

"I'm not having Mother's Day this year," said Janice, "I'm seeing my mother on Saturday, so Sunday is my day, and both my girls are away."

"Next Sunday it is then," I said. "My children won't mind. I'll let John know."

"Where do we stand legally?" Owen asked. "Do we have a legal opinion yet? He suddenly chuckled. "Jail time doesn't appeal to me. I tend to like my freedom!"

"So do I," I said. "I told my boss this week I was planning to do this, but I may be arrested for doing it."

Owen looked stunned. "You told your boss?"

"What did she say?" asked Janice.

"She called the big boss over, and we had a three-way conversation," I said. "They're cool with it. Basically, they are concerned it will be rather stressful for me and gave me the option to take the next day off. All I have to do is let them know when I think the show will be aired."

"Wow! Normal people still amaze me!" said Owen. "I'm not used to good bosses anymore. I always expect the worst." He sounded quite cranky, not like him at all. "That's what comes of working for so long in such a toxic atmosphere. It ruins your perspective."

"There's nothing wrong with your perspective, Owen," I said, "you saw things, horrible things, as they really were."

He nodded, and his smile came back. "Have either of you found a lawyer yet?"

Now it was my turn to smile and nod. "Prosecution *was* a bit of a worry for us," I said, getting back on track, "but it's not anymore. Wait 'till you hear this!"

"Yes!" said Janice beaming. "I have some excellent news!" She looked like the cat who had just eaten the cream. "I had an appointment this week with a Barrister who worked on the Fitzgerald Inquiry and the Christopher Skase prosecution, so he should know what he's talking about."

Owen was impressed. "That's high profile! How did you find him?" He paused and then shook his head in amazement. "How does anyone find a Barrister with that kind of experience?"

I laughed. "Incredible, isn't it?" I was grinning as I spoke. "It just so happens Janice and this Barrister both volunteer their time at the same Community Centre."

Janice nodded and began to explain, "When I said I needed some legal advice, they set me up with an appointment straight away," she giggled. "I had no idea about this man or his expertise until a few days ago. We had never met because we work on different days. Anyway, I told him our problem, and he's given us some advice."

"Excellent advice!" I said.

"The short of it is we can't be prosecuted for anything we've told the ABC because we are revealing lies and deception," Janice explained.

I was nearly jumping off my seat. "We're not in breach of the Act!" I said. "The Act was set up to protect Australia and its interests. We're not betraying Australia - we've trying to protect Australia. We're not breaking the intention of the Act. We can speak out, even publicly, against corruption without fear of prosecution."

"As long as we don't use specifics," said Janice.

"Like correct names or exact places," I explained.

"And we can be more direct in what we say," said Janice. "Dayle, that's the Barrister, said we should be bold in our descriptions."

"You know how we always say 'fudged' or 'manufactured'? Well, he told us to tell it like it is and use strong words which everyone understands like 'lying', 'misleading', 'deceptive', 'falsified'," I said. "He told us we should never use just one description if two will fit."

"We can say all that?" Surprise was written all over Owen's face.

I laughed. This was such good news.

"He said every time we make a claim we should give a short example of that thing happening." Janice continued. "For example, we could say they 'showed utter contempt for the courts and the rule of law when they refused to allow a staff member to attend jury duty, threatening her with dismissal if she attended'."

"Short and to the point!" I said, smiling, "an accusation and two testaments to the truth of the accusation in just one sentence."

Now it was Owen's turn to laugh. "This is fantastic!" he said, "lessons in legalese!"

"Who would have thought?" I laughed.

"There's a whole lot more," said Janice, "but I'll email it to you."

"I think if we can speak openly about the bullying being used to cover the falsification of data and the corruption of ASIO records, without being prosecuted, then others might realise they also can step forward without reprisals," I said.

"Wow!' said Owen. "I'm blown away." He was noticeably stunned. "This is much better than I thought it would be."

"I can't wait for next Sunday," Janice said. "I just want to tell it like it is!"

"I'm hoping the ABC will handle this well enough for things to change for the better," I said.

"How much is this legal advice going to cost us?" asked Owen, still smiling.

"Nothing! It's a miracle of provision," I said, smiling broadly. "When God provides, he provides the best."

"Dale is offering his advice as a community service," Janice confirmed. "And just in time too!"

"What do you think the odds are of us finding an experienced Barrister, with his particular field of expertise, willing to give us free advice at this exact moment in time?" I said, speaking seriously.

Janice looked serious.

Owen shook his head.

"This has God's hand all over it," I said, "It's a miracle! Pure and simple! The same kind of miracle which got Janice and me into DSA in the first place. God is in this! He's been leading us all from the beginning, and now he's providing protection for us."

"Amazing!" said Owen chuckling again. "I'm so happy right now. I'm on a real high."

"And do you know what?" I asked, though it wasn't a question, "we don't have to worry about hiding our faces. We have absolutely nothing to fear."

"They could shoot us!" suggested Janice.

"What, all of us?" I laughed. "Wouldn't that look a little suspicious?"

"The people who set this up are not very bright," grinned Owen, stating the obvious, "or they wouldn't have done what they've done."

"I guess they would have to gun down John and his crew at the ABC as well," I said.

"And Dayle," said Janice

"Bit of a blood bath!" said Owen.

"Hmmm...probably not an option," I concluded as laughter took over, and our conversation turned to the sheer nonsensical absurdity of our experience within Australia's so-called 'intelligence' community. Talk about a misnomer!

Our story goes to air

John and his crew of two arrived at my home at 10am on Sunday 8 May 2011, Mother's Day, and it was action stations immediately. The sound and cameramen rearranged the furniture, found power points and set up their gear. They had so many cords running across the floor, I wondered how they remembered which one went where; they all looked the same to me.

John handed out different lists of questions to Owen, Janice and me, and we all went to the dining room to study them and practice our answers. Janice phoned Dayle who gave us sage advice as to the best way to present our specific viewpoints and then asked to speak with John. It was all 'go'.

Four hours later, it was over, and we were exhausted.

None of us was nervous about being filmed, though we had warned John our faces might break his camera. We were instead consumed with saying the right thing and getting our message across clearly, but it was extremely difficult to tell if we had been able to do that. We'd answered the same questions so many times and in so many different ways that at the end of the day it was impossible to know if we'd said the right thing. Plus, we didn't know which versions of our answers John would use for his story. Would we come off looking genuine or like cranks and idiots? We didn't know.

The story would not be aired until the following Monday evening, so we had to wait eight long self-questioning days to see what John would do with the information we had given him. Meanwhile, John plied Crystal and us with probing questions via email, sometimes ten a day, checking details, and pedantically making sure he was getting every little fact correct. I admired his professionalism, no wonder he was successful, Defence investigators could benefit from following his example.

The big day arrived. Monday 16 May 2011, a date to remember. Janice was in Western Australia, with her family but as nervous and excited as I was. We had all spent a week wading through the options, going over the 'what-would-we-do-ifs'. Now there were no more 'what-ifs'.

Lateline came on, and I held my breath. "Defence staff told to fake security checks - orders from the top. They say fake security clearances have left a gaping hole in Australia's National Security. They say that information was invented to fill in gaps on security applications, including top-secret-level clearances sent to ASIO."

- "Sometimes applicants didn't give the city they had gone to in a certain country, so you would just pick a city, sometimes they would write Asia, so then you'd just pick an Asian country and certain things like that." Owen.

- "There was a large percentage of applications that came my way that had gaps...that had problems that needed the applicant to be phoned - I would think about 25 per cent." Janice.

- "Information like where you live, or previous employment…DSA didn't care about that stuff. We were told to just make it up, put in some dates, put unemployed for periods which were missing, addresses, just put the area address, or find a street or make up some information, any information, to fill in those gaps." Owen.

- "I put a few problem applications aside and took them to a manager. Problems with their addresses, their workplaces, or they didn't give all the information about relatives or didn't supply certificates for a change of name. I was told these words, 'be creative'. Monica.

- "The pressure is on you to process them and get them out quickly, so if you don't meet that pressure and get your numbers up, then you're going to lose your job." Owen.

- "In May 2010 an investigation was conducted, but Mr Snowden said in a letter that the investigator was unable to find any evidence of bullying or harassment." John.

- "I explicitly told one of those investigators that information in top-secret clearances had been fabricated." Monica.

- "A spokesman for Defence Minister Stephen Smith has told *Lateline*, "Defence has in place a rigorous vetting and quality assurance process." John.

It was the main story and took up most of the hour, but I don't remember breathing again until it was over. It was so good, so shocking, so well presented, I was speechless. I looked at my son Martin, seated on the lounge on the other side of the room, gave a big smile, jumped up, threw my hands into the air and yelled out, "Yes!"

John was a genius! A true artist! He had taken a little bit of this and a little bit of that and created an exact picture. And he hadn't betrayed us. He hadn't let us down. I felt like dancing. Janice must have too, because she phoned me almost straight away, in awe of what we had just seen. Then through the laughter, the re-hashing of the program started and gradually what we had just done began to sink in. Defence was not going to like this story. They were not going to be happy…

No response from Defence

We expected Defence to come gunning for us immediately. So did John. But it didn't happen.

The day after our shocking allegations aired, there was silence from Defence. Nothing! Not even a squeak! Just after my lunch break, John phoned me at work.

"Thank you so much, John, for the way you presented our story," I said. "It was brilliant! It said everything we wanted said."

"I was happy with it," said John. "But I'm surprised we haven't heard anything from Defence." He sounded disappointed. "It's definitely unusual. They normally respond straight away."

"Nothing at all?" I asked. "Why do you think that is?"

"I don't know." He said. "I haven't seen this happen before. This story is important and yet they are not saying anything. I'm going to ring Minister Smith's office and see if I can get a response."

Okay, so he was warning me he was going to provoke a response from Defence. Strangely, I didn't mind at all. "Let me know what they say," I said, "you know, forewarned and all that..."

"Do your bosses mind if I phone you back?" he asked.

He was so considerate. "No, John, they don't, I assured him. "They actually offered me the day off if I felt I needed it." He couldn't see that I was smiling. He didn't realise how much I appreciated working with decent people. "They understand my present situation. Call me anytime."

Later that afternoon, John called me back.

"Smith's office said they don't have any reason to comment," he said.

"You've got to be kidding me!" I was shocked. I shook my head. "No reason?"

"They said you didn't provide any specific examples of clearances being compromised, so there's nothing for them to comment on," said John.

Specific examples? Did they want us to provide evidence? Wouldn't stealing paperwork send us to jail? "Can you understand this, John?" I asked.

"No," he said. "It doesn't make sense. We'll have to wait and see what happens over the next few days. Meanwhile, I have some good news for you."

I laughed. "Oh, do tell!"

"Have you checked out the online comments on our website? There are plenty, and most of them are 100% behind you three," he said.

"Wonderful!"

"That tells me a lot," he said, "it shows your story has touched a nerve."

"Well, the Department of Defence always denies everything." I said, "People have been crying out for justice for years, decades! They never listen, and justice is never done! Nothing ever changes."

"I think they might have to change this time," said John, "too many people are coming forward."

"What do you mean?" I asked

"I've also been directly contacted by quite a few people who claim to have worked with you at DSA, and they are confirming everything you guys have told me," John said. "They've given me their names but want to remain anonymous, and that's not a problem, I'll keep them anonymous," he hesitated for a second, "but I'd like to run the names past you to see if you know them; to see if they actually did work with you."

"Not a problem, John. I won't betray their trust either," I said.

"I'll send you an email, I think there are about eight so far," he said. "And when I spoke to them I could see they clearly knew what they were talking about."

"Eight!" I laughed, this was more good news. John read out the names on the list he had compiled, and I was amazed. "Those people are all Defence staff, John, they're not contractors. I'm amazed! I didn't realise just how much support we had. I thought they were all against us, but it seems many of them also want the bullying and corruption to stop, even if they're not game to say so publicly."

"This kind of story usually gives others the courage to come forward, but that's a significant number," said John.

"It certainly is!" My mind flitted over all the people I was working with at DSA, both agency and Defence. I'd sat beside most of them, two days here, a week there, so I knew all their names and faces. Eight of them were heroes in disguise. I couldn't help feeling proud.

"I guess their coming forward has made you feel a little more confident, John," I said.

"Yes, it has, I think we need to keep going with this story though or Defence is just going to bury it with some internal inquiry."

"Keep me posted, John," I couldn't help chuckling with delight. "This is getting good!"

Suddenly, the denials come in like a flood

The next day the denials began. The first of a series of official denials came in the form of statements from the office of the Minister for Defence as a direct result of John Stewart's enquiries.

- "In response to questions from *Lateline*, a spokesman for the Defence Minister has told us, "There is no evidence to suggest that security clearances have been compromised."
- "The Government takes allegations of the fabrication of information in security clearances extremely seriously." Minister Smith.
- I'm advised, these allegations are not true, and that's the advice provided by Defence. (Brendan O'Connor MP on Sky Channel.)

When I heard we had been publicly called liars, my response was immediate. I laughed long and hard! Far from being crushed, or hurt, I knew what they were saying was ludicrous - stupidly ridiculous. Minister Smith said there was no evidence, but that was totally absurd. Paper evidence was useless for unless a paper application was checked against the information actually entered into the database, no discrepancies would be seen. What DSA staff 'made up' was not on the applications, it was not in the paperwork, it was in the Defence database. There was heaps of evidence in the database, all investigators had to do was look! The sobering question was, would they bother looking?

Besides a lack of paper evidence, the main problem Defence had with our public 'revelations' was that we were not pointing the finger at them. We were not accusing them so much as confessing what we had done ourselves. We had gone on air and said we had passed false information, through their database to ASIO! So now, how were they going to prove we hadn't provided false information?

We said publicly that we had broken the law, and they said publicly that we were lying and so hadn't broken the law! This put them in a no-win situation!

The reality was, if they prosecuted us, the corruption would be seen. If they ignored us, the public would smell a rat. They obviously didn't know what to do, which is why they were stalling; using denials to fend off the press while their lawyers worked overtime.

That same day a spokesperson for ASIO also responded to our *Lateline* revelations by publicly supporting the Defence position. It would be several months before the ASIO publicity machine would wake up to the reality of the situation and revise their stance.

- "ASIO understands claims of inappropriate vetting practices have been reviewed by the Department of Defence and have not been substantiated."
- "ASIO takes allegations such as these very seriously and will work with the Department of Defence as required."

When I saw these statements, I immediately wondered when our claims of inappropriate vetting practices had been reviewed. It was evident from the ASIO statement they had been told Defence had already reviewed our claims. But when did they do that? The previous investigation was limited to management practices, so when had Defence reviewed our complaints about National Security?

Had Defence lied to ASIO? Again?

That afternoon Minister Smith announced he had asked the Inspector-General of Defence to investigate our allegations of inappropriate vetting practices within DSA.

Hold on! Didn't ASIO just tell the media that very morning a review had already been done? Then why another one? Hmmm, confusing, to say the least!

- "Any allegations of fabrication of information in security clearances will be investigated by the Inspector-General of Defence." Minister Smith.

Meanwhile, that evening, Cassie emailed us, and her short and interesting 'insider' view made us all howl with laughter. Vault-window mentality had its advantages for us, that was for sure.

- "We had a meeting on Monday to advise us not to talk to the media. That means everyone became aware there would be something about DSA on the ABC, and because of that I imagine most people at work watched it." Cassie

No wonder there were so many comments from DSA and ex-DSA staff after the program had been aired! DSA advertised it for us! We couldn't stop laughing!

Dayle goes the extra mile for us

The next day I came home from work to find a message on my answering machine from an investigator for public defence with the Inspector-Generals office asking me to contact him. That was quick! The investigation was announced one day and begun the next. Hmmm, probably some legal advice would be good.

I contacted Janice, still in Western Australia, and asked her to phone Dayle on our behalf, for there was no point in us all phoning him, to find out what we should expect from this investigation. Janice called him immediately, and he was available. Amazing! His short, sharp, strongly suggested advice was not what we would have expected.

“Firstly, congratulations on not being scared to say and do what was clearly right,” said Dayle.

“Thank you,” Janice replied and got straight to the point. “We have been contacted by investigators from the Office of the Inspector-General of Defence.”

“Have you spoken to them yet?” asked Dayle.

“No, they just want to set up a meeting.”

“Not a good idea. Not even with an independent third party present.” There was no hesitation in Dayle’s response. He obviously knew what he was talking about.

“Why is that?” asked Janice.

“You’re not protected from prosecution. Speaking with them can leave you vulnerable. You’ve given them plenty of opportunities to discuss these issues, and they have hurled them back in your face each time. The safest place to give any further evidence is in the Senate,” Dayle said.

“A Senate Inquiry?” asked Janice. “How do we go about that?”

“Find a Senator who will take this issue seriously,” said Dayle.

“Okay, but what do we say to these investigators?” asked Janice. “They want a response straight away.”

“Don’t speak to them!” said Dayle emphatically. “You interview them!”

Janice laughed nervously. “What do you mean?”

“Ask them, ‘What is the purpose of your call? What is your rank or public service grade? To whom do you answer? Who will see this report? Do you agree to pay all our legal expenses?’” said Dayle, “and then tell them you have been advised the safest place to discuss these issues is in the Senate.”

Janice laughed again, this time with delight. “Not quite what they will be expecting.”

"Let me know how you go," Dayle said, winding up the conversation.

"Thanks, Dayle," said Janice, "I will."

It was clear from Dayle's advice we had been walking blindly into a massive trap. This investigation into our 'allegations' looked so proper, so logical, so correct, yet if we participated in it, we could very well end up in jail. And Minister Smith thought this was a good idea!

The immorality of the Defence machine, and all its little operators, never ceased to amaze me. This ruse was about to fail. But what would they try next? We were on a roller-coaster ride now, and there was no getting off until the ride stopped.

The day after receiving Dayle's warning we were again phoned by the investigators from the office of the Inspector-General of Defence, so of course, we took Dayle's advice and interviewed the investigators. When we asked if they would pay our legal expenses, each of us was told the same thing. "Oh, ah, um, I can't make that decision, I'll need to get back to you."

Our response to their hesitation was to tell them they need not get back to us as we'd been advised by our barrister not to disclose anything without Parliamentary protection.

They didn't ring us back. We never heard from them again. It was such a hoot - us interviewing them! What a turnaround!

We couldn't wait to tell Dayle about the outcome of his wise counsel to us, so we asked Janice to phone him on our behalf again and let him know how pleased we were with the result. When she called him, Janice discovered Dayle was doing more for us behind the scenes than we'd thought. He'd been speaking to the Defence lawyers.

"I spent some time on the phone with an internal Defence lawyer trying to establish a workable background to permit you to speak to a Defence appointed review," said Dayle, getting straight to the point.

"A new review?" asked Janice.

"I haven't seen any terms-of-reference for the current investigation," said Dayle, "and I believe in the worst when there is no evidence of a new found intention to throw a klieg light on the secrets and lies."

Janice chuckled, 'klieg light' what a graphic picture it painted.

"You need someone who is independent and can look afresh at the allegations while ensuring you can never be persecuted or prosecuted for whistle-blowing," he said.

"Oh, that would be good," said Janice

"If it occurs, it will only be with your consent," said Dayle, "and the consent of each of the persons who may wish to come forward."

"Other people?" asked Janice.

"You should consider identifying to me a group of persons whom you trust, who share common experiences with you, and who can point particular fingers at specific bits of gross impropriety," Dayle explained.

"Well," said Janice remembering the large number of the vetting personnel who had come forward, "there are quite a few of us now, and certainly some of them can point to specific horrendous examples."

"Good! If you present me with an outline of what they might say, I could ensure your group gets immunity."

"Oh wonderful," said Janice, fumbling with pen and paper, "I'm just going to jot this down."

"Don't worry," said Dayle, "I'll forward you an email."

"Excellent," said Janice putting down her pen.

"I have also asked for the right to cross-examine the agents for Defence as part of the mix of evidence before the tribunal or other statutory body empanelled to hear your grievances and requests, if any, for redress."

"Thank you, Dayle." Janice's head was beginning to swim. Legal jargon was not her forte. "I can get a list together, when would you need it?"

"I think the Defence stuff can stew a little more at least until the end of the week," Dayle said candidly, "nothing in Canberra ever move's at the speed of even a sleepy gazelle."

Janice laughed softly, she liked the way Dayle played with words; he was so very expressive. "I like your turn of phrase Dayle," she told him. There was no flattery in her voice, just honest observation. "You are very good with words."

"I'm paid to be good with words," Dayle said simply. "They are the tools of my profession."

"Of course!" Janice responded; glad he was on our side and secretly thinking she would hate to have him opposing her in a courtroom.

"You may have to figure out what, if any, fiscal redress each of you separately seeks," said Dayle.

"Oh!" said Janice slightly taken aback. "Well, we have thought about the money side, but only in passing," she said, "we three have agreed that seeking compensation would diminish what we are doing."

"How so?" asked Dayle.

"People might think we are doing this for the money," Janice explained. "We're not! We're doing it because it needs to be done. And we don't want anything, including compensation, to get in the way of the outcome we're working towards. We want to stay focused."

"Understood!" Dayle responded.

"The bottom-line is Dayle, this is not about us." Janice continued, "it's about Defence thinking they can treat Australians like filth on their shoes and get away with it. It's about them thumbing their noses at Australian law. It's about all the Australians they are putting at risk, including our trusting military."

“They are accountable to Australian law!” Dayle said as if there was no argument to his statement. “The Department of Defence has no power to act illegally and to allow it to do so would be a criminal offence.”

“I can’t see anyone with the courage and authority to pull them into line, Dayle.” Janice was getting a little angry, “certainly not our elected ministers. ‘Illegal’ doesn’t seem to mean anything!” Janice decided to calm down and change the direction of her thinking. “Can I ask you a personal question?”

Dayle remained silent.

“Why are you doing all this for us?”

“Because I think it’s a good cause,” Dayle said without hesitation.

“So, we are on the same page,” Janice said simply. “Thank you for everything you are doing for us Dayle, I’ll pass your comments along to the others.”

Dayle was a God-send, another answer to our prayers, no doubt about it. A miracle of protection from God! He was the right person in the right place, at the right time. Taking his advice had literally kept us out of jail. Now he was ‘going the extra mile’ by expertly convincing the Defence lawyers we needed a forum free from prosecution or persecution. He amazed us! He was not only fighting a not so small battle for us behind the scenes but was offering his usually expensive services free of charge, passing them off as a mere good deed. We couldn’t help but thank God for him.

Organised and ready

Emails became our primary form of ‘instant’ communication within our expanding group. So I emailed Janice and asked her to convert Dayle’s email string to a word document so we could send it out as an attachment to everyone who had come forward.

Within 24 hours, Janice was back from Western Australia, the emails had gone out, and everyone was aware of Dayle's advice and what he was doing for us behind the scenes. No matter what we were about to face, we were organised, and we were ready.

- "Isn't this amazing and wonderful? It really is our time to shine and the fact Dayle is willing to cross-examine is so cool. This is so overdue. Someone up there is looking after us." Crystal.

- "Dayle has confirmed our suspicions. Of course there are no terms-of-reference. Why would Defence pay a legal team thousands of dollars to find out what *they* have done wrong? They know what they've done wrong - it's just another 'internal investigation' dressed up as something else, and we've all already been through one or more of those." Linda.

- "Kate contacted me, and she is in contact with Leah, they have both spoken to John. I've passed on Dayle's advice. I will get in contact with Jim, our good friend in the DSA saga, to see if he wants a piece of the action and also Rosie. Do you remember her? She worked in the basement and never stopped smiling. Can you guys think of anyone else?" Owen.

- "Jade told me that when she saw the news story, she just burst into tears and cried all the way through *Lateline* - she thinks you are all heroes. Doesn't that just break your heart?" Crystal.

- "I just wanted to personally write and say you three have taken a huge step which I hope will help a lot of us! You have started something I was just too scared to start myself, but something I have thought of often. You have my full backing when the time comes." Jade.

- "Moira has also spoken with John, asking to remain anonymous." Crystal.

- “It’s amazing how many have jumped on board. It’s also good to hear about the legal help you’re getting. Keep me posted of further developments.” Jennifer.
- “The best news is that Crystal, Linda and Jade have all spoken to John, asking to remain anonymous, but confirming our story. Linda is rounding up others as well.” Monica.
- “Janice is in contact with Cassie, and I am in contact with Donna and Jennifer. It’s just a case of being ready for the next round, knowing what we want to say, getting our facts in place.” Monica.
- “This is AWESOME!” I so would like to talk to this independent inquiry to tell our stories, pending of course when Dayle negotiates the terms by which we can speak without persecution or prosecution.” Owen.
- “We’re not pressed for time. It is all rather early stages at this point, and Dayle is still checking things out and making enquiries; whether it is a review or a Senate inquiry - the more of us, the merrier. This is a BIG learning curve for us all.” Janice.
- “I’m jumping out of my skin. This is amazing, and you have no idea how I feel. I so hope it also includes the bullying and harassment eventually - as that is how they got us to do what we did, and some of us have paid so dearly for it.” Crystal.
- “I’ve decided to explore the Senate angle. I’ve just made an appointment to see Senator Clair Moore’s assistant, Meredith Newman, at 8am on Wednesday morning. She’s local, and I’ve been told she cares about the treatment of workers in the workplace. Does anyone have any questions you think I should ask her about a Senate Inquiry?” Monica.
- “Can I come too?” Crystal.
- “You don’t have to ask. I’ll meet you there at 7.30am. See you Wednesday.” Monica.

Wednesday came around quickly. It was good to see Crystal's smiling face again. It had seemed such a long time since we had sat in the bar and agreed the media was the way to go. In reality, it was only a few months, but here we were again, face to face, planning another mission, and our friendship was echoed in our silent hug.

"The best thing about today is seeing you again," said Crystal with genuine warmth. "You look awesome!"

"For someone going through the mill, you look pretty wonderful yourself!" We were both grinning from ear to ear. "It's a shame we won't have time to have a coffee afterwards."

"No, but I guess there will be other times," Crystal's voice changed slightly as she began to get down to business, "what can I expect from today?"

I took a deep breath. I wasn't exactly sure. "I want to find out about the correct procedure to follow and what we need to do to instigate a Senate Inquiry."

"Will it involve giving proof upfront?" Crystal sounded nervous, "you know we can't do that."

"They would know that too," I said, trying to reassure her. "Remember what it was like with Brett?"

Crystal nodded.

"This will be the same," I said gently. Poor Crystal. DSA had obviously taken its toll on her. She was even more suspicious of everyone now then she'd been two months ago. "They're not going to try and trick us, Crystal, they're going to try and understand."

Crystal's hands developed a nervous tremor, and I knew she was desperately trying to overcome her fears. "Do they know how many of us there are now?"

Poor Crystal, she was afraid they would all be betrayed. My poor terrified friend. She'd been at DSA way too long! All I could do was reassure her.

"Not yet, and I won't be giving them any names," I said firmly. "It's all about consent, Crystal, no one needs to come forward unless they want to." I smiled, and lightened the mood by mocking DSA, "I don't believe in coercion!"

Crystal laughed in relief and took a deep breath, "Okay, then let's do this."

We gained the information we needed about Senate Inquiries, and then Meredith turned her attention to Crystal's ongoing bullying situation. She was so concerned about the number of horrendous accounts just tumbling freely, without emotion, from Crystal's memory, she asked permission to personally contact the Minister's Office that day to ask why nothing had been done in response to Crystal's formal requests for protection, copies of which had been handed to her. Crystal was so grateful for this little bit of support she was flat out holding back the tears.

We left Senator Moore's office content we had done what we needed to do. And after a brief hug and fond farewells, we both headed off to commence an otherwise normal working day.

In the scheme of things, our visit to the Senator's office may have seemed insignificant, but the timing was perfect. We didn't know it, but everything was coming to a head - quickly!

In just one short week, Defence's 'terms-of-reference-free' investigation had been exposed, the witnesses refused to cooperate, a barrister was asking questions, the ABC was asking questions, and now a Senator's office was asking questions. The pressure was well and truly on Defence!

The whole situation was volatile, all it would take now was one little spark, and the entire thing would erupt into flames.

Suddenly, the spark appeared in the form of a real-life example of what we had been warning about - a clearance gone wrong!

Only God could have provided such perfect evidence, at the right time and in the right way. For us, it was another miracle.

It came to light that one of the men guarding the highest official in Queensland (the Queensland Premier, Anna Bligh), a man with unlimited access to every room in the Queensland Parliament building, had actually been wanted by Interpol for seven years, and yet the clearance process which gave him unlimited access to the Parliament, didn't pick it up. It was all over the news!

Kaboom! The whole thing erupted! What an incredible mess!

> *A man wanted across the world has been found guarding Premier Anna Bligh and the offices of the most powerful people in Queensland."*
> (Courier Mail Headline, May 2011)

Defence was

beginning

to back-peddle!

CHAPTER SEVEN

Undeniable problem? Cover it up!

The investigation by the Inspector-General of Defence into our allegations must have been one of the shortest high-level investigations in Australian Defence history. It was abandoned after just nine days.

Since we three whistle-blowers would not speak with the investigators, they had no other choice but to abandon it. They had no one to investigate! Those nine days were not wasted though and in that short time there was so much evidence uncovered which proved what we had said on *Lateline* was true, the Minister for Defence, on the 25 May 2011, announced via the ABC that further action would need to be taken to redress the security breaches they had discovered.

Stephen Smith's humiliating public admission that our allegations may, in fact, have some substance, was followed by a second admission that there was evidence Defence had previously been told by us about the problem some twelve months earlier, but had overlooked the importance and truth of our statements, which he said they now regretted.

These admissions, together with a few uncomfortable questions from Senators, prompted two new investigations. Minister Smith ordered an immediate internal review of DSA, and the Prime Minister, Julia Gillard, took the responsibility for the investigation of our claims out of Defence's hands and gave it to a truly independent body.

The Prime Minister asked the Investigator General of Intelligence and Security (IGIS), Dr Vivian Thom, to conduct an 'inquiry into allegations of inappropriate vetting practices by the Defence Security Authority and related matters'. This independent investigation was announced in the Senate on 30 May 2011, just two short weeks after our first appearance on *Lateline*.

Defence was in trouble, but they were not going to go down without a fight. At the same time as the new IGIS investigation into our allegations was announced, the Assistant Secretary of Defence, Stephen Merchant, disclosed to the Senate that Defence had only been checking the applications 'touched' by 'those' whistle-blowers. He made us sound dirty, as if we were saboteurs who had deliberately done damage to applications in order to cause embarrassment. They were admitting there was a problem, but now it appeared they were going to try and focus the blame for it onto us. No wonder our savvy barrister had warned us to avoid them.

Minister Smith admits there is a problem

The news that a Queensland government security guard, who had been on Interpol's most wanted list since 2004, had nevertheless been guarding the offices of Queensland Parliamentarians, was received as a shocking kind of wake up call. It showed that what we had been saying all along was true, checks were not being done as thoroughly as they should have been.

The big question people were beginning to ask was, 'how many more are there out there?' How many indeed! How many, they wondered, had 'slipped through the net'? Could there be others? Could there be terrorists? These were questions no one could answer.

Defence had no choice now but to admit there was a problem. But would they? As long as I had been alive, I had never seen Defence back down. They always held their ground until their opponents either gave up or died, proving the accepted idiom, "no one wins against Defence!"

But, at the end of May 2011, the power of that old saying was broken. The unthinkable happened. Defence capitulated! Minister Smith contacted the ABC and made a shocking public announcement. What we had said on *Lateline* was true! Unbelievable! Finally! How wonderful!

I first heard about Stephen Smith's humiliating announcement from John Stewart. He phoned me at work just after lunch and told me the good news.

"Stephen Smith has just announced that you guys weren't lying!" said John. His voice was more animated than usual. This news had surprised even a seasoned investigative journalist.

I couldn't believe what I was hearing, "What do you mean?" I asked.

"He's just gone on air and admitted there are problems with the clearances," said John.

My mouth dropped open. "No!" I said, shocked, "He's admitted it?" This was incredible news. I was stunned.

"He admitted to two of your three allegations," said John. "He also said Defence knew about it last year and didn't do anything about it."

"He's backed-down?" I still couldn't believe it. "Defence never backs down!"

John laughed. It was the first time I'd heard him laugh. "I want to do another story tonight."

"You said they admitted to two out of three, what didn't they admit to?" I asked.

"That it's still going on," said John, "they say it was confined to DSA and hasn't carried over to AGSVA."

Now it was my turn to laugh. "Well we know that's not true!"

"Do you think you could do another interview for us tonight?" John asked. "I think we need to respond to these admissions."

"Not a problem, I can do that," I said, but my head was still trying to grasp the impact of what I had just learned. "Do you know what this means, John?"

John was silent, waiting for me to continue.

"We can't be prosecuted!" Laughter began to bubble up from somewhere deep inside, and I knew I would not be able to contain it. "We can never be prosecuted for these allegations now...because of these admissions!" I began to laugh. This was just the best news ever!

"I will try to get a TV crew to your place tonight, though it might be a problem because of the State of Origin football coverage," John said, "there may not be any crews available."

"I'll see if I can round up Janice and Owen," I said, "they're going to whoop for joy when they hear this. I'm so elated, John. Nine days! They backed-down in just nine days!" I was laughing again. "That's got to be some kind of record for Defence."

"Look, I just want to say congratulations," John's tone was sincere. "This is an unusually good result. I certainly wasn't expecting them to back down, and to do it so quickly means they must have found a truckload of evidence to prove what you're saying."

I found it difficult to respond, I was laughing with joy. I felt so light I just wanted to jump up and down and spin around and scream out "Thank you, Lord!" but I couldn't, I was at work. I had to contain myself.

I stopped laughing and let John know what I wanted to say that night. "Crystal and I visited Senator Moore's office this morning, John, to get some information on how to get a Senate Inquiry going," I said. "That was Dayle's suggestion, and he seems to know the best way for us to proceed. So tonight I'd like to take the opportunity to call for a Senate Inquiry."

"Not a problem," John responded, "We'll talk later."

From the moment our conversation finished, it was all go. I had to get permission from my bosses to go home early so I could go over the transcript and work out my responses. They were wonderful, as usual, and had no problem with me leaving work early. I couldn't get hold of Owen, so I phoned Janice and asked her to get hold of him and to meet me at my home that evening. I emailed 'the group' and let them know they should watch *Lateline,* and I phoned Meredith at Senator Moore's office and told her our news.

"I haven't received any media releases to that effect," Meredith said, "but I'll keep an eye out and let you know if I hear anything."

That afternoon, Meredith sent me the transcript of Minister Smith's announcement. There was no official media release, just his appearance on the ABC.

When I arrived home, several emails from John awaited me. He couldn't get a crew. We would have to be interviewed at the studio. The ABC would pay for the two-way cab fare to the combined Channel 10/ABC Studios at Mount Cootha on the outskirts of Brisbane. I had never been inside a television station before, so this was going to be a new experience; and a little daunting!

I wrote out my responses to Minister Smith's admissions, sent them off to John and got ready. He responded he didn't have time to organise any questions for Janice and he knew we hadn't been able to contact Owen, but told me Janice was welcome to go with me to the studio. When Janice arrived, we had just enough time for a quick coffee before piling into the taxi for the hour-long drive.

At the studio, I had my makeup done by a professional, a definite improvement, and was then positioned at a spare news desk with a green screen behind me. It was almost surreal. John asked questions through a speaker connection as he was still in Sydney, and it felt strange giving my answers to a fixed position on the blank computer screen in front of me. I answered questions for about ten minutes, and then it was over. We were bustled back into another cab and were home in time to watch *Lateline*.

How exhausting! But it was worth it! This program was even better than the first one. Both Janice and I thought it was explosive!

- Minister Smith had said only Defence personnel clearances were affected. We said this was not so as we were also doing clearances for civilians...
- Minister Smith said it was an old DSA problem which didn't carry over into the new AGSVA. A current DSA worker said AGSVA was now worse than DSA by double...

Janice and I whooped when we heard that! John backed up that statement by showing a letter of complaint written to the Minister about AGSVA just two weeks earlier stating how bad it was. We didn't know about that complaint - this was someone outside our group - wow! This didn't look good for Defence or for Minister Smith!

We were so happy about these new revelations we couldn't stop laughing. It was all so amazing to us, a bit of a blur really. It was like were in the back seat of a limo, watching everything outside flash past. Who else could have brought all these various loose ends together at the same time, so neatly, so perfectly, but God? We were on cloud nine! This was fantastic! We were enjoying the ride.

The next day the emails began again. This time they were all about John. Minister Smith had not liked his interpretation of events, and so John was now in the firing line as well. Yet, he had the courage to continue standing with us. We thought he was wonderful.

- "John, *Lateline* was great! Stephen Smith actually admitted to the bullying and harassment and what Monica came in and said afterwards was fantastic - about our only avenue being a Senate inquiry - and fairly said not said in an intimidating way. This is something they just will not want, but what other option is there?" Crystal.

- "I thought overall, it was better or had more punch than the first one. I am waiting to see what happens from here." Linda.
- "John, I was on such a high last night and do so appreciate the brilliant way you put it all together. Keep up the good work because we SO need your voice to get the truth out there!" Janice.
- "John, that was excellent. You put it together beautifully. I loved it. You are so good at what you do!" Monica.
- "I got a hard time from them yesterday. They reckon I took the minister out of context. They said his statements related to clearances only, not bullying." John.
- "We know the context was correct, John! I believe, eventually, they will have to admit we've stated the truth about everything all along." Janice.
- "This is just another fact the Minister has gotten wrong. How many are there now, John? So many! If anyone has taken anything out of context – they have! Defence has taken our complaints about discrimination and constant bullying way out of context, dismissing them as mere management troubles. Not so!" Monica.
- "I want to keep talking to people ex-DSA. ASIO reckon they have no problems with DSA. That is laughable." John.

Uncovering the source of the problem

The following Saturday, I met Crystal for coffee in a small, out of the way, pastry shop in the inner city. She was still nervous about being seen in public with me, so we took a table amongst swaying palms in the brick-wall enclosed tropical garden out the back.

We settled ourselves on black padded chairs under a canopy of maroon umbrellas near a gurgling water feature and ordered a small selection of deliciously fresh and exotically different pastries to share. There was no one else sharing this tiny slice of paradise, so it was perfect for us.

"Can you believe this week?" I asked, slicing a warm honey and almond pastry in half and sliding the halves onto the two separate plates provided.

"Oh, these look delicious," said Crystal, reaching for the pastry on the plate nearest her and drawing it to her side of the table. "Ooooh, and still warm..."

"What a great little oasis," I said, relaxing back into my chair, "you can almost feel the serenity."

"I was blown away by the Interpol story," said Crystal coming straight to the point.

"It couldn't have come at a better time..."

"John asked me if DSA did his clearance," said Crystal, giving me a seriously meaningful look.

I understood that look. The analyst look! The look you give when you know it is entirely unethical to comment. "What did you tell him?" I asked.

"That I couldn't tell him even if I knew."

I nodded. "I told him the same thing."

"I think it's hard for him to understand there is still a line we can't cross," said Crystal. "But the good thing is there are some things we *can* talk about."

"And need to..." I agreed.

"You, know, Monica, four years ago it was not like this," she said. "Four years ago we could ask questions, learn and everything was transparent. That has all changed, and to sit there and publicly say it does not go on since AGSVA was rolled out is a disgrace. AGSVA has simply made it worse."

"Why did it all change?" I asked, "do you know?"

"It seems to me it all suddenly went pear-shaped just before an Australia-wide review of all the vetting agencies was done in 2008, which led to the new clearance processes being introduced," she explained.

"A review?" I asked.

"The review found DSA, along with all the other vetting agencies, didn't have the structure, focus, skills or capability necessary to meet Australia's security needs," Crystal continued.

"But it had up until that point?" I asked.

"Yes," said Crystal. "Everything was going smoothly. Vetting was being done on time, and there was no bullying. DSA was a genuinely nice place to work."

"What happened?"

"We got a new CSO, and he wanted to do away with all the individual vetting agencies, and create one centralised agency."

"AGSVA!"

"Yes! That review was used as the basis for arguing we needed AGSVA, a centralised vetting agency for the whole of Australia."

"Hence the competition, to see which State would be chosen as the central office," I said.

"That's when everything started to change, the new procedures began to be introduced, and the bullying started. It was slow at first, but by the time you came it was in full operation," said Crystal.

"This explains everything," I said.

"Don't take my word for it," said Crystal, "I have an article here," she handed me an old newspaper clip, and I scanned it as she kept speaking.

> *Under the new CSO, DSA would become largely a policy, threat assessment and security advice co-ordination agency, with security clearances off-loaded to another agency.* (The Australian, 30 Aug. 2008)

I shook my head. "All this has been about moving clearances out of DSA?"

Crystal nodded. "It's about setting up a new centralised agency," said Crystal. "That's why I think it's all being rubber-stamped at the highest levels," said Crystal.

"So that's why no one wants to know," I said. I finally understood.

"That review told everyone at the highest levels, way back in 2008 there were major problems with clearances," said Crystal. "And yet, we've just spent a year and a half knocking on Defence doors telling them a serious problem exists with clearances only to have Stephen Smith go on television pretending to be ignorant of the problem! He knew all along!"

"And they had the nerve to call *us* liars!" I said.

"On that subject, I got a call from his office yesterday." Crystal looked like she was saving the best for last.

"Smith's office?" I laughed. "When were you going to tell me this?"

She smiled back at me. "I'm telling you now! But I'm a bit thirsty, do you mind if we get another coffee?"

It was now lunch-time, and so we ordered more coffee and a light lunch. Had we actually been talking for two hours? It felt like ten minutes.

"So why did the Minister's office phone you?" I asked while we waited for our order.

"About my complaint of 'unacceptable behaviour'," she said. "We were on the phone for a while, and I told them plainly the bullying of staff was still continuing, not just towards me but other staff as well."

"Were they interested?" I asked, "or was it just a 'we-have-the-Senator-on-our-back-so-we-have-to-look-like-we-care' call?"

Crystal laughed. "You got it in one," she said. "I gave him enough detail to get him interested, told him about agency staff being moved if they talk to Defence personnel..."

"That's still happening?" I asked.

"It's never stopped! Nothing has changed since you left Monica. I feel sad for the new people. It's such a shock for them," Crystal said. "Anyway, the guy from the Minister's Office told me that kind of behaviour was not acceptable."

"Yes, well, we've all heard that before..."

"I told him it was drip fed intimidation which goes on all day, every day." Crystal continued, "I let him know how intimidated and scared I am all the time and asked him if he could arrange to have me transferred out of there. He said he couldn't do that."

"Of course, more games!" I was starting to feel angry.

"Then he told me I'd made some serious allegations," said Crystal, "you know how they say it like it's a threat and you're going to be in serious trouble for making any allegations at all, well that's how he sounded."

"Yeah, right! Has he already forgotten what has been in the news lately?" I wondered how many times one could beat one's head against a brick wall before going insane. "They definitely don't want to know, do they?"

Crystal shook her head, "no, they don't!"

"They want their brand new, bright and shiny, money-making AGSVA," I said, "but it's not bright and shiny; the rot continues..."

"He asked if the illegal falsification of documents is still happening, even after the move to AGSVA, so I told him it was worse, but I didn't give him any details."

"And?"

"He wanted to know more, but I wouldn't tell him," said Crystal, "I said the only place I will feel comfortable talking openly is in a Senate Inquiry."

I nodded. Good on you, Crystal! Now they know why you've been to see a Senator. They know you mean business!"

Our lunch arrived, and we turned our conversation to more pleasant things. But I couldn't help wondering just how obtuse Defence could pretend to be and for how long. How could the Minister's office continue to deny the problem, while the Minister himself was openly telling the media the problem existed? What a farce! It was fairly obvious that, despite public admissions, Defence had no intention of doing anything to stop the rot.

I remembered Dayle's words *'The Department of Defence has no power to act illegally and to allow it to do so would be a criminal offence.'* Minister Smith would know that, and yet, despite everything he'd been told, everything that had happened on his watch, it was evident that under his hand the breaches of law within DSA would continue, without abate! Our only hope was the Senate!

The Senate starts asking questions

Two days later, our claims were being discussed in the Senate. When we found out, we were stunned! How does one get a Senate Inquiry without having a Senate Inquiry? The Senators were already inquiring! They were asking the hard questions and forcing the issue. Awesome! We were in a daze. Everything we were wanting was happening for us! Talk about timing!

How many miracles can one expect in one saga? This was number four! First was my stunning entry into DSA, then Dayle was provided when we needed someone with his skill-set, then came the exposure of an international criminal with a clearance, and now questions in the Senate.

Apparently, the Senators wanted to know if Australia's security had been compromised, and more personally, if their individual safety had been compromised. They spent thirty to forty minutes discussing the problems facing Defence because of the issues we had raised on *Lateline*, which had been highlighted by the real-life example of the parliamentary security guard wanted by Interpol.

This would have been a great outcome to boast about if we'd been able to plan it, but of course, we didn't plan it. None of us had prior knowledge the Senate was discussing DSA until John phoned me at work after the meeting and told me what had happened.

"Hi Monica," I recognised John's voice as soon as I answered the phone, "have you been able to watch the Senate Estimates?" he asked.

"Hi John," I responded, "no, I haven't. I'm at work and don't have access to television, and anyway, I wasn't aware it was on."

"The Senators put a bit of pressure on Defence today," he said, "they asked some good questions."

"So, what was the mood?" I asked. I couldn't help but be sceptical, but I was so hoping John would give me some good news, "were they for or against?"

"I think the Senators were pretty strong actually," John explained, "and it seemed to me like Defence was trying to play it all down."

"What kind of questions were they asking?" I tried to sound casual. I didn't want to seem pushy.

"They wanted to know if DSA was doing checks for ministerial staff," said John, "They said that in the light of what has happened recently there seems to be good reason to ask questions about the security process."

I started to laugh, a happy sort of chuckle, "So the right people are starting to ask the right questions..."

"You should download the transcript off the net. I think this is important," said John.

"You don't have a transcript, John?" I asked, knowing he would give me one if he had one on hand.

"No, I only have a video copy," he said, "I'll have to wait for the Hansard to become available."

"Okay," I said, "I'll ask Janice to download it."

"It might take a few days for it to appear on the Senate Estimates website, but when it does, it will give you a lot of detail about the response from Defence. It goes for about thirty to forty minutes. There is quite a lot there."

"Oh, excellent! Are you doing another story, John?"

"Stephen Merchant, the acting Secretary of Defence, did most of the speaking for Defence. I'm going to run some of his comments on *Lateline* tonight. Just a brief mention."

"Let me know if you want me to respond."

"Thanks, Monica," John said. "I think Defence know there are big problems at the AGSVA and they are trying to fix them before the Inspector-General of Intelligence and Security finds out."

Hello, what was that? A new investigation? "Hold on John, before who finds out?"

"The Inspector-General of Intelligence and Security is now doing the inquiry," John repeated, "not the Inspector-General of Defence, you didn't know about this?"

"No, it's the first I've heard."

"They are not Defence," said John, "they're an independent authority, so it will be interesting to see what they find."

"John I'm in the dark here," I was painfully aware he was looking for information from me, but instead I was the one receiving the information, "I need to read the transcript otherwise I just don't know what to tell you."

"No worries, I'm only doing a brief mention tonight. We'll talk again after you've read the Hansard."

"Thanks for the 'heads-up' John."

When I got home that evening, I did an internet search to see what I could find out about the IGIS. What I found out was impressive and, as it turned out, accurate.

The Inspector-General of Intelligence and Security (IGIS), currently Dr Vivienne Thom, along with her small, hand-picked team of investigators, was Australia's Intelligence Agency watchdog. Her office was superior in authority to the Defence Department and all Australia's security organisations, including ASIO. Her authority came, not from the elected Government, but from the Attorney General and her reports were for the Prime Minister's eyes only. If the Prime Minister chose not to make any particular IGIS report public, it remained a secret document.

Dr Thom's role as IGIS was elite, so elite the role of IGIS had its own Act, the IGIS Act, which gave the Inspector-General immense power to compel people to appear before her, equivalent to that of a Royal Commission. This was great news for us! It meant we could speak openly and honestly without fear of prosecution.

Suddenly, we had everything we wanted. The Senators were asking all the right questions, and we had an investigative forum which had the clearance and clout not only to hear what we had to say but to investigate our claims properly and instigate changes where necessary. Things were definitely looking up! What a difference a few days made! This was fantastic news! The only problem was Defence didn't like it!

Defence throws mud on the evidence

When I watched *Lateline* that night and heard Stephen Merchant's comments, I realised Defence was not going to simply admit they had done the wrong thing and fix the problem. Instead, they were going to try and save face instead - by blaming us!

Defence couldn't claim anymore that we were lying, or that the problems didn't exist, because their own cursory examination of files had shown the problems were there; and a real-life example meant they couldn't brush it under the carpet. But neither could they face admitting they had made such a colossal mess of Australia's National Security! So they had to find a way to dodge the inevitable bullets, and they found it! Or so they thought! In the Senate, they strongly implied the damage was limited to clearances handled by just three supposedly incompetent people. We three whistleblowers!

> *"From the examination of the packs that were touched by the three contractors who appeared on Lateline, we estimate that about 1,500 clearances were touched by those contractors."* (Stephen Merchant, Senate, 30 May 2012)

How predictable! How transparent they were! We had seen this coming way back in the garden when we were sitting around the yellow cloth, wondering why Defence wanted to hire extremely short-term agency staff to do the work we did. There had only been one answer then, '*so that agency staff could get the blame if something went wrong*' and that answer had just been proven correct. It was only theory way back then, but now it had become a reality.

Didn't they know how see-through they were? This was not a good look for Australia's intelligence community!

Stephen Merchant's carefully chosen words were derogatory and highly offensive to us, and were supposed to be! 'Touched' was a colourful word when used the way it was used against us in the Senate. It made us sound dirty; as if anything our vile hands 'touched' would be tainted. It conjured up a picture in my mind of investigators wearing white coats, face masks and protective gloves, picking up our filthy clearances with tweezers so that our germs wouldn't contaminate them. It also made 'those contractors' sound like we were different from all the other contractors and somehow creepily contagious. Good one, guys!

Yet, the only thing different about us was that, of the one hundred and fifty or more agency staff who had passed through DSA during 2009 to 2011, we were the only three who had publicly admitted the problem existed. We were doing Australia a massive favour by sticking our necks out, but here we were, being crucified for coming forward.

The emails began to flow again, mainly from John, who was full of questions and keen to gauge our response to Mr Merchant's statements.

- "They are basically arguing the only clearance packs which need to be re-checked were packs done by you three. I asked Defence Media if those 1500 checks included other staff as well. Their official written response to the ABC was, *The 1500 clearances are those which Defence records show were 'touched' by the three former DSA contractors.*" John.
- "I think it's pretty obvious they are coming after us now, John…want to say we are the only ones who 'filled in the gaps' and falsified documents since they are only looking at the ones we 'touched'." Monica.
- "Blaming us...I guess that is to be expected…but can't they see the writing on the wall? They are going to look so stupid when the truth finally comes out." Janice.
- "Defence said they only needed to re-check the clearances done by you three…not by anyone else. Were there only 1500?" John.
- "There were tens of thousands, John. My estimate would be at least 40,000 maybe more. Looks like they're still just trying to water it down...cover it up." Monica.
- "The number of affected clearances is too high to be blamed on just three people. The proof is in the database." Janice.
- "So why are they only checking the ones done by you three?" John.

- “No one else has gone public! There weren’t any faces to the statements about AGSVA and the confirmation letter that you read out on 25th, John, so they are completely disregarding them!” Janice.

- “They don’t know who the others are, John, or how many. So, of course, they’re going to point the finger at us! Very cowardly of them though, it takes courage to admit when you’re wrong. It’s terrible for us to see just how lacking in courage our Defence bureaucrats are - what hope Australia?” Monica.

- “They are SO into the bullying mentality it seems to be beyond their little grey cells to realise that if only three of us were dodgy, then it was mighty peculiar of us to reveal it on *Lateline* and so advertise to the world our own incompetence! Ridiculous!” Janice.

- “Do you think it could be just classic Public Relations - damage control?” John.

- “Definitely damage control. I think they are running - but running around in circles. Have you ever heard of a high-level investigation being ordered one week and cancelled the next? Just laughable!” Monica.

- “But do you think the new inquiry might be better than the last one?” John.

- “Yes, I do. This is a statutory body - the forum we have been waiting for! No fear of persecution or prosecution! Completely independent - and answerable only to the Prime Minister - not Defence! It’s good news for us, John.” Monica.

- “I checked with Dayle…he agrees.” Janice.

- “The whole process of security clearances for both Defence and non-Defence applicants has been one of systematic corruption for at least two years - longer according to Defence staff. All the applications done over the past two years need to be re-done because *all* of us were deceived by management into believing ‘filling in the gaps’ was a normal process.” Monica.

- "It's entrenched behaviour, John, and all the clearances were affected. When you calculate the number of applications done over two years, you'll find the number which need to be re-checked. It's not rocket science!" Janice.
- "Is that why Merchant is saying, 'I think it's important we don't jump to worst-case conclusions here...'?" John.
- "Absolutely! They already know...they just don't want anyone else to know they know...including the Senate, obviously." Monica.
- "The Defence advantage is that no one wants to believe it...not even the staff who still work there... most of them still can't believe they've been doing anything wrong...they believe it's okay to falsify documents as long as they are just following orders." Janice.
- "They are very good at convincing staff that lying and deception are normal. Here's hoping the Senators will see through the lies. We certainly need them to keep asking the right questions. We need a Senate Inquiry!" Monica.
- "Thanks, guys." John.
- "No probs, John." Monica.

Contacting Senator David Johnston

When the Senate Hansard proof became available a few days later, Janice downloaded it and sent a copy to me. Before I had a chance to read it, she phoned.

"We've found our Senator!" she sounded as if she had just won the lottery.

Her excitement was contagious, but I had no idea what she was talking about, "What do you mean?"

"It's in the Hansard," she explained, "there is one Senator who is asking all the right questions."

I still didn't know what she was talking about, so I opened the Hansard document on my computer screen. "What page number are you looking at?"

"Page 32, I looked him up, he's not just a Senator, he's the shadow minister for Defence!" said Janice, sounding very pleased with herself.

As she was talking, I was reading, and I liked what I was seeing.

Senator Johnston's questions were clear, direct and to the point, but more than that, he sounded keen to get answers and was quick with further comments when he didn't like the answers given. "Great find Janice, I think you're right!"

"I know he's the Shadow Minister, so he's obliged to ask questions, but I think there's something more." Janice continued.

"I can see what you mean," I agreed. I was reading his questions and comments. It may have been his role to play 'devil's advocate', but that was precisely what we needed. "He certainly gets to the point, exactly what we need! What State is he in?"

"Western Australia," said Janice.

"Too far away for an introductory visit..."

"I was thinking of sending him an outline of everything that's been going on." Janice continued.

"Okay, but our approach has to be in line with his portfolio," I said.

"What do you mean?"

"He can only act within the bounds of the authority afforded by his office," I continued. "We can't throw everything at him because he won't be able to use most of it."

"Can't we just ask him to lead a Senate Inquiry?" said Janice.

"No, we have to give him something he can use, something which will help him do his job, and I think that something is in the Hansard. Have you noticed the answers that were given to his questions?"

"Yes, not entirely accurate," said Janice. "Reading them made me quite angry."

"Exactly!" I said. "They're lying to the Senate! They don't want the Senators to know the truth."

"I thought it was an offence to lie to the Senate," said Janice.

"That's our reason for writing," I said.

"To let Senator Johnston know he's been lied to?" asked Janice.

"Yes! Maybe we should put the whole sorry saga into a report," I said, 'there's so much of it."

Janice laughed, "It's going to be a mighty big report."

"Not if we limit it to the questions and answers in the Hansard," I said. "We could do two reports, yours and mine, two different viewpoints of the same pack of lies."

Janice agreed, "yes, let's do it."

Over the next few days, we each went over the Senate transcript with a fine-tooth comb. Senator Johnston had asked some probing questions, but the answers given by Stephen Merchant and the DSA Chief Security Officer (CSO), Frank Roberts, were not accurate at all. They were, in fact, totally misleading. Yet how would the Senators know Defence was lying to them unless someone else came along with proof of those lies? So that was the information we decided to collate and send to Senator Johnston; proof that what the Senators had been told was not true.

Each of us wrote up a statement of the things which were being said in the Senate showing, with documented evidence, what had transpired over the past two years and how the things being reported as fact conflicted with the reality we had experienced every day while working within DSA. When they were done, we met for celebratory coffee at our usual place, our local Christian Bookstore.

"I've been thinking that before we send these reports we should 'test the waters' with a short letter," I said.

"Way ahead of you," smiled Janice, "I've already written one. In fact, I sent it off a few days ago. I just got so 'hot under the collar' when I was reading the lies, I couldn't help writing straight away."

"Did you get a response?"

"Yes! Not from Senator Johnston, but from his Media Advisor, Rebecca," said Janice, "just a general 'thank you for your email' response, but at least it is a response."

"Excellent! I've also been thinking he doesn't need both of us writing to him. It would probably be best if we followed the procedure we used with Dayle."

"Do you want me to be the 'front' person again?" asked Janice.

I nodded. "Yes, you're good at that kind of thing. And you've already got the ball rolling."

Janice beamed. "I have, haven't I?"

The IGIS Investigation begins

The following week we were each contacted by Dr Vivienne Thom, Inspector-General of Intelligence and Security, first by letter informing us she would like to interview us, and then by phone to personally invite us to speak with her about our concerns. Her tone was so nice, so pleasant, it was hard to imagine just how much power this one woman had.

I had read the IGIS Act. I understood the legalities attached to that simple phone call. Dr Thom's formal powers included the authority to 'compel' people to appear before her. Once we had been notified of a meeting time, it was an offence to fail to comply with such a notice. The Act was very clear; six months jail and a $2,000 fine for anyone failing to appear once they had been asked to appear before her.

In short, if any of us who had been requested to appear before her now failed to turn up to the meeting she set we would go straight to jail. No questions asked! Wow!

The interview would be conducted under oath and, though less formal than a courtroom, the Inspector-General had far more power than a judge. Being interviewed by her was akin to giving evidence before a Royal Commission.

Though we welcomed the freedom to speak openly about everything we had experienced, we each were well aware, and in awe of, her immense authority.

"Do you think they will muzzle us?" asked Owen. We were standing in the car park outside the Springwood Community Centre. It was nearly time for our 'pre-IGIS interview' appointment with our Barrister.

Janice nodded. "I was wondering the same thing. Once we tell them what we know, we might not be able to talk about it to anyone else ever again."

"Yes," said Owen, "confidentiality and all that..."

I shook my head. "No! I don't believe they could do that. We can check that one with Dayle, but I don't believe they could stop us from telling our story. This is our story! We are the ones who have made the complaints. These are our complaints! If we don't like the way this is handled, then we are free to take our complaints elsewhere. *We* have requested this, not the other way around!"

"You're right!" nodded Owen.

"Well, that may be true, but I'm still glad I have sent everything through to Senator Johnston," said Janice.

"Have you sent yours yet, Monica?" asked Owen.

"No, not yet, it's finished, all fifteen pages, but I am still rechecking the facts. I want to get it to him before the IGIS interview," I said, "if the IGIS freeze our interview information at least we will know we can still quote what we told the Senator."

"It's nearly time," said Owen referring to our interview with Dayle, "do you think we could pray before we go in?"

He didn't have to ask twice. We needed Godly guidance now, more than ever before. There in the car park, we linked arms and prayed. The truth is we were not sure what to expect from the IGIS. Up to this point, all we had seen from any authority was lies, deception and trickery. Ministers were covering things up as a matter of course, the law was being broken daily, and no one in authority wanted to know about it, the top people in Defence and Defence Security were lying to the Senate and legal traps were constantly being laid for anyone who wanted to say, 'hey, this is wrong'.

The stark reality was we three were currently being set up by Defence to take the fall for their mess.

It was not so far fetched for us to believe the only reason we were now being asked to appear before the IGIS was so we could be forced to stop talking to the media, and everyone else, about the gaping hole in Australia's National Security. We honestly didn't know what to expect.

Furthermore, we were not sure whether our meeting with the Inspector-General of Intelligence and Security would take the form of interview or interrogation. So prayer was our most sensible course of action. It kept us focussed and calm and got each of us through the next few days.

Our individual, two-hour interviews with one of the most powerful people in Australia, came and went.

Thankfully, it was not an interrogation!

Personally, I thought Dr Thom was a sweetheart. She was not pushy or overbearing, and her manner with me was both professional and kind. What a change of pace from the brutal horror I had become used to when dealing with Defence officials.

Though I am still under oath not to reveal anything discussed in that meeting, I was assured by Dr Thom, and Dayle, there was no confidentiality clause. We were all free to continue speaking about our concerns to each other and to the media, albeit within the bounds of established law.

Finally! Someone who was playing according to the rules! It was a bit of a shock, really. At first, I was not sure how to handle it. It took me a while to just relax and trust Dr Thom was on the straight and narrow and would not be using her powers to promote or cover Defence corruption.

Defence tries to blame us - again

While the IGIS investigation was in progress, things were quiet. Everyone, it seemed, was waiting to see what the IGIS would find. Everyone except Senator Johnston!

In September Senator Johnston sent out a media release insisting Minister Smith immediately make public the findings of the previous investigation - the 'nine-day' wonder - done by the Inspector-General of Defence.

- "The Parliament needs to get to the bottom of this. In Senate Estimates, in May, the committee was assured by Defence officials and the government that this was a bit of a storm in a teacup, but it is clear I was misled."
- "This is not what I was told by a whistleblower, but I took the evidence of the Defence officials at face value."

- "The Minister needs to explain exactly who is being held accountable for this unbelievable set of circumstances where Defence has potentially left our bases and embassies vulnerable to security breaches."
- "The security breach is now so serious that the Minister has recommended the Prime Minister refer the Inspector-General of Defence's report to the independent Inspector-General of Intelligence and Security for investigation."

During those few quiet months, it had gradually become apparent to everyone involved, Defence, the Senate, Ministers and the media that the scale of the problem was so widespread and had been going on for so long it could not possibly be attributed to three short-term contractors.

Amazing! We didn't have to defend ourselves; God was doing it for us!

The Minister for Defence, Stephen Smith, now had no choice but to finally admit publicly there were serious problems, affecting a massive number of clearances.

We had said all along there was an extreme risk to Australia's National Security because tens of thousands of clearances had been corrupted. Now, finally, Minister Smith was publicly saying the same thing.

> *"I don't want to put a figure out to alarm people, but as a general rule of thumb, the security vetting agency will see in any year somewhere between 40,000 and 50,000 security assessments done. So we are not talking about every assessment being done, we are only talking about those affected by deficiencies in procedures."* (Minister Smith, ABC Sept. 2011)

He didn't want to alarm people? The numbers were huge! He was only giving numbers for one year, yet the problem had been going on for at least two years, maybe even more. He was talking upwards of 100,000 possibly compromised clearances!

We knew the ratio of affected clearances was about 40% of the total, so the real figure would probably be around 40,000, as we had suggested, 20,000 per year, yet the only way they could separate the affected files from the non-affected files was to painstakingly re-check the paperwork for every single clearance - upwards of 100,000 - by hand.

The problem was enormous!

Nevertheless, to our gob-smacked amazement, Defence continued to try and play it down. The facts were impossible to hide, they couldn't deny the risk anymore, and they could no longer blame it on us, so they came up with yet another new tactic, one which nevertheless put the focus back onto us...again! Unbelievable! When were they ever going to give up and just fix it?

They began to belittle our part in the clearance process, making our role sound so insignificant as to not have any effect on the end result. This made our allegations seem naive and unwarranted, despite the confirmed size and seriousness of the risk to National Security.

Their turn of phrase made us seem like we didn't understand the full process, that there were checks in place we were unaware of and secret 'workaround' agreements with ASIO to which we were not privy. It didn't seem to matter that the workarounds they mentioned didn't actually exist. Who would know? How could the media check?

- "I think it is important to understand that the errors made were essentially errors at the beginning of the data entry process, and there are very many layers to the security assessment." Stephen Smith.

The 'errors' in the process (bounce-backs from the ASIO database) were always at the end of the process. Always! Again, Minister Smith was deceiving the public.

From the very beginning of this saga, all levels of Defence had continually misled the Australian people about the seriousness of DSA's breach of security.

- We had said many security clearances were compromised; riddled with false data or approved despite missing information. Defence representatives told the media what we were saying was not correct. Then (oops) evidence was found that many security clearances had indeed been compromised.
- We had said we told a previous investigation about the risk to Australia's National Security. The minister told the media we had only mentioned it 'in passing'. Then (oops) both the media and the Senate were shown we had detailed our concerns in writing and had been completely ignored.
- We had said security guards were a definite risk. The minister told the media we were wrong; that the risk to security was extremely low. Then (oops) a man who had been wanted by Interpol for seven years was found working as a security guard for the Queensland Parliament. And people began to ask, "How many more are out there?"
- We had said there were multiple thousands of corrupted clearances. Defence representatives told the media and the Senate they would only need to check the clearances 'touched' by 'those' whistleblowers. Then (oops) a thorough investigation showed the number of corrupted clearances was so high they were afraid to tell the Australian public the truth.
- We had said the false data could not be detected once entered; not even by ASIO. The minister was now telling the media there were 'many layers' of checks and balances we didn't know about. (Oops) Minister Smith was about to find out he was wrong again! When was he ever going to get his facts right?

Thankfully, none of the Defence rhetoric had fooled the media for a minute, and they continued to ask probing questions; questions the Minister for Defence could not answer. "How worried should the Australian public be?" How worried indeed! Good question!

"Minister Smith, we're talking about serious maladministration; at this point, a remedial process is only just getting underway, checks which are only just starting. How worried should the Australian public be?"
(Ali Moore ABC Lateline, 20 Sept. 2011)

Did they really

think

they could fool ASIO?

CHAPTER EIGHT

ASIO deceived? Nah! They knew!

During the gap between Senate meetings, May to October 2011, 'workarounds' became the new media buzzword. Instead of talking about ways to plug the gaping hole in Australia's National Security, Defence told the media fabricated phrases like 'Fake Street', 'Green Street' and 'Unknown Street' were used to fill gaps in information as a matter of course.

They gave the strong impression there was nothing wrong with 'making things up' and implied all workarounds used had been approved by ASIO.

Ironically, this very tactic proved our point! We had said DSA staff had been deceived into believing 'making things up' was okay; that it was standard procedure. And now Defence was using the same deception on the Australian people, telling the Senate, the media and everyone else, very convincingly, it was okay to make things up, it was procedure. ASIO, however, was not amused!

ASIO denied any knowledge of the 'Fake Street', 'Green Street' and 'Unknown Street' style of workarounds supposedly approved by them for use within DSA, stating they were not aware of them, and no such approval was documented.

The ASIO denial of the publicised DSA workarounds had a profound effect. Defence had been caught in a lie.

In September 2011, it was announced on *Lateline*, that both the head of DSA, Frank Roberts, and the acting Secretary of Defence, Stephen Merchant, had written to the Senate revising their statements about workarounds. They had both admitted the procedural workarounds they had referred to previously did not officially exist.

That same night it was announced that Stephen Merchant had suddenly resigned his position as Deputy Secretary of Intelligence and Security and, despite his 34 years with Defence, would not be seeking any future position within Defence or the Intelligence community. A few minutes later, when questioned in a live interview, Stephen Smith, Minister for Defence, claimed he had no knowledge of this high profile resignation.

The ship was sinking, no doubt about it. There was nothing left to do now but jump ship or drown. Drastic career choices were being made, and the IGIS investigation had not even been concluded, let alone released.

The corruption continues unabated

On a beautiful, sunny midwinter's day, the original four gathered for a catch-up picnic in Brisbane's historic Botanical Gardens. I pulled out the yellow cloth and threw it over one end of a rectangular picnic table. The girls smiled. This was familiar territory.

After we had unpacked our baskets and the table was laden with tasty goodies, we poured our drinks and settled in for some good conversation.

Jennifer opened the subject, "So, how are things in DSA land, Cass?"

Cassie smiled, a shy kind of rueful smile, "Nothing has changed," she said, "well, not for the better anyway."

"Are you saying things have gotten worse?" I asked.

"You could say that," Cassie said.

We waited. We knew Cassie wasn't trying to be evasive. We understood it was difficult to go from not being allowed to talk about work at all, to talking openly; it was a completely different mindset, and she would just need a moment to adjust.

"It's so confusing," she said, "I don't want to sound paranoid, but I think they have been deliberately mean to me."

"Not surprising, since you're our friend," I said.

"You could never sound paranoid to us," said Janice, "we know what they're like."

"What did you do?" asked Jennifer. "You must have done something or said something they didn't like."

A rueful grin slowly spread across Cassie's face, "Yes I did, actually. I stood up for you guys." Seeing the inquisitive looks on our faces, Cassie explained. "A few weeks ago the CSO, Frank Roberts, came through and asked the agency staff if we had ever filled in the gaps or had ever been bullied. He said we could see him privately if we didn't want to speak openly."

"So you bit the bullet?" I asked.

Cassie nodded. "When I went to see him, he asked who had told me to fill in gaps with 'fake street', 'green street' etc. and if we were ever given any printed procedures. I told him I'd never heard of those streets and that agency staff had to fill in gaps, and it didn't matter what we used to fill them. I also told him how you guys were bullied and about other bullying I've seen."

"Ooooh!" said Jennifer, "he wouldn't have liked that."

"Oh, no, he was nice," said Cassie, jumping to his defence, "he didn't know about any of this."

We all laughed and shook our heads. "He knows everything Cassie," I said, "He's known about all of it, right from the beginning."

"He's the top cocky, Cass, he's the one who ordered it and wants to cover it up," said Jennifer.

Cassie shook her head. "No, he didn't seem like that."

"He's currently lying to the Senate and the media about workarounds, Cassie," I said, "he's probably fishing for proof the workarounds were official."

"Oh, that makes sense," Cassie said, with understanding dawning on her face.

"What do you mean?" asked Janice.

"I guess that's why the Defence staff are all running around like chooks without heads trying to find old procedure notes. I thought it was just because the CSO wanted copies." Cassie was finally beginning to see.

Janice and I glanced at each other and grinned. This was excellent news! We had written to the Senate via Senator Johnson about the non-existent workarounds, and now the Senate was obviously asking the right questions.

"They won't find anything," Janice said.

"The thing that tickles me is the irony!" I said, "DSA never write anything down, and that's the problem now! It's because they don't write anything down that they don't have any proof for their own statements!"

"Without documents," Janice continued, "the Senate will know they've lied."

"Not very bright, for an 'intelligence' organisation, are they?" said Jennifer chuckling.

"Well, I'm glad I'm out of there now!" said Cassie, dropping a bombshell in her quiet and casual way.

We all stopped talking and turned to face Cassie. "When did this happen?" Janice asked.

"Yesterday! I came in, and someone else's purse was on my desk." Cassie continued. "They told me desks were reserved for permanent Defence staff, not agency. So, I didn't have anywhere to sit."

Janice nodded, "sounds familiar..."

"How long has this been going on?" asked Jennifer.

"A couple of weeks."

"Did it begin before or after the CSO spoke to you?" asked Jennifer.

Cassie's eyes registered understanding, the penny had dropped. "It was just after..." she said, slowly realising the CSO had betrayed her confidence. Betrayed *her*.

"So what's been going on Cass, what have they been doing to you?" asked Janice.

"Well, I was officially told by email from the agency that I'm regarded as an underachiever because I'm not reaching target," she stopped and smiled. "The target is now twenty per day."

"Twenty a day!" gasped Jennifer, "no one can do twenty a day! I was flat out doing ten!"

"So, you don't check information against the previous file anymore?" I said, remembering my eighteen per day record; only possible because I didn't check anything at all.

Cassie shook her head. "That's the new rule, we don't have time to check anything, all we do is push them through and send the ASIO report," said Cassie.

I was flabbergasted, "they're up to their ears in investigations, being scrutinised from every angle, and they're still doing this?" I couldn't believe they could be so impervious to decency. "What's wrong with these people?"

"How many were you doing, Cassie?" asked Janice.

"Not many at all," Cassie continued, "I haven't had full access to the database for the last two weeks, so I had to fiddle and get around problems all the time. Just completing one was a nightmare."

"Let me guess," said Jennifer, "no one wanted to know about your database problems."

"Bingo!" smiled Cassie, trying to make light of the situation. "I went to the agency team leader who was too busy to assist, so I went to the Defence IT person, who sent me back to the agency team leader for instruction, who again was too busy to assist. It became a daily routine. I felt like a nuisance that no one wanted to know. So, yesterday, without a desk, or proper database access, or any semblance of assistance, I got the message and resigned."

"Déjà vu," said Janice. "You're in good company."

"I have a confession to make," I said, "I already knew."

Now everyone was looking at me in surprise, so I didn't keep them in suspense. "Crystal emailed me last night and told me Defence staff were officially informed you were let go because you had been speaking to Defence personnel without permission."

Cassie's relaxed smile disappeared as she realised they had not just betrayed her confidence and deceived her, but they lied about her as well.

"Are they still enforcing that?" asked Jennifer, "after all that's happened?" She shook her head, dumbfounded.

"Way to go, Frank!" I said, speaking into the air. It was so easy to see that this typical DSA punishment had been ordered by the CSO and tailor-made by senior DSA staff to fit Cassie. How stupid did he think people were?

"Horrible, horrible, place..." said Janice.

The media finally catch on

Cassie had just confirmed to us the bullying of staff and corruption of data was still continuing, even after all the complaints, all the media coverage, even after multiple and continual, tax-payer funded, investigations. It was beyond understanding – simply mind-boggling! Her personal experience showed that both the bullying and corruption of data was now, in fact, even more intense within the new AGSVA than it had been in DSA.

On top of that, the head of DSA, Frank Roberts, the man who took control of DSA in 2008 and announced he didn't want security clearances done by DSA anymore, the man who, alongside Stephen Merchant, had lied to the Senate about the corruption of data; this man was still pretending to agency staff he was ignorant of what was happening in regard to bullying and the corruption of applications.

What was it going to take to stop this corruption? Didn't these people care about the security of our military who were putting their lives on the line, trusting that the people around them were also trustworthy? Didn't they care about our bases, our airports, our embassies? Didn't they care that ASIO was being fed so much miss-information they wouldn't be able to sort the truth from the lies?

The worst thing about this whole mess was the knowledge that it was, absolutely, disgustingly, without a doubt, deliberate!

At the same time he was pretending to the DSA/AGSVA staff he was ignorant of the problem and 'innocently' asking if anyone had 'filled in gaps', the head of DSA, Frank Roberts, was being quoted in the media as saying 'workarounds' were a monitored and acceptable part of the security process.

As you would imagine, the media came knocking on our doors to find out if we agreed with the official Defence position. We didn't!

- "Contrary to statements made to the Senate by Mr Stephen Merchant and Mr Frank Roberts, 'workarounds' were not discussed with agency staff during the time of my employment," said Janice to Dan Oakes from the Sydney Morning Herald pointing out the fabricated data was unsupervised and haphazard.
- "The Minister for Defence, Stephen Smith said whistleblowers had only been involved at the beginning of the clearance process." Dan Oaks said, more as a question than a statement.

- "That's the very point!" Janice responded, "When the early stages have errors, errors that haven't been flagged by previously accepted workarounds, how can anyone working in the following stages recognise the error and follow them up?" If ASIO is looking for agreed workarounds and not finding them, how can ASIO know what is right and what is wrong?" (SMH July 14, 2011)

The headlines began to roll:

- Govt ignored faked security clearance claims!
- Fake data used to rush 'top secret' clearances!
- Defence led up 'fake street'!
- Illusory entries were workarounds!
- Contractor challenges Defence testimony!
- Years of faking of Defence security clearances!
- Thousands of security clearances compromised!
- Defence admits need to re-check clearances!

The ABC radio reporter, Michael Edwards, was also asking about 'workarounds' and interviewed Senator Johnston and me by phone on live radio.

- "We were not told about 'workarounds'. The information we entered, whether it was true or false, once introduced, couldn't be checked by anyone else down the line unless it was flagged as a problem. We didn't flag anything." Monica.
- "Opposition Defence spokesman David Johnston says he's almost too frightened to think about the possible ramifications," Michael Edwards.
- "We have embassies, foreign dignitaries, all coming to Australia, all being the subject of people with security clearances doing rudimentary and fundamental jobs like servicing the aircraft and doing all these sorts of things, it is very concerning that this problem has come to the point that it has because it was ignored for so long." Senator Johnston.

Despite the media coverage, the questions from the Senate, and an investigation being conducted under the authority of the Governor General, Defence continued to bury its proverbial head in the sand, and Minister Smith continued to publically support the false testimonials to the Senate of both Stephen Merchant and DSA CSO, Frank Roberts.

> *"A spokesman for the Defence Minister, Stephen Smith, says that Senator Johnston's assertions are baseless and the Government has taken the matter very seriously since the allegations were first raised."* (John Stewart ABC Lateline, 19 October 2011).

The Department of Defence was so bull-headed! So determined to betray Australia and Australians. When was it going to end? How was it going to end? Incredible!

ASIO backs away from the Defence claims

While the media was running with Defence's 'ASIO knew about workarounds' propaganda, the reality behind the scenes was that ASIO was not amused! The ASIO heads began to distance themselves from the Defence claims by making direct statements, not to the media, but to the IGIS and the Senate.

Prior to the completion of her investigation, and because of the statements made to the media by senior Defence officials, Dr Thom directly asked ASIO to forward relevant documentation to her and to answer a few questions like, "Was ASIO aware of the workarounds and, were they documented?" The response from ASIO to Dr Thom was swift and very clear:

- ASIO has not now, and has not previously, agreed to such workarounds."
- "ASIO's position now, as in the past, remains that full and accurate information is required by ASIO to undertake its security assessment role."

- "Further, because the prescribed workarounds were not known or agreed to by ASIO, ASIO was not in a position to know that modified information was being sent and therefore that it needed to be 'corrected'."
- "ASIO's advice is that the impact of many of the workarounds described is 'potentially significant'." (IGIS report, page 46)

From this information, Dr Thom concluded, *"There is little doubt the integrity of the data that has been passed from the DSA to ASIO during the period 2008 to 31 August 2011 has been undermined."* (IGIS Report, Page 47)

Though we had no idea at the time this was all happening in the background, the reality was the truth was breaking through. And it was as undeniable as it was shocking. While Defence was telling the Senate and the media the workarounds they said they used, which didn't actually exist, were monitored and agreed to by ASIO, ASIO was about to tell the Senate that workarounds were not an agreed or documented process.

The October Senate Estimates Committee Meeting had now become pivotal. Everyone involved was waiting with bated breath; Senators, Defence, ASIO, the media and, of course, we whistleblowers, to hear when Dr Thom would release her full and final report. Even if it was completed in time for the Senate hearing, it still could not be released without the direct approval of the Prime Minister, Julia Gillard, and time was ticking.

As the days passed, it became clear the Prime Minister would not be receiving the IGIS report in time to read it, evaluate the contents and decide if it should be made public or remain a secret document, prior to the Senate Estimates hearing. So until the Prime Minister decided it could be made public, not even Senators were privy to its contents. Nevertheless, the Senate hearing would provide valuable intelligence on when and if Dr Thom thought the IGIS report could be completed and released.

Suddenly the game is over. Checkmate!

The phone rang at work, and a familiar voice greeted me, "Hello, Monica, is this a good time?"

"Hello, John." How casual we had become, like old friends. "Perfect timing, how can I help?"

"There's been a bit of a breakthrough," John sounded like he was holding back information, and finding it hard to contain his enthusiasm, so I knew our story was going to air again, "Both Stephen Merchant and Frank Roberts have retracted their statements to the Senate about workarounds."

I gasped. I didn't see this one coming! "They admitted they lied?" I nearly fell off my chair.

"They each put it in writing," he spoke in a casual tone, but this was huge! "We have the letters, and we are going to air tonight."

"Both of them?" I couldn't get my head around this, I was astounded! "Together?"

"It's good for you guys," John continued, "everything you've said is being validated." He paused then continued, "if this were a game of chess, this would be 'checkmate'." I could tell he was smiling.

I laughed, a quiet, sort of stunned laugh. "This is... this is unbelievable John!"

"Merchant wrote...here, let me read it to you," said John. '*On May 30th, I advised the committee that process 'workarounds' used by DSA to overcome the inflexibility of computer applications were documented and managed... However, contrary to my understanding at the time of the estimates hearing, there was no single document or instruction that recorded all of the 'workarounds'. The controls in place to manage and record the process by which data was adjusted by staff were regrettably ineffective and in some cases non-existent.*'"

"Frank Roberts was similar...'*On 30 May I advised the Committee...that contractors used accepted entries; "Green Street, Fake Street and Unknown Street". Subsequent investigation indicates that the use of these entries was not agreed either internally in the vetting centre or with ASIO.*' "

"Finally!" I was almost dumbfounded. Almost! "John, what happens when people in responsible positions get caught lying to the Senate?"

"I guess we'll just have to wait and see." John was non-committal, as usual; he was an excellent reporter and very rarely gave a personal opinion.

"We're just going to be interviewing Stephen Smith tonight, want him to comment on these high-level retractions and the real effect of a lack of workarounds on the ASIO data systems."

Wow! What a story! Though I was pleased I was not going to be before a camera again, I knew this was not just a 'heads-up'. John was after information.

"Without workarounds, John, there is no way ASIO can possibly tell the true information from the false. Totally impossible! These admissions show the false DSA data couldn't help but corrupt the ASIO database!"

"From what we are reading in these letters, ASIO didn't know about the workarounds."

"Exactly as we have been saying, John, we didn't know about them either, seems they were so secret, nobody knew about them!" I couldn't help laughing at the absurdity! How stupid! How vault-window mentality! How DSA!

"Senator Johnston is now asking how many approvals ASIO has done based on false information."

"Good question, John! The cold, hard reality is that if the false data entries had been mere 'workarounds', none of the DSA clearances would now need to be re-checked. Workarounds would be recognised as workarounds, and there wouldn't be a problem."

"That makes sense," said John.

"The fact that Defence has ordered clearances to be re-checked means they *know* there weren't any workarounds. They know! And it also means ASIO now knows they've been sent a whole lot of false information."

"So, we only need to know how big the problem is, how many clearances need to be re-checked."

"Yes, well, how do you go back and re-check every clearance done over two or three years. Do you know how much that is going to cost, John? I don't even know if it's possible."

"So they won't be able to be done in six months."

I laughed again. "Absolutely not, John! We're talking a minimum of two years of clearances hurried through the process by a full staff. Proper re-checking of all those clearances will not be able to be done by a handful of people in just six months."

"Have you heard when the IGIS report will be released?" asked John, "will it be made public?"

"No, not a clue," I said, "I think Dr Thom might give the Senate a heads-up during the October Senate Budget Estimates hearings. The program seems to indicate a portion of time has been set aside for her to speak, but who knows? Only the Prime Minister can approve a public release of her report."

"Thanks, Monica."

John didn't tell me he had inside information that Stephen Merchant had not just apologised to the Senate but resigned his position as Deputy Secretary of Intelligence and Security. After 34 years with Defence, he had suddenly, inexplicably, chosen to quit his senior intelligence position and find employment outside Defence.

That night, on public television, when Minister Smith was asked by Ali Moore on *Lateline* to comment on Stephen Merchant's sudden departure, he claimed to have no knowledge of the Deputy Secretary's resignation.

- "I understand Stephen Merchant, the Deputy Secretary for Intelligence and Security, who indeed referred to workarounds in those Senate Estimates hearings, I understand he's announced he is leaving his job. Was he told to leave?" Ali Moore.
- "Well, that's...I don't have that advice. I met with the Deputy Secretary of Intelligence and Security today. I've been working closely with Mr Merchant on this matter, and I have not seen..." Minister Smith.
- "But will someone be held accountable? Will someone be held responsible?" Ali Moore.
- "I've had no discussion with Mr Merchant about his intention or any suggestion that he would leave Defence. He's the Acting Secretary of Defence, and he seems to me to be very comfortable and keen to continue his work." Minister Smith.

Two days later a spokesman for Minister Smith announced to the media that Mr Merchant was stepping down from his position, but his resignation was unrelated to the security clearance furore.

Of course! Checkmate!

Our 'checkmate' victory came quietly

There was no fanfare; no official recognition; no public announcement of any kind. All we had was the knowledge Defence had totally run out of excuses. They had no more moves! They could no longer deny the problem. They could no longer blame us. They could no longer diminish our roles. They could no longer hide from the truth. Their only course now was to face facts and deal with the problem. It was game over for them. Checkmate indeed!

On public television Defence had admitted total liability for tens of thousands of compromised clearances, senior Defence officials had apologised for misleading the Senate, and the Acting Secretary of Defence had resigned.

Senator Johnston had taken up the reigns and was carrying our fight forward in the Senate, and the IGIS report, which we trusted would also confirm everything we had said, was due to be completed any day. Our fight was over! We had thoroughly and completely won!

We had started our battle with the understanding that no one wins against Defence, yet against all the odds, three insignificant people had done the unthinkable, we had won our battle not just against Defence, but against Defence Intelligence. Their multiple denials of the problem had not only been shot down, they had been smashed to pieces, and in such a short space of time! It had only been six months since we first aired our concerns on *Lateline*. How in awe we were of our God and his amazing power!

The emails flowed, and the phone rang continually; friends, family, and acquaintances all contacting us to tell us how proud they were of us and how wonderful to see our victory. When the phone calls ceased that night, I emailed John and thanked him for the impressive way he had handled our story. This was his victory as much as ours.

Even now it is hard to put into words the kaleidoscope of feelings which whirled continually that evening; shock, realisation, laughter, tears, amazement, humility, joy, thanks and gratitude mixed with memories of people, places, events, threats, betrayals, surprises, disappointments, prayers and of course victory. So much to absorb! No wonder everything felt so surreal.

The next day, despite my mental elation, physical exhaustion hit me like a brick. I wasn't expecting it. I couldn't control it. Yet it completely enveloped me, so that I couldn't even speak.

I didn't know I was so emotionally exhausted until I arrived at work and people who had seen the *Lateline* program were coming up to me beaming and congratulating me on what we had done and the surprising outcome. I was so overwhelmed with their good-will I couldn't respond. I couldn't even say 'thank you'. I tried to smile, but instead, my eyes filled with tears which quietly rolled down my face, despite the fact I felt happy, and so appreciative of everyone's kind encouragement.

My bosses took me aside. "We want you to go home, Monica. Take a couple of days off, you need a break."

"I didn't realise it would hit me like this," I said, "I'm so sorry."

"No, don't apologise," said Jodie, who had been my supervisor for many years before I went to work for Defence, and who had opened the door for me to return to State Government work after I left Defence, "it's a big thing you've done. I'm just surprised you didn't break down earlier."

I let out a grateful sigh, "we've been pushing this for nearly two years, and now suddenly we don't have to push anymore. We've won! Nobody wins against Defence!"

"Are you going to seek compensation?" asked Bernie, she was the kind of person who would help me do so if that's what I wanted to do.

The tears stopped, and I shook my head, "No. This has never been about compensation. We did it because it was the right thing to do. Going after money now would just make me feel cheap." Clever lady – good question – got me to stop crying!

"Is the investigation finished?" Jodie was trying to be practical, an excellent antidote to the emotional.

I shook my head again, "No, not yet, but I'm sure it will only confirm how bad this whole deception has been."

"Will there be any more TV interviews?" I think Bernie was concerned that I may not be able to handle another one.

"I guess there will be a little mopping up to do involving Senator Johnston and the IGIS report, but I think the ABC stories will centre on people in authority now more than on us. I am happy about that because they should be taking responsibility and explaining to the Australian people how it is all going to be fixed." I suddenly stopped talking, sat back in my chair and chuckled. I was back...and I was on to them...

My bosses were watching me intently.

I gave them both a look which acknowledged I understood what they had just done and they both grinned at me like Cheshire cats.

"Well," said Bernie to Jodie, "I think she's ready to go home now, don't you?"

"Indeed, I do," smiled Jodie and rose to give me a hug.

The hugs were genuine. It was so very nice to be around normal, decent people.

An unexpected kindness

On my way out of the building, I ran into another work colleague and Christian friend, Jane, who, though she was employed by the same Department, was now located on a different floor. We didn't see much of each other but to keep in touch we would often have lunch together and use those times to pray about any pressing needs.

"Monica! Are you going home?" asked Jane with surprise in her voice.

I was crossing the foyer heading towards the front of the building, but when I heard my name being called, I stopped and turned into the direction of the voice, only to see Jane walking towards me with her arms out ready for her usual "kiss on the cheek" greeting. "Jane! What a lovely surprise!"

"I'm just on my way to lunch," Jane said, and the invitation to join her hovered unspoken in the air.

"Would you like some company?" I asked immediately, knowing what the response would be.

Jane beamed. "I would love it!" she said, linking arms with me. "Where shall we go?"

"What about that nice little Asian place around the corner which sells those great big bowls of delicious soup?" We'd been there before, and it was never crowded before noon. I looked at my watch, it was only 11am.

"I take it you started early today, Jane?" I said.

She nodded. "Yes, 7am! I like starting early, that way I get home in time to cook a decent meal for the family."

Jane was a Samoan Australian, an island beauty, with a strong, hard-working husband, three very pretty adult daughters and a strapping son who was still in high school, so her home life was as busy as her working life.

"What about you?" she asked again, "are you on lunch? You look like you're going home," she said, glancing pointedly at the tote bag I was carrying.

"I am going home," I said, smiling at her candour and immediately saw the questions begin, one after another, in her eyes. "No, I didn't get the sack," I chuckled. "No, I am not sick, and no, there's no problem at home."

"What then?" Now concern was written in her eyes.

I couldn't help grinning, we weren't going anywhere until I gave her a clue! "It's nothing bad, Jane, just the opposite. Did you see *Lateline* last night?"

She shook her head, "No...so this is about Defence?"

I nodded, "I'll fill you in over lunch."

When we reached the cafe, we ordered our soup, chose our table and settled into our seats. It was a large open sidewalk cafe, and there was quite a lot of inner-city street noise, ideal for us as it ensured our privacy.

As usual, we started our meal with prayer, and then I began to fill Jane in on the latest happenings with Defence and what had been revealed on the *Lateline* program the previous night.

I couldn't hide the joy I was feeling, and because Jane was a fellow Christian, I also told her how wonderful God had been to us, how he had led us every step of the way and intervened on our behalf in order for us to gain this 'giant-slaying' victory.

"This is wonderful, Monica, it deserves a celebration." Jane was beaming, filled with joy for us. "How are you all going to celebrate?"

"The three of us are going to have a celebratory brunch on Sunday morning," I said, smiling.

Jane's eyes filled with tears.

I stopped laughing and stared at her, speechless. I had no idea why she would be upset and was a little taken aback. "What's wrong, Jane?" I asked gently.

She took a moment to gather herself so she could respond. "I am overwhelmed," she said, and the tears started to flow again. "Monica, when the Prime Minister does even a little thing for this country they all go out and have a special gala dinner. You have done something huge, and you're just going to celebrate with a small breakfast?" She shook her head as if to say that was not a good thing.

I was watching her, listening to her, dumbfounded.

"You could have just saved Australia from disaster, and you haven't received any official phone calls, any thanks," she was dabbing at her face with a tissue as she spoke, "not even a bunch of flowers."

I hadn't considered any of this, so I remained quiet.

Jane reached down and rummaged in her bag, pulled out her purse, took out some money and scrunched it into her fist so I couldn't see how much she was holding. Then she reached across the table and took my hand. "You're not paying for your celebration."

I started to object and began to pull my hand away, but Jane was holding on firmly, though gently and she pressed the money into my palm.

"This is not me giving you this, accept it from God. You have all, the three of you, done this unselfishly, for him. Let him do this for you..."

Now it was my turn to be overwhelmed. The tears flowed again. What a pair we made. Sitting in an open cafe on a main street in Brisbane at midday, holding hands, tears running down both our faces, we must have looked a sight, but it didn't matter. This had become one of the most memorable days of my life!

The end of an era

Two days after our 'checkmate' victory was announced to Australia via *Lateline*, I woke to an early phone call. "So you are home..." said a familiar voice.

"Crystal," I said hearing, the smile in her voice. "You saw *Latelin*e..."

"Yes, it was awesome! You three should be so proud of what you have achieved."

"We three?" I questioned her. "There were four major players in this particular battle last time I counted!" I realised Crystal must have been feeling a little bit left out because people only saw the three faces on the telly. They didn't know about Crystal and her brave behind-the-scenes support. "You, me Janice and Owen, Crystal, the four of us won this."

I have tossed up whether to go public, and a few others are thinking about it, but I know I can't. Even now, it will still cost me my job." Crystal's voice began to shake with emotion, "you three did what we couldn't do. You made it all real."

"Crystal, your behind-the-scenes confirmation was pivotal. Without it, I don't know if we would have been able to achieve such a resounding victory."

"Monica, things have finally changed at work because of all of this." Crystal became a little guarded in what she was now saying. Her tone had become professional, which told me she was not able to communicate with me as freely as she used to about vetting arrangements. I understood. I had lived through the old regime with her, but I no longer held the security clearance to know about the new changes. "It's almost back to the way it was before everything got so screwed up. The correct procedures are beginning to be enforced again. Too many heads have rolled."

"That's right, so many have rolled," I said and began to list the people I knew who had suddenly decided to ditch their long-held careers or take permanent 'leave' when the klieg light had passed their way. 'Pandora, Jack, Erik, Con, Stephen Merchant..."

"Plus two more you don't know about, head people at DSA in Canberra, one has just resigned outright, and the other has suddenly taken holidays just before a critical Senate Estimates, a bit unusual, so no one expects him to come back," added Crystal.

"Sounds like he's doing an Erik!" I commented.

"I guess they know what's coming," said Crystal.

"Yes, and it's about time," I responded. "This is only the beginning, Crystal."

"The IGIS investigation has got the hierarchy scared. The leaders are walking on eggshells." Crystal's tone was matter-of-fact. "Even after the investigation is finished, everyone is expecting AGSVA will be monitored for quite some time. They can't keep doing what they have been doing, and they know it."

"This is a good result, Crystal."

"It is! It really is! Let me know if anything else happens," Crystal said, winding up the conversation.

"I will," I responded.

As I hung up the phone, I felt so proud of all the people who had risked so much to achieve this victory. The agency staff were pretty much out of Defence reach, but Crystal had gone the distance within Defence, knowing the cost, and personally paying it continually for over eighteen months. Though she had been severely pressured to give up the fight, she had hung on until we gained the victory.

In my lifetime, and even to this day, I have never met anyone as brave as Crystal.

Our friendship needed to change now. She was no longer free to speak to me about her work in the new AGSVA. I understood, but her bravery, honour and kindness, even in the face of adversity, were etched in my mind and on my heart. I couldn't admire her more.

Senator Johnston questions Defence

The Senate Estimates hearing of October 2011 finally began, and it was announced that the IGIS investigation had not been completed and would need to be extended for another month.

This was a good sign for us; there was apparently too much evidence of corruption for a short investigation. We rejoiced. Good on you, God! No wonder Defence staff were shaking in their boots and jumping ship.

It was clear the information from ASIO had reached the Senate, and the Senators were aware ASIO considered the workaround fiasco to have had a 'significant impact' on National Security, though it wasn't directly discussed. The spokesperson for Defence was still Stephen Merchant who, though he had resigned, was required to face this hearing despite his resignation, and Senator Johnston did not spare him but continued asking all the right, albeit very uncomfortable, questions.

- “The Minister, on 21 September, almost a month ago, said: ‘Allegations about poor security processes were first raised in passing in the course of an investigation into harassment and bullying.’ Is that entirely correct?” Senator Johnston.
- “I think that...was a reference to the fact that it was raised in an indirect, in passing way, in the report we received from Miss Trent.” Stephen Merchant.
- “Three Ministers were told of these practices.” Senator Johnston.
- “I readily concede, and the Minister has said this, that it was unfortunate that ah, that ah, and it was not right that we did not follow through appropriately to that reference in Miss Trent’s report.” Stephen Merchant.
- “Not only did you not follow through, three Ministers did not follow through on matters which require us to now re-do 20,000 plus vets...of security that is of significant importance.” Senator Johnston.
- “The first that came to my attention, about the fact that there were inappropriate practices being alleged in the vetting process, ah, was actually the *Lateline* program of 16 May this year. And that, of course, has initiated all this subsequent action.” Stephen Merchant.
- “Well, you can see my problem. It’s good enough for the producer of a television program to elicit the matters, but when they are directly taken to three Ministers of this government, and everybody sits on their hands and does nothing, and here we are today with a massive administrative issue. One has to say and ask the question, ‘Does it take a television program to get anything done, or to get any attention to these sorts of matters?’ Because the only action that has come about is because of a TV programme.” Senator Johnston.

- "Senator, I'm not aware they were raised in such explicit terms to Ministers." Stephen Merchant.
- "I'm told on the 23 June 2010 that a letter to the then Minister Griffin specifically made that Minister aware of these security issues, together with the bullying, but specifically of these issues. I'm told Miss Trent's report adverted to these security issues in 2010. I'm told that on 7 July a letter from Minister Griffin to Mr Raguse, the then member for Forde, indicated he was aware of the matter. A letter from Minister Snowdon, on 26 October, indicated that he was aware of the matter. Now it strikes me that these Ministers are aware of the matter, and here we are today with this problem, and it's been sitting around waiting for a television program." Senator Johnston.
- "Senator the references in my recollection were about the awareness of allegations of inappropriate management practices, ah, at the vetting centre...it is my sincere wish that we would have got onto it much earlier, so that we didn't have to have the issue aired on *Lateline* before we picked it up and um, and then started to look at it, and, of course, that's what we've done since." Stephen Merchant.

The problem could no longer be denied by Defence for it was obvious the Senators had been advised our allegations were true. It was also obvious neither the threats to National Security nor the bullying had been taken seriously by Defence for both had been fobbed off and treated as 'management practices'.

At this stage, no one knew how big the problem was, how many years it had been going on, or how many clearances had been compromised.

Though Defence had downgraded the annual figure of 40,000 to 50,000, announced on *Lateline* by Minister Smith, to a collective 20,000 by the time it got to the Senate, it was apparent the actual figure was unknown, and Defence was playing down the extent of the damage to save face.

Only the long-awaited IGIS report would be able to shed much-needed light on the real size and effect of this great betrayal of the Australian people.

It was now well over two years since I had first dipped my toe into this foul swamp. Finally, everyone was about to find out how deep these murky waters were and how wide an area they covered.

> *"We are going to find out from the Inspector-General of Intelligence and Security the depth and length and breadth of how severe this problem is, and I think it's very severe."*
> (Senator Johnston, Lateline, 19 Oct 2011)

An enemy

could not have done

a better job of sabotage!

CHAPTER NINE

Accountability? Um! Yeah! Sure!

When the IGIS Report was finally released by the Prime Minister, Julia Gillard, in February 2012, it was beyond severe, it was scathing. It not only confirmed everything we had said but proved we whistleblowers had only seen the tip of a huge and deeply buried iceberg. According to the detailed report, the corruption was, in fact, so widespread and had been going on for so long, that much of the damage done had become unfixable.

The IGIS report recommended thirteen sweeping changes to Defence security vetting, but the first recommendation surprised us. The Defence Department, who for the past eighteen months had continually publically implied we were either lying, stupid or criminal, had been ordered to put in writing, to each of us, that what we had said about the corruption of data from the very beginning was, in fact, true.

ABC's *Lateline* was the first to air the details of the IGIS report and opened their program by announcing to Australia that we three whistleblowers had been vindicated; that what we had been saying all along had been proven to be true. They reported that the Inspector-General of Intelligence and Security had found the integrity of the data in the DSA and ASIO databases had been undermined, if not compromised.

The next day, in an address to Parliament, Senator Johnston publically honoured the service we had done for our Nation. He told the Parliament, Australia owed us a debt of gratitude for coming forward. Finally, our efforts had been acknowledged!

Senator Johnston's amazing address to Parliament on our behalf was not the end of the story for at the next Senate hearing in May 2012, he tabled nine Questions on Notice in Parliament to the Minister for Defence regarding the ineffective outcomes of the first 2010 investigations.

Though answers to Parliamentary Questions on Notice are usually given within thirty days, the Minister for Defence didn't respond in thirty days or even sixty days. So we waited...

While we were waiting, the results of the DLA Piper investigation into a flood of bullying complaints against Defence was released, and it was damning. The Government immediately announced a $40 million compensation package for victims, which they pointed out was to come out of the Defence budget.

With a barrage of bullying complaints coming from every angle, Stephen Smith finally did what had never been done in Australia's Defence history. On behalf of Defence, he publically apologised to the Nation for the bullying culture within Defence, promising reform. The media labelled this day 'an historic day'.

A short while later, well before the end of his term of office, Stephen Smith suddenly announced his resignation. He told the media he would be leaving the political arena at the end of his term and would not in future seek re-election to public office.

We were three months out from a Federal election. It was my hope there would be a change of government and the new Minister for Defence would use his position and power to bring about the changes necessary to make sure this kind of betrayal of Australia and Australians would never happen again!

The IGIS report is released

On the morning of 8 February 2013, we three whistleblowers were individually notified that the Prime Minister, Julia Gillard, had decided to approve the official release of the full IGIS report. It would be made public, first to Parliament and then to the media the same day. This notification came by phone, via an AGSVA agent.

"Is this Monica Bennett-Ryan?" The emotionless voice was unreadable.

"Yes, it is, how may I help you?" I answered with a professional tone, expecting the call to be work-related.

"This is agent Jones from AGVSA, letting you know the IGIS report is being released today and a copy of the report will be hand delivered to you prior to the release."

I was taken aback. I didn't know how to respond. We had been waiting for months to hear when the IGIS report would be released, and now suddenly, on the morning of the release, we were being rung and told we would each need to be available for a sudden hand-delivery.

"Hand-delivery?" I said. Though I wondered why the report would need to be hand delivered, I knew I couldn't ask the agent. He wouldn't tell me. I just needed to keep it simple. "Where is this going to take place? When?"

"I can bring it to your place of work at around 3pm this afternoon," the agent remained emotionally non-committal. "I also have a letter for you from the Secretary of Defence which needs to be delivered at the same time."

The Secretary of Defence? Why would he be writing me a letter? While my mind wondered, I continued the conversation, "I'm afraid you can't bring it to my place of work," I said, remembering what I had previously been told by my bosses about conflict of interest, "you will have to bring it to my home, and I won't be there until 5pm."

"5pm it is!" he said and hung up the phone.

As I hung up the phone I realised, I hadn't given AGSVA my new work number, yet they not only knew where I worked but my current in-house phone number as well. I smiled to myself. It wasn't long ago they had told a Minister they couldn't find some of us. Did anyone ever believe anything they said? Mad if they did!

I wondered if John Stewart knew about the report's release, so I opened my email to send him a 'heads-up'. Too late! There were already several messages from him asking me to contact him about doing another interview in my home that evening.

Okay, things were starting to get a little hectic, I would have to contact Owen and Janice and see if they could come over to my house that evening, check with my bosses about going home early at short notice, then prepare a response to a report I hadn't begun to read. Still, we had been waiting for this day for a long, long time, besides I wanted to know what was in the letter from the Secretary of Defence. Why was he writing to us?

The phone rang again. It was John. I filled him in on my conversation with the AGSVA agent. "I will send the questions to your home email and will need your responses back to me by 5pm if possible. When will you be home?" I could tell John was more anxious than usual; this was an unusually tight deadline.

"I'm going to ask my bosses to let me off now, straight away." I was making an executive decision, and I wasn't an executive, but I couldn't see they would object. They all knew how important this report was to me and how long I had been waiting for it to be released. "I should be home in less than two hours. Do you have a copy of the report yet John?"

"No, not yet! Can't get my hands on it! I was hoping you would have yours."

Poor John, how could he ask the right questions without a copy of the report? "I won't have mine until 5pm, but maybe Janice will get her's earlier."

"If I can get hold of a copy I'll send it to you."

"Thanks, John, talk later..." I could hear from his tone he was under pressure, a breaking news story, but no facts to report, no questions to ask, no time to develop a response. Hopefully, Janice would receive her report earlier and send him a copy.

I didn't have to wait long to find out; half an hour later John phoned back and told me Janice was not receiving hers in time either. "Don't worry about rushing to prepare for an interview tonight. I've run out of time. I'll just run with Senator Johnston's official response."

"Okay, John."

When I hung up the phone, I breathed a sigh of relief. The pressure was off. All I needed to do now was go home a little early and wait for the AGSVA agent to hand-deliver my copy of the report and the mysterious letter from the Secretary of Defence.

Defence writes an apology

The agent arrived at my home at 5pm as arranged. After checking I was the intended recipient, he handed me a copy of the IGIS report and a sealed envelope and departed. I closed the front door, walked over to the lounge, sat down and stared at the two items in my lap. What were they going to say? Which one would I open first? Defence had not been kind to us, so I put aside the letter from the Secretary of Defence and opened the IGIS report.

It was 64 pages long, so I did what most people do when they want to fast track their understanding of a large document – I went straight to the recommendations. There were thirteen, laid out over two pages, and as I read the first one, my mouth dropped open in shock. I couldn't quite grasp what was written...it was not what I had expected... not even close!

These recommendations were not mere suggestions, they were akin to enforceable orders. Knowing that, this first recommendation left me speechless.

> Recommendation 1: *The Department of Defence should write to the three Lateline complainants and acknowledge that their allegations in respect to data-entry were true.* (IGIS Report, page 6)

Understanding slowly dawned. Ah! So that was what was in the letter from the Secretary of Defence. After all Defence had done to us, the denials, the false accusations, the traps, the slurs and the attempted public humiliation, the Secretary of Defence had been ordered to put in writing to each of us that what we had said from the very beginning had been true all along. How wonderful for us! How humiliating for them!

I closed the IGIS report and picked up the letter. My hands shook a little because I still didn't trust them. Would they actually obey this direct order? Or would they word things in such a way we would still be able to be blamed for something? I opened the letter.

> *"Evidence provided to the Inspector-General's Inquiry confirmed that the substance of your claims was true: both contractors and the Australian Public Service Employees working in the vetting centre were entering incorrect information into the vetting process. Further, this corrupted information was then used by ASIO to conduct its security assessment checks. The Inspector-General concluded that the integrity of the data in both DSA and ASIO had been undermined if not compromised."*

It had started well, but then came the put-down.

> *"The security vetting process involves a range of other subsequent checks including personal interview, multiple referee checks, financial checks, a police records check and often a psychological interview for high-level clearances."*

Really? How many times did we have to tell the authorities in Defence the same story, over and over again? *We* did the paper checks, the financial checks and police record checks. They were not done 'further down the line'. *We* did them! That's why we blew the whistle! That's why this was all so very bad! There were no more data-entry checks after they left our hands! That was the whole problem! How could it be that the Secretary of Defence, even after all this time, still didn't get it? I was angry now, but the final comment made me wish I had never opened his letter.

> *"It is regrettable that it took your appearance on National Television to bring attention to these inappropriate practices."*

So, there it was. They were only sorry we made it all public! How embarrassing for them! Poor dears!

Apparently, there were no regrets about the enormous amount of damage which had been done to individuals, to Australia, to the military, to National Security, to ASIO's records; damage which would take years to fix. No regrets at all! And no regrets about the tremendous waste of time, effort and tax-payer money so willingly squandered by Defence. It seemed their only regret was we had made it public.

I folded the letter, put it back into its envelope and firmly resealed it. Then I opened my filing cabinet and put it into the very back file - out of sight, out of mind. As far as I was concerned that official insult could stay there forever and rot. I never wanted to look at it again.

The whole tone of the letter seemed childish and out of keeping with the authority carried by such a high office. It reminded me of a typical playground scene: A child is forced to apologise to another for doing the wrong thing but doesn't want to apologise. So he puts his head down, shuffles his feet and grumbles 'sorrrrr-eeee' albeit with a nasty undertone. Everyone around him knows the child is not sorry; they know he's only saying the words because an adult is making him say them; and everyone also knows, until the 'sorry' is genuine, it doesn't mean anything.

It was clear the only reason the Secretary of Defence had acknowledged the truth of our claims was because he had been ordered to do so, yet the ongoing Defence 'attitude' towards us had clearly not changed.

Why was it so difficult, I wondered, for someone in Defence to simply say, "Thank you for coming forward. Thank you for what you've done." Unbelievable!

Accountability takes courage! It was so disheartening for me to see blatant cowardice being displayed by so many Defence officials throughout this whole sorry saga.

Australia-wide, public vindication

That night to my surprise, *Lateline* blasted our vindication across Australia. The story that went to air was about how we three whistleblowers had been vindicated. I was stunned. When God vindicates, he goes all out!

Australia was told, in no uncertain terms, we three whistleblowers had told the truth right from the very start; that the problems we pinpointed were not easy to now fix and that Defence had been ordered to implement immediate changes to their vetting practices. I was in awe! I watched the program in stunned silence.

- "Three whistleblowers who claimed thousands of Defence security checks had been compromised have been vindicated after an official report found their allegations to be true. John Stewart reports:"
- John Stewart: Last year three whistleblowers told *Lateline* thousands of security applications had been fabricated to speed up the checking process. They said that information was invented to fill in gaps on security forms, including checks on private security guards working on Australian military basis, Australian staff working in embassies overseas and air marshals and senior public servants with access to sensitive information.

- At first, the Defence Department denied the claims made by the three whistleblowers. But today the Inspector-General of Intelligence and Security found, "Evidence provided to the inquiry confirmed that the substance of the allegations was true."
- The Inspector-General also found that some security databases still contain fake information. "The Inspector-General found that the integrity of data in both DSA and ASIO had been undermined if not compromised. Modified data entered the databases, and some persist today."
- David Johnston, Opp. Defence Spokesman: Given that 5,000 of the 20,000 are top secret security clearances, embassies, members of Parliament, other sensitive areas, one would not be able to sleep at night confidently given that the Inspector-General has completely savaged the process and those participating in the process.
- John Stewart: The report recommended sweeping changes to Defence security vetting and told the Defence Department to write to the three whistleblowers and acknowledge that their allegations about false data entry were true."

The phone rang. I knew it would be Janice. "Well, did you see it?" she said, abandoning her usual greeting.

"I am in awe! How amazing! This is so much better than I thought it would be, and I haven't had a chance to go through the report yet."

I could feel the joy breaking through, and I realised I had been a little emotionally numb. "What did you think?"

"Loved it!" said Janice. "I think it's very nice to be publicly vindicated, but it's rather strange that those telling the truth and wanting to put a stop to the corruption are the ones who need vindication, while those doing the corruption and lying about it are not even reprimanded!"

"True!" I nodded, chuckling at Janice's observations.

"This feels so good, Monica," Janice said. "It's over, it finally is over!"

"I'm going to give the report a thorough read tomorrow. Senator Johnson said the report had 'savaged' the vetting process so I can't wait to see what the IGIS found. I haven't emailed our thanks to John, yet," I said,. "so I'll do that tomorrow, as well."

"Are you working tomorrow?" asked Janice

"No! My bosses have given me the day off." I chuckled again. "I guess they remember my last 'day after' experience.

Janice laughed. "Yes, well, I imagine we will be on the phone most of the day...lots of congratulatory phone calls...and people to thank."

"Yes, I think we will be quite busy," I laughed. But my mind was still re-running the *Lateline* report, and my heart was thanking God. What an amazing result!

A shocking and unexpected number

I was too awake to sleep, so I opened the IGIS report and began to read. Senator Johnson was right, the IGIS report was not only scathing, it had savaged the entire DSA/AGSVA vetting process. What the investigators found was, in a nutshell, widespread disorganisation and chaos. Processes which didn't exist, workarounds which didn't exist, lack of training, lack of qualifications, poor management skills, inadequate agency contractual arrangements and inadequate system upgrades.

The investigators had gone over everything done in DSA since 2008 and every accusation made by us with a fine tooth comb. They were thorough! They shone the light into every little dark corner and in doing so had found what we had been saying all along was correct.

Worse, they found the corruption of data was on a broader scale than anyone could have guessed. Defence had given the Senate a generalised figure of 20,000 checkable paper applications which they estimated would have been compromised. Applications which were now, they said, beginning the long, slow process of being rechecked. Yet, the IGIS investigation showed that checkable paper applications were not the only applications which had been compromised! The number given to the Senate did not include the high number of electronic applications (ePacks) which now could *not* be re-checked or corrected!

- "Potentially the most significant outstanding issue is that remediation will not resolve all data issues – particularly those relating to the unauthorised and unaudited access to the current electronic vettee pack where it seems likely that it will not be possible to identify the missing or inaccurate information." (IGIS report page 5)
- "I was advised that DSA staff have access to a password reset function, intended to be used when an applicant loses their password." (IGIS report page 58)
- "It was apparent from some staff interviewed that this permission was neither sought nor documented." (IGIS report page 58)
- "...over half of the ePack2 submissions may have been modified in this way." (IGIS report page 58)
- "...the use of this practice is of significant concern in that it bypasses all security and audit controls." (IGIS report page 58)
- "The range of data changed via this method appears to be unidentifiable and given it occurs at the first step of the vetting process, has the potential to significantly undermine the remainder of the process." (IGIS report page 58)
- "...these changes cannot be picked up via a comparison of the paper and electronic versions" (IGIS report page 58)

This was shocking indeed! Besides the corrupted paper applications, at least fifty per cent of all electronic applications had also been changed in some way, and now no one was able to tell how they were modified or who modified them!

At first, I was stunned the problem was at least twice as big as Defence had at first stated. Then, I was horrified at the amount of false information which had been fed to ASIO as truth on a regular basis over so many years - information the IGIS report confirmed could not be picked us as inaccurate if it was not flagged as inaccurate.

I wondered how any intelligence organisation in this country could do its job of protecting us from terrorists when the information they were relying on to be accurate was nothing more than a honeycomb of fantasy.

As I kept reading my shock slowly turned to anger. Even though the people directly responsible for this unspeakable betrayal of Australia and Australians had been identified and were named in the report by the Inspector-General of Intelligence and Security they were nevertheless not going to be officially held accountable.

> *"While I have found that a significant contributing fact to these problems was lack of management oversight I have decided that there is no evidence of sufficient weight that any person was guilty of a breach of duty or of misconduct to justify referral to the Secretary of the Department of Defence."*
> (IGIS report page 52)

I couldn't get my head around it! The inner workings of the greatest intelligence scandal in Australia's history had been exposed for all to see and yet those who had been found to be responsible were not even going to get their hands slapped!

Everything we had said had been proven to be true and yet the people who planned all this, organised it, and ruthlessly enforced it were not going to be held accountable in any way. I couldn't believe it! I couldn't take it in!

The Inspector-General had told us many times she did not have a mandate to investigate bullying. And now I knew why.

The evidence which would show the deliberate, callous and outright criminal nature of the deception played out in DSA in order to enforce the 'maladministration' would have been found, in abundance, if a legitimate investigation into bullying had been conducted.

> *While not the direct subject of this inquiry, it has been difficult to untangle the allegations of inappropriate vetting practices from the accusations of bullying and harassment at the NCC, as well as poor management in general. The report would be incomplete without some observations in this area.*
> (IGIS report page 37)

The exclusion of bullying from the IGIS investigation was significant. If the bullying, harassment, intimidation and coercion of DSA/AGSVA staff had been investigated, the deliberate nature of the maladministration would have been seen and prosecutions would have followed.

The IGIS investigation found it *difficult to untangle* corrupt vetting practices from the coercion which enforced them, yet, because bullying and harassment were not part of the terms-of-reference for that investigation, no *evidence of sufficient weight,* which would have justified criminal prosecution against those responsible, was ever uncovered.

The above comment from the IGIS should have been enough to open an investigation into the bullying culture prevalent within DSA, but this never happened. Evidence of coercion for criminal purposes was excluded even from the highest investigative body in Australia.

Was this why no legitimate investigation into the bullying at DSA/AGSVA had ever been conducted? An investigation into bullying would have revealed a mine-field of evidence of deliberate corruption ordered by those in high places.

My mind raked over the five letters we had sent to Minister Griffin back in 2010. Our barrister told us there was enough evidence to prove a breach of Section 13 of the Code of Conduct in those letters alone, yet even though Minister Griffin ordered an investigation into our allegations, the DSA hierarchy manipulated his order into an investigation of 'management practices', and our allegations of bullying were never investigated.

Despite the lack of investigation, Defence had spent the last two years telling the media and the Senate that an investigation into our complaints of bullying had definitely been conducted, during which complaints about National Security had only been 'mentioned in passing'. That whole statement was an outright lie! Our allegations were never investigated. The bullying was *never* investigated! It still hasn't been investigated!

Instead, on receipt of Minister Griffin's order, DSA hired a 'management consultant' without any legal expertise or proper security clearance. No one ever picked up on it, the word of the Defence officials was always taken as Gospel. No one ever asked, 'can we see the results of that investigation?'

That is, until Steven Merchant finally admitted the truth to the Senate about the initial investigation into our claims of bullying and illegal vetting practices, *"references in my recollection were about the awareness of allegations of inappropriate management practices."*

Now, in the light of the findings in the IGIS report, I could see the reason DSA pushed so hard to avoid any investigation into bullying. Finding actual evidence of coercion would have proved too dangerous for the few at the top who were responsible for this betrayal of Australia.

The IGIS report itself was welcome and thorough and honest to the point of shredding forever Defence excuses regarding the corruption of clearances, but sadly it was also limited, and it was the nature of that limitation that denied justice to everyone who lived through the brutality of DSA.

Without evidence of coercion, the deliberate and criminal nature of the callous deception of staff to enforce illegal and corrupt practices would never be seen.

What do you do? Where do you go for justice when you live in a country whose highest officials, though they see the corruption, can't or won't punish those who promote and sustain that corruption with brute force?

I was so angry, I couldn't even speak.

Telling John what I thought about the outcome

I couldn't speak, but I could write. Late as it was, I sat down at my computer, opened an email and began a letter to John Stewart. I was furious, and so I just let my emotions tumble out onto the page in front of me. It was like a relief valve had been opened.

When I finished, I felt better knowing I had been able to express some of my anger, but I also knew enough not to send it to anyone until I'd calmed down.

The next day, after re-reading what I had written, I decided to send it, unchanged, to John Stewart with a copy to Senator Johnston.

Hi John,

When I wrote this I was angry, so I put it aside, calmed down and re-read it. You can hear the anger - but it still says what I want to say. I don't know if it will be useful to you or not, but you can always delete it. :) Here goes...

You are always asking me if there is any terrorist who has slipped through the net. I'll tell you who slipped through the net, John. The people who have done this...

- *They have lied to Ministers!*
- *They have lied to the Senate!*
- *They have perverted investigations!*

- *They have lied to ASIO!*
- *They have lied about ASIO!*
- *They have falsified people's personal data!*
- *They have ignored Australian workplace laws!*
- *They have forced staff to lie to ASIO!*
- *They have forced staff to falsify personal data!*
- *They have completely ignored Parliament approved procedures for vetting!*
- *They have compromised Australia's security in such an effective way it will take up to a decade to undo the damage!*
- *They have thumbed their noses at every authority in this land! And...*
- *They are not being prosecuted!*
- *They are not even being sacked!*

Instead, they are being patted on the head and told: "there, there, it's all right, you're not to blame, no one is - we understand - it just happened."

Maybe this should now be the defence used in court for every criminal act committed in this country from this time forward...

- *You murdered someone? Don't worry, we understand - no one is to blame - it just happened - this is Australia - we don't care about the law.*
- *You want to rob a bank? No problem! Steal a car? Of course - you won't be Robinson Crusoe!*
- *You want to be a terrorist? Come to Australia, we make it easy for you!*

Law? What law? Where are the people who are supposed to uphold our laws?

To work with DSA, I had to endure an invasion of my privacy. A ten-year check of my personal life to prove I was an upstanding Australian citizen with a clean criminal history. Then the first thing they did when I passed their test was force me, through the use of threats and deception, to break the law and betray Australia - to enter into criminal activity - falsifying people's personal data and lying to ASIO. Without even touching the rampant bullying side of it, this is a clear breach of the law. A criminal act!

> *A corporation shall not, in trade or commerce, engage in conduct that is misleading or deceptive or is likely to mislead or deceive.* (Trade Practices Act – Section 52 [1])

I was misled and deceived, and I was forced to mislead and deceive (and I am only one of hundreds). ASIO was misled and deceived. Every applicant whose data was corrupted was also misled and deceived by DSA/AGSVA. They trusted them with their personal information, and they were betrayed.

The law was broken, deliberately and continually, over and over and over again for years. And now, they beg innocence through ignorance? If they are not prosecuted lawlessness wins.

How can terrorism destroy our society any more than this deliberate act of betrayal?

What are our officials afraid of - a compensation lawsuit? Australia can't afford that! If every affected person in this scenario entered into a class action, there would be 30,000, 40,000, 50,000 people or more. That is not reasonable or desirable as far as compensation is concerned.

Instead, what every one of us would want to see, I believe, is justice. The law needs to be upheld and applied to those who have done this to us and to Australia. Everyone involved in this needs to see that the law actually counts for something in this country.

- *The Ministers who turned a blind eye need to be removed from office, permanently.*
- *The heads of DSA/AGSVA need to do jail time.*

What is the point of laws if they are not upheld? This is not a small matter. And a pat on the head just won't cut it.

The law is the net, John, they are the big one, and they're getting away...

Thank you for all your help. Monica.

A few hours later Senator Johnston's media advisor, Rebecca, responded to my email, requesting my permission to use some of my sentiments in the Senator's address to the Senate that afternoon.

Of course, I gave my consent. I was honoured. It was nice to know that even in my raw emotional state my opinion had some value and had been taken seriously by someone who actually had the power to effectively use some of what I'd written.

Honoured in Parliament

When Rebecca emailed the Senate Proof of the Senator's Ministerial Statement to the Senate dated 9 February 2012, I was utterly taken aback, honoured and humbled. Though I was at work and reading it on my work computer, I gasped out loud several times.

I was so shocked at the sheer volume of praise Senator Johnson was laying on we three whistleblowers, that his comments took me completely by surprise.

- In March 2010, three whistleblowers raised the issue of corrupted vetting practices. Defence's response and the response of the Members of Parliament was to simply ignore them.

- It was not until the *Lateline* program, in May 2011, raised these issues that the whistleblowers were taken seriously.
- These whistleblowers were treated with contempt. They were derided and treated as cranks. They have now received the Inspector-General's report.
- The first line of that report is that there should be an acknowledgement that what the whistleblowers said from day one was true and correct.
- We owe them a debt of gratitude.
- These three might have been in breach of the law disclosing what they disclosed.
- The parliament owes these three brave people a great debt of gratitude for coming forward in the circumstances.
- The simple question that we all must ask is: who is accountable? Who is responsible? There is nobody that this government has pointed to as being responsible. It is always a review, adverse findings and 'we'll fix it now'. Nobody is accountable.
- This is an absolute disgrace. (Full version pages 7-9)

When I finished reading my face was dripping with tears, and I couldn't speak. I thought of so many other whistleblower horror stories that I'd heard about over the years, and all I could think was I had never known of any whistleblowers anywhere in the world who'd been honoured the way we had just been honoured, in the highest forum in the land. I was overwhelmed.

In calling for accountability, Senator Johnson had just taken the responsibility for seeking justice off our shoulders and placed it onto his own.

We had fought the good fight. We had won the race. We had brought everything out into the open.

Yet, despite the enormity of what had just been revealed - a gaping Titanic-sized gash under the surface of Australia's National Security - there was still no accountability. It was just 'maladministration', which is not criminally prosecutable. How pathetic! I remembered again what Dayle had told us right from the very beginning:

> *The Department of Defence is accountable to Australian law! It has no power to act illegally and to allow it to do so would be a criminal offence.*

How many people in the highest places of government, I wondered, just in this one scandal, had allowed DSA/AGSVA to remain unaccountable for the breaking of Australian law?

Now that everything was out in the open it was my hope Senator Johnston would continue our battle in the Senate and open the doors for a proper investigation into the bullying within DSA/AGSVA.

It finally felt extremely good to pass the baton to Senator Johnston whose words of praise on our behalf would echo in my heart for a long, long time. *"We owe them a debt of gratitude. The parliament owes these three brave people a great debt of gratitude..."*

Thank you, Lord!

Poetic justice

A few months later, in the Federal Election of 2013 not only did the Liberal Party win power but to our great surprise and delight Senator David Johnston was chosen as Minister Smith's replacement and was sworn in as Australia's new Minister for Defence on 18 September 2013. Janice called it 'poetic justice'.

He had fought the good fight for us in the Senate and battled Defence bureaucrats boldly and effectively. And now he was in the position to actually make a difference.

He showed his intention to do just that by accepting his new portfolio with a promise of *"a new defence white paper within 18 months and a root and branch review of the defence organisation"* (The Australian Sep 14 2013).

He kept his word!

Immediately things began to change and the first most, noticeable change, was the change to our National Security. Not only were our borders being suddenly protected but it was announced that our National Security would be reviewed. The first line of the proposed new Act stated, *"National Security is the highest responsibility of Government."* (National Security Legislation Amendment Bill [No. 1] 2014).

"It's about time National Security was recognised as the highest responsibility of Government," Janice shared in an email to me. "What a shame DSA never seemed to be aware of that small fact."

Under the new Minister for Defence, the military was suddenly being supplied with new personnel and equipment; and projects which had previously been on hold or cancelled were given the go-ahead. It was like the military was being given new life.

Furthermore, there was talk of a Royal Commission into the findings of the DLA Piper Report. Compensation had been paid to victims, but only a Royal Commission could get to the heart of identifying and naming the perpetrators of the violence which had cost so many so much.

This was good news! Victims' compensation was not enough. It would never be enough! A Royal Commission would bring the perpetrations to account. It would bring justice! And only justice could bring healing.

The people now in authority in this country were taking responsibility, and making all the right suggestions. So it looked like; finally, Defence was going to be made to bow to Australian law and accept accountability for their illegal activities.

Hopefully, the new AGSVA, under the monitoring eyes of the IGIS appointed auditors within the Attorney-General's Department, would now forego the financial pressures placed on them by money-hungry 'recruitment' agencies, and instead abide by the *National Security Amendment Bill* and actually make Australia's National Security, rather than money, it's highest priority.

Change, good change, was well and truly beginning to happen. We couldn't have hoped for more.

We had entered this warfare in July 2009; it was now July 2014. Finally, after five long years, we could relax! For us, it was over! It was time to enjoy life again...

Have not I commanded you?
Be strong and courageous,
do not be afraid or dismayed,
for the Lord your God is with you,
wherever you go.

(Joshua 1:9)

POSTFACE

Dear readers,

My warmest thanks for taking the time to read this book. It is my sincere hope it will inspire and encourage those experiencing oppression to take hold of their faith and make a stand against injustice.

This book is about faith, trust, courage and the willingness to stand up for what is right no matter how daunting the obstacles may seem. It is about not trying to do it all at once but slowly taking one step at a time until the job is done. It's about not giving up and not giving in. It's about knowing the word of God is reliable and trustworthy and will never fail those who follow it's precepts. It's about faithful friends, both seen and unseen, and more than all the above, it's about my faithful God and Saviour, who continually led and guided the events, like a shepherd herding sheep and defending his flock from unseen attacks.

There can be no victory without a challenge, no triumph without effort. God calls his people to be overcomers, but we can't be overcomers unless we first have something to overcome. There are plenty of evils in this world. Look around! Choose your battle, and enter in with the courage of Joshua. Once God gives you his word, your victory is assured.

I began this battle with a word from God. *Write the vision, make it plain, so that he who reads it will run with it. (Hab.2:2)* and my testimony today, is that God made those words come to life before my eyes as I watched people in high places take notice of everything we whistleblowers wrote, even when some of them wanted to ignore us.

What I learned, like a truth burned into my heart, is that God's word never fails. At no time in history has God ever failed to get the victory. Therefore, when he gives his word and sends his people out to fulfil his word, victory is assured, despite the way things may seem along the road.

There are many sad stories about whistleblowers who are damaged or even destroyed by the battles they endure, and my heart goes out to them. But that was not our experience. We three whistleblowers were all, and are still, dedicated Christians. We were not damaged or even harmed by this battle. Though sometimes we felt daunted by the mountain in front of us, most of the time we went through our days rejoicing as we watched in awe as our God removed obstacles out of our way. And though there were also times when we were staggered by the evil our eyes were seeing, what we saw, heard and experienced didn't destroy us, far from it, it made us appreciate the unchanging nature of our holy God and trust him more.

I personally felt like I'd been thrown into the pages of Scripture and was experiencing exactly what the patriarchs of old experienced. I saw God *use what was weak to confound the wise (1 Cor.1:27)* so that I could say, *"when you think I'm weak, look out, for that's when my God is strong through me (2 Cor.12:10).* Today, I know I can directly identify with the stories of old, as these few examples show;

- When the Philistine army sent Goliath, their biggest, strongest, most experienced warrior, to challenge the armies of Israel, God answered them by sending a boy. He had no sword, no spears, no armour, just a slingshot and faith. And that was enough to win the victory! (1 Sam.17)

- When the Syrians surrounded Jerusalem and were starving the people of Israel, God answered their challenge by sending four very weak people who were literally falling apart, four lepers. When the lepers, holding each other up, set out towards the enemy camp, God made their footsteps sound like a vast army, and the Syrian army fled. The victory was the Lord's! (2 Kings.7:3-20)

- When Australia's Defence Intelligence took a stand against truth, honour and obedience to God's law, God answered them by sending what they least expected; a grandmother and her friends! We challenged the might of Defence without a scrap of evidence to back our claims and watched as God brought them to their knees. The victory was his!

If you think you are too weak, or too insignificant or too small to stand against the evil you see, think again. *God is able to do exceedingly abundantly above all you can hope or think* (*Eph.3:20*). And he will! Your weakness is the opportunity he needs to display his strength. It is my joy to encourage you to stand up for what is right, and my hope and prayer is that you will be able to trust in the Lord with all your heart, all the days of your life that he gives you on this earth.

Monica Bennett-Ryan

If my people,

who are called by my name,

will humble themselves and pray,

and seek my face

and turn from their wicked ways,

I will hear from heaven and forgive their sin,

and heal their land.

(2Chron.7:14)

SPECIAL ACKNOWLEDGEMENT

There are a few exceptional people I want to thank, for without their constant and trustworthy prayer support, we wouldn't have had the victory we had. These people, I believe, moved the hand of God.

Without fail, every week for the three and a half years this long battle raged, we six met together in the loungeroom of Rod and Sharon McCormack's home. Along with them, Bronwyn Bye, Miriam Wentworth and Katherine Dengate, held up my arms when I was tired or overwhelmed, supported me, encouraged me, and lifted up every aspect of this battle to God in prayer. We laughed together, cried together, sang, repented, rejoiced and earnestly prayed the word of God into reality.

I could trust them! I often needed to suddenly phone them and ask for prayer, and every time I did, I knew without a doubt they would stop what they were doing and pray with all their might.

They were in the background through every step of this process from beginning to end. They were praying behind the scenes when I wrote my first letter, met with Brett Raguse, was interviewed by the ABC, or newspapers or radio, when I faced the intimidating IGIS panel and when Senator Johnston was taking our concerns to the Senate. Their strong prayer support was with me where ever I went and whatever I did. The knowledge they were praying for me gave me the confidence to stay strong.

So I want to thank you personally, my friends, for your invaluable faithfulness and fellowship during this time. I couldn't have done this without you.

The LORD is my rock,

my fortress, and my deliverer.

He is my shield and my salvation.

I will call upon the LORD,

who is worthy to be praised;

so shall I be saved from my enemies!

(Psalm 18:2-3)

CPSIA information can be obtained
at www.ICGtesting.com
Printed in the USA
LVHW110327271222
735873LV00022B/168

9 780994 325631